AN INOFFENSIVE
REARMAMENT

Frank Kowalski Jr., congressman-at-large from Connecticut, in his Washington, D.C., office, 1959
Courtesy of the Kowalski family

AN INOFFENSIVE REARMAMENT

THE MAKING OF THE POSTWAR JAPANESE ARMY

COL. FRANK KOWALSKI
EDITED AND ANNOTATED BY ROBERT D. ELDRIDGE

NAVAL INSTITUTE PRESS
Annapolis, Maryland

This book has been brought to publication with the generous assistance of Marguerite and Gerry Lenfest.

Naval Institute Press
291 Wood Road
Annapolis, MD 21402

© 2013 by Carol Reidy, Barry Kowalski, and Robert D. Eldridge
All rights reserved. No part of this book may be reproduced or utilized in any form or by any means, electronic or mechanical, including photocopying and recording, or by any information storage and retrieval system, without permission in writing from the publisher.

Library of Congress Cataloging-in-Publication Data
Kowalski, Frank, 1907–1974.
   An inoffensive rearmament : the making of the postwar Japanese Army / Col. Frank Kowalski, Robert D. Eldridge.
       pages cm.
    Summary: "Col. Frank Kowalski served as the Chief of Staff of the American military advisory group that helped establish the National Police Reserve, the predecessor to the Japan Self-Defense Forces during its first two years of existence. His work provides a detailed account of the manning, logistics, and personalities involved in standing up—on short notice—of a force of approximately 75,000, while sharing insights about the diplomatic, political, legal, and constitutional challenges his headquarters and his Japanese counterparts faced in rearming Japan in the wake of the sudden outbreak of the Korean War. Published in Japanese in 1969, this is the first English version of this edition, and includes a biographic section about Kowalski"— Provided by publisher.
   Includes bibliographical references and index.
    ISBN 978-1-59114-226-3 (hardback) — ISBN 978-1-61251-373-7 (ebook) 1. Japan—Defenses. 2. Japan—Armed Forces—History—20th century. 3. Japan—Military policy—History—20th century. 4. National security—Japan. 5. Japan—Foreign relations—United States. 6. United States—Foreign relations—Japan. I. Eldridge, Robert D. II. Title. III. Title: Making of the postwar Japanese Army.
   UA845.K68162 2014
   355.00952'09045—dc23
                                                            2013031916

♾ Print editions meet the requirements of ANSI/NISO z39.48-1992 (Permanence of Paper). Printed in the United States of America.

21 20 19 18 17 16 15 14 13   9 8 7 6 5 4 3 2 1
First printing

CONTENTS

	Editor's Preface	vii
1	Grace of Heaven	1
2	Japan before Korea	11
3	Basic Plan	21
4	Constitution Bans War	33
5	Yoshida's Views	45
6	Struggle for Control	56
7	Advisers and Operations	73
8	Organizational Problems	84
9	Leaders Fashion Armies	96
10	*Seishin Kyōiku*	109
11	*Yobitai*	121
12	Confusion and Conflict	132
13	The Imperial Military	146
14	Dawn of a New Era	158
15	Conclusion: A Critique	171
	Notes	183
	Index	189

EDITOR'S PREFACE

About the Book

The memoir you have before you is the detailed account of the early years of the postwar Japanese military covering the years 1950 through 1952, when the National Police Reserve (Kokka Keisatsu Yobitai), or NPR, and then the National Safety Force (Kokka Hoantai), or NSF—both predecessors to today's Japan Self-Defense Forces (Jieitai), or JSDF—were established. The author, Frank Kowalski Jr., a colonel in the United States Army, served as the deputy chief, Civil Affairs Section, General Headquarters, Supreme Commander for Allied Powers, and then chief of staff of the Military Advisory Assistance Group (MAAG) in Japan. The MAAG was tasked by General Douglas MacArthur to stand the NPR up following the issuance of a letter from MacArthur to Prime Minister Shigeru Yoshida on July 8, 1950, authorizing the Japanese to establish a force of 75,000 men and expand the Maritime Safety Board by an additional 8,000.[1] The manuscript was completed in 1966, eight years after Kowalski had retired from the Army and three years after he had left Capitol Hill, having served two terms in the U.S. House of Representatives as a member of Congress from Connecticut.[2]

Like most military men, Kowalski moved around a lot, but according to his daughter, Carol, he was careful to preserve his papers throughout his moves and travels. In fact, "he kept records on many ideas of his early on," she recalled.[3] Kowalski reiterates this himself in the preface to the Japanese version of the book, saying that he kept memos and notes of conversations and ideas of important things and events from a young age.⁴ He kept such good records, in fact, that his son, Barry, was able to donate a significant collection of his papers to the Library of Congress in 1990. The papers, which cover the years from 1925 to 1976 and the bulk of which focused on the period between 1948 and 1963, were processed in 1992 and made available to researchers at that point.

It was with these records, his recollections, and his notes from the time that Kowalski wrote his original manuscript, comprising 321 typed pages and handwritten additions. The only copy the family had was one Kowalski gave to his daughter, Carol, to whom he inscribed on the manuscript's cover, "To Carol-Helene, my daughter, who I know can write a better book."

Carol suggests that he began keeping copies of important materials related to the NPR in the summer of 1950, and he then continued to collect information as he followed the progress of the NSF and then the JSDF and the development of Japan's post-1952 defense policies through various channels, connections, and the press. Katsuyama Kinjiro, who worked in Kowalski's command as a translator and interpreter and later became a close friend, remembers Kowalski asking him about the concept of the book and getting his thoughts.⁵ When he actually started working on the book is unclear, but his daughter, who helped in his office in the spring of 1965, remembers Kowalski making several trips to the Japanese Embassy, then at 2520 Massachusetts Avenue in Washington, D.C., probably to gather materials and to see about possible interest in the book in Japan.

His manuscript, translated by Katsuyama,⁶ was published in Japanese in March 1969 by Simul Press.⁷ Katsuyama said later that the translation took nearly three years to complete because he had moved to the United States in 1959 and did not have all the Japanese-language materials at hand; he had to have them sent to America.⁸ The Japanese version of the book is still consulted by scholars forty-plus years later.

It is unclear if Kowalski, who died in 1974, intended to publish the book in English, as no full version of the manuscript resides among the donated papers at the Library of Congress.⁹ He did leave among the papers, however, an incomplete version of the first several chapters and a detailed table of contents, including notations about the approximate number of words and an overview of each of the chapters. There was no cover letter attached, so it is uncertain if it was meant as a submission to an American publisher.

Having referenced in my own research over the years the Japanese version of the book, which was reissued by Chuo Koron Shinsha in 1999 as the eighth volume in its series on the occupation period,[10] I thought there would be great value in getting the memoir published in English. Since Kowalski had made the effort to write his memoir in the first place, I believed he would have wanted it published in English too, and so I approached the family after several years spent looking for them. Even though his family's recollection is that he seemed to focus on a Japanese audience, as mentioned above, they felt he would have wanted the memoir to be published in English as well and blessed my efforts to seek an English-language publisher. Fortunately, the Naval Institute Press, with whom I had published the English translation of the Iwo Jima–related memoir of Major Yoshitaka Horie (who served on the staff of General Kuribayashi Tadamichi),[11] expressed a strong interest in publishing the volume, for which I am particularly grateful. I especially would like to express my gratitude to the Kowalski family as well for supporting this project and for the wealth of background information they provided, some of which is used below in a short introduction of the late Colonel Kowalski. I would also like to thank the staff of the Library of Congress, who assisted me over the years during my research trips and in making contact with the family. Finally, thanks go to Courtney Dowse for assistance in typing the manuscript in a quick, efficient, and positively bright manner. An intelligent and mature young lady, she has a promising future in whatever career she chooses to dedicate herself.

The original book is divided into seventeen chapters. Because more than forty years have elapsed since it was written, I decided not to include two chapters (15 and 17, titled "Power and Potential" and "A Cooperative Security" respectively) that were in the original manuscript. These chapters discuss the events following 1952 to the mid-1960s and U.S. policy in the region, which takes away from the main focus of the book, which is the period of the early 1950s. I have included this editor's preface to provide background on the book and about the life and times of Kowalski.

In editing this book, I came to realize and better appreciate the valuable contributions Kowalski made to his mission at the time, in addition to producing this account. Kowalski provides details about the manning, logistics, and personalities involved in standing up, on short notice, a force of approximately 75,000. He also provides insights into the diplomatic, political, legal, and constitutional challenges his Headquarters and his Japanese counterparts faced in navigating this new course for Japan in the wake of the sudden outbreak of war on the Korean Peninsula in June 1950. In light of these limitations, the path for rearmament had to be slow and "inoffensive" while psychologically and materially contributing to Japan's internal defense. Kowalski's account is balanced, a blend of both criticism and praise, of all of those involved, including himself. Kowalski, who later served in Congress, was a highly intelligent Army officer who had served in local military governments in western Japan. He was expecting to be deployed to Korea in the summer of 1950 when he was tapped for a secret mission to create a new Japanese army while having to call it a police reserve. An honorable man, he was pained by the subterfuge he and his government, working hand in hand with the Japanese government, had to play in order to establish this needed organization, which was seen as going against the "antiwar" article of the postwar constitution. Kowalski believed that many things were mishandled, but he also viewed the "quiet and reasonable approach" of the rearmament program as successful in allowing the NPR to "adequately and effectively" provide for the urgent defense needs of not only Japan, but also the United States, which had a quarter million dependents left to fend for themselves in Japan in 1950.

Kowalski noted that there has always been a tension in the postwar U.S.-Japan relationship over Japan's not doing enough to contribute to the bilateral alliance and international security. This book will not end that debate, but it does provide greater context and historical understanding of what factors existed at the time. This is a particularly important topic to Japan watchers and alliance managers as Japan is re-examining its defense posture today, both for its own needs as well as to strengthen its still complicated relationship with the United States, its only alliance partner.

This book is also important for those in the U.S. military, whether they are involved in Japan or not, or equally important, if they are involved in the training of foreign militaries (or nation building, for that matter). While Kowalski's focus is not the reconstruction of Japan as a whole after World War II, he does talk about the importance of building of a professional military within a democracy in which the dignity of the individual soldier is upheld and the principles of civilian control are maintained.

Kowalski's memoir begins with chapter 1, "Grace of Heaven." In it, he discusses the destruction that befell Japan as a result of World War II and the role of the occupation forces in the early postwar years on the eve of the Korean War. He names the chapter after the reported comments by the then prime minister, Shigeru Yoshida, who felt not only that the war in the nearby Korean Peninsula would help Japan's economic recovery, but that it was a "God-given opportunity for an accelerated peace treaty and eventual independence for the nation." But Japan was also a "military vacuum" as a result of occupation forces departing for Korea, which forced General Douglas MacArthur, as supreme commander for the Allied powers, to order the rearmament of Japan, "contrary to international agreements at Potsdam," Kowalski writes, "in violation of instructions from the Far Eastern Commission, in contradiction of the noble aspirations of the Japanese Constitution, and with little help from his own government."

Chapter 2, "Japan before Korea," looks at the degree of domestic instability, including communist activities in Japan, before looking at the apparently successful efforts to combat it. Ironically, this success left the United States overly confident and militarily unready when the North Koreans attacked the South.

Chapter 3, originally titled "Initial Rearmament Plan," was renamed "Basic Plan" by Kowalski as he finished his manuscript to reflect the formal name of the document. In any case, both titles would be correct—it was the basic plan for the initial rearmament of Japan. This chapter examines the basic plan that was developed in conjunction with the decision to direct Japan to organize a national police reserve force of 75,000 to preserve security in Japan after U.S. forces departed to fight on the Korean Peninsula. Kowalski describes his personal involvement in the plan as well as the professional and ideological rivalries that existed within the General Headquarters, Supreme Commander for Allied Powers, or GHQ SCAP, over this plan and the rearmament process in general, including which offices and individuals would be involved.

Chapter 4, "Constitution Bans War," discusses the prohibition, including the various phrases considered in the drafting of the postwar constitution, against possessing a military that went into effect in May 1947 and the efforts to justify the establishment of the NPR in light of the constitutional ban on the use of force to settle disputes.

Chapter 5, "Yoshida's Views," introduces the opinions of Shigeru Yoshida, Japan's long-serving prime minister during these years, on the establishment of the NPR and its political leadership. His views greatly informed the cabinet and Kowalski's Advisory Group as it worked to create the NPR. Yoshida and his government expressed strong concerns about the influence of militarists in the country. He possessed a "genuine horror of the military" and opposed the dispatch of the NPR to Korea.

Chapter 6, "Struggle for Control," discusses the struggle in GHQ SCAP and within the Japanese government over the question of using former Imperial Japanese Army officers in the NPR. General Charles A. Willoughby, MacArthur's intelligence chief, played a major role in trying to control the appointments of key Japanese. The chapter introduces how the struggle spread to former militarists.

Chapter 7, "Advisers and Operations," discusses American organizational problems and includes Kowalski's personal experiences and anecdotes. The United States, according to Kowalski, not only organized but commanded and controlled the new Japanese army. This was particularly true in the hectic first days, weeks, and months.

Chapter 8, "Organizational Problems," examines American efforts to teach Japanese officials the theory and practice of U.S. civilian control over the military as the NPR was being established. Kowalski discusses the relationship he had with Keikichi Masuhara, a former prefectural governor, who was appointed the first director general of the NPR, the "dignified" de facto first minister of defense of postwar Japan.

Chapter 9, "Leaders Fashion Armies," discusses the problems of leadership, who the leaders were, and their thinking and behavior. It concludes that neat uniforms, saluting, articulate officers, sharp commands, and even modernness do not necessarily make a fighting force. Nevertheless, Kowalski was proud of the Japanese civilian leaders, the U.S. advisers, and the leadership at the company and battalion levels. They learned, listened, and rapidly acquired basic military knowledge and skills. Kowalski found that the challenge was to make the NPR into a modern military and maintain the traditional fighting qualities of the Imperial soldier without militarizing the force ideologically like the prewar Imperial Army had been.

Chapter 10, "*Seishin Kyōiku*," introduces the Japanese style of military education called "*seishin kyōiku*"—spirit, heart, guts. *Seishin kyōiku* was considered the essence of the fighting Japanese soldier. Japanese civilian leaders felt that the men in the NPR lacked this strong sense of dedication and mission, seeing, as General Hayashi, chief of the General Group, said, "no spirit in their eyes." The challenge for them became to blend the Japanese ethics found in *bushidō*, or way of the samurai, with the "new, still unfamiliar, precepts of democracy" and civilian control.

Chapter 11, "*Yobitai*," discusses the *yobitai*, the new Japanese soldier, his thinking and behavior, and the views of the people and the press concerning the new soldiers. Because the NPR was organized in "pseudo-secrecy," finding a name acceptable to the Japanese for the soldiers, many of whom believed they were becoming police reservists, was a problem. In addition, owing to this initial secrecy, the NPR had difficulty identifying with the people, and this started a decades-long effort to win the hearts and minds of the public. This chapter cites stories both positive and negative concerning public opinion toward the NPR. Kowalski also describes his efforts to impress upon the NPR leadership that they could not tolerate the force's members acting in a high-handed manner toward Japan's citizens in a democracy, as these actions would affect public opinion toward the NPR.

Chapter 12, "Confusion and Conflict," describes the ambiguous nature of the NPR in its formative days. Though it was armed with artillery, tanks, and aircraft, the prime minister refused to acknowledge in Diet interpellations that the NPR was an army. Other cabinet members took a similar line, which caused the opposition parties to raise more questions. Kowalski notes that criticism was heard from both the Left and the extreme Right about the way rearmament was proceeding. For example, the Left objected to the reported pressure the U.S. government was placing on Japan to rearm, while the Right challenged the U.S. dominance in organizing, training, and equipping the forces. Kowalski cites a variety of public opinion surveys regarding the degree of rearmament necessary, and he ends the chapter with an anecdote about Yoshida's strong desire not to strengthen the NPR beyond 110,000 until well after the end of the Korean War for fear of being drawn into that or other conflicts in East Asia.

Chapter 13, "The Imperial Military," examines the remnants of the Imperial Army and the challenges former soldiers had with accepting a democratic Japan and an NPR that was limited in its roles, missions, and political-legal power. In particular, Kowalski looks at some of the Rightist groups and efforts of some of the former Imperial military officers to exert their influence in the creation of the NPR.

Chapter 14, "Dawn of a New Era," discusses the various social and political changes Japan had undergone in the early postwar years to become an established democracy before it returned to the international community of nations in 1952. The NPR, which became the National Safety Force (Hoantai) in October of that year, had come to embrace civilian control, and the people had come to accept the existence of the NPR despite the radicalism that was caused by the Communist Party and its supporters.

Chapter 15, "Conclusion: A Critique," serves as the concluding chapter. In it, Kowalski reviews the political, social, and legal challenges involved, from a U.S. as well as Japanese perspective, in establishing the NPR as well as the development of the Self-Defense Forces, created in July 1954. He acknowledges mistakes the U.S. and Japanese governments made along the way, feeling that the two governments "trampled upon the Japanese Constitution, deliberately confusing the truth and sadly violating moral commitments." At the same time, he is critical of the Socialist and other opposition political parties for refusing to recognize the "dangers facing the nation," adopting a "rigid political stance," as well as "confus[ing] the electorate and in the end achiev[ing] little of positive value." Despite the various challenges and problems at the time, he argues that this "inoffensive rearmament," in which, "within the limitations imposed by the structural deficiencies of the Constitution, Japan [developed] a small, modern, highly effective military establishment and a significant armament industry," helped to build the foundation for Japan's later prosperity.

Please be aware that Kowalski's occasional use of the words "now," "today," and "currently" throughout the text refer to the late 1960s, when he wrote the book, and not necessarily to the present in 2013. Please also note that Japanese names appear as Kowalski wrote them, in Western order (personal name first followed by family name), rather than the traditional Japanese style of family name first followed by personal name.

About Kowalski

Frank Kowalski was born in Bristol, Connecticut, on October 18, 1907, to Polish immigrants Frank and Mary Kowalczyk. Both were originally from Warsaw, although the family name of Kowalczyk (meaning "blacksmith") is Belorussian and the mother's maiden name, Miller, was Germanic. Frank (Sr.) came to the United States in 1901 through Ellis Island, and Mary, short, stocky, with dark hair, came in 1902, also through Ellis Island.

Frank did not have any siblings, but there was another child, Josephine, in the family who had lost her parents and was taken care of by the Kowalskis. She was like a sister to him. Frank Sr. was an illiterate foundry worker, and little Frank spoke Polish at home until he went to school at age seven. Presumably, his English was limited at that time, but he studied hard. According to his daughter, Frank's mother was "a dynamic force to him. She often told him he could become King of Poland."

The Kowalski family was poor, but just as Dwight D. Eisenhower, for whom Frank would later work, observed of his own family's economic situation, they did not know they were poor. Growing up on a farm, young Frank was rewarded with healthy exercise and a work ethic stimulated by daily chores and forced responsibility. He milked two cows daily, first at 5 a.m. and again in the evening. As a blizzard approached late one day, delaying his parents' return from work and errands, eleven-year-old Frank milked all fourteen cows by himself.

His mother used to share stories of Poland, its history, and all the Catholic cultural rituals. Unlike his father, Frank's mother was literate, and she would read to all the Polish residents in the area who were not. It was his mother who sent Frank to the Alliance Preparatory School, a Polish parochial boarding school, in Erie, Pennsylvania, for an education that included learning about Polish history, culture, language, and customs. He was able to attend the private school on a sports scholarship, playing both baseball and football. He became quarterback and led a team that included bigger and much older young men who had returned from World War I. According to his son, a 1922 photo shows Frank standing upright and relaxed with a smile on his leather-helmeted face behind the rest of his teammates, all crouched in three-point stances: "It's obvious that he is the boss and brains of the outfit."[12]

Frank was sixteen when his mother died at the age of fifty-five. He was "plucked" from the school, according to his daughter, "by his father who wouldn't pay." At the public school in Meriden he went to upon returning to Connecticut, a chemistry teacher recognized Frank's mathematical and scientific gifts and got to know his family circumstances. He suggested the United States Army enlistment program, which allowed for enlistees to try for the U.S. Military Academy at West Point through an examination.

When things became bad at home with his alcoholic father and new stepmother, Frank ran away and enlisted in the Army in 1924 right after Christmas. He was seventeen but lied and said he was eighteen, a falsehood that later caused problems when he was going for retirement. He continued to study hard, using library textbooks and past examinations to teach himself the core courses he had missed in leaving high school. After eighteen months of study, he successfully passed the test and received an appointment to West Point in the summer of 1927. He eventually graduated in 1930. His daughter wrote, "I always felt this leap forward was the greatest risk he ever took and forged his greatest success—an appointment to West Point. His move to Congress was less a stretch than that effort. I often used his story to help boys in high school who struggled with handicaps of life."

On trips back to Meriden during his time at West Point, Frank occasionally visited Helene Amelia Bober, a childhood friend three years his junior. The connection seems to have been that Helene's parents were from the same village in Poland as Josephine's future husband, Vincent Scotniki. At the time, Helene, who had already graduated from high school, was working in the office of the mayor of New Britain, Connecticut, a small city in the central part of the state nine miles southwest of the capital city of Hartford, close to Meriden. Because of its large Polish population, the city was and apparently still is called "New Britski."

Frank's first assignment was Fort Holabird, Maryland, an Army installation established in 1917. After he had purchased a car and was able to make the drive up to Connecticut, he began seriously "courting" Helene. She even traveled to Baltimore, chaperoned by Josephine, to see him. Their relationship became particularly intense in the summer of 1931, and they got married on October 20 of that year.

Their first duty station together was Fort Sam Houston in San Antonio, Texas, where they moved after the wedding. There Frank led an infantry machine-gun platoon in maneuvers against the cavalry, helping to establish the supremacy of firepower over horsepower. Next he commanded a platoon of motorcycles through an upstate New York winter, attempting to execute one of the Army's various plans to replace the horse with the motorcycle.

In 1936, as part of two postgraduate study opportunities he would get, he was sent to the Massachusetts Institute of Technology in Cambridge, Massachusetts, where he earned his MS in mechanical engineering. His thesis concerned the armored plating of tanks, perhaps due to his then being in the Armor Branch.

In 1937, after he had switched to the Ordnance Branch, he went to the Aberdeen Proving Ground in Maryland. While there, he experimented with a variety of weaponry and new technology, including the prototype of a tank-piercing bullet. One day, a bullet ricocheted 180 degrees off the side of a tank and imbedded itself in Frank's cheek between skin and bone, giving him a permanent scar.

"Despite having shot himself," his son recalls, Frank "gathered several patents and membership in the fledgling American Rocket Society, a life-long avocation, tinkering as an inventor."[13]

Subsequently he changed to infantry and was sent to Fort Benning, Georgia, to study at the infantry school. It was there that the Kowalskis' first child, Carol, was born in September 1938. Around this time Frank was also promoted to captain.

In 1938, Frank found himself in Anniston, Alabama, and then later in Tampa, Florida, as an engineer to help construct McGill Field. This assignment was followed by time at Fort Campbell, Kentucky. As war approached, he returned to the Armor Branch and was sent to Pine Camp (later Fort Drum), New York, in 1941 into 1942. With the North Africa campaign developing, the family went to Palm Springs, California, in 1942 for desert training. The Army then sent Frank to Fort Leavenworth, followed by Fort Campbell, and then back to Leavenworth for Command and Staff School in 1943–44.

By this point, Frank was extremely frustrated about having not been sent into combat. From Leavenworth, Lieutenant Colonel Kowalski (he was promoted to full colonel one year later) was sent to work for General Dwight D. Eisenhower, the commanding general of the European Theater of Operations, where he worked in the G-3 Division for Civil Affairs and Operations. He landed on Omaha Beach on June 20, 1944, and soon thereafter was in Paris. He then traveled over France before going east to Poland (Krakow, Warsaw, and Czestochova) and Czechoslovakia. He collected data to help the people establish civil government.

The Kowalskis' second child, Barry, was born in August 1944 at Hartford Hospital. Frank was not there for the birth as he was in London and Scotland for part of the war. Nevertheless, his time in Poland was especially meaningful for him.

Kowalski returned to the United States in autumn 1944 and went to the Pentagon and then to Columbia University to prepare for going to Moscow as a military attaché. The family also began to prepare, purchasing warm clothing for the Russian winter, shots, and Russian-language training. But their plans were abruptly canceled. Kowalski had developed stomach problems during the war years and had become quite ill; he entered Walter Reed General Hospital for a subsequent stomach operation. The Russia assignment was canceled because in case of an emergency the nearest suitable hospital was in Stockholm, Sweden. Seeking treatment in the States proved to be a good decision as Kowalski underwent a second operation shortly thereafter that removed his entire stomach. He left Walter Reed a gaunt skeleton around Christmas 1946, after nearly eighteen months there.

Kowalski's next assignment was at the Pentagon, where he served until he went to Japan in January 1948. The Kowalski family followed him in June. He served in the military government in Kyōto Prefecture, Japan's former capital, until October 1948 and then in the military government in Ōsaka, Japan's second largest city at the time, until September 1949. Next he served in the Chugoku area, in Kure City, until the spring of 1950, when he was sent to Tōkyō to work under Major General Whitfield P. Shepard, the chief of the Civil Affairs Section at General Headquarters, Supreme Commander for Allied Powers—General Douglas A. MacArthur's headquarters. It was shortly after this that Kowalski was given the task of standing up the postwar Japanese military, which is covered in detail in this book.

Kowalski left Japan with his family in June 1952, several weeks after the end of the Allied occupation and the restoration of Japanese sovereignty. After enjoying a couple of months of leave, he went to Fort Knox, Kentucky, where he was post commander, a job his daughter said he "hated and arranged for a transfer to Fort Meade after only two months." He did not like the new job, assisting with reserve officer's training, either, and he moved to Camp (later Fort) Pickett, near Blackstone, Virginia.

One issue that was complicating things at the time was McCarthyism, which was greatly damaging morale in the U.S. government. Kowalski's daughter, who was fourteen at the time, recalls the arguments between her father and mother over her father's refusal to sign "the pledge." At the height of the "Red Scare," the military was requiring its colonels and generals to sign a "loyalty oath," which Kowalski was unwilling to do out of principle. "'God damn it,' he would howl at Mom, 'I swore an oath to protect and defend the Constitution when I was a cadet. No one has the right to question my loyalty after all these years.' Colonel Kowalski never signed a 'loyalty pledge' and I am not sure how he avoided the threatened consequences," Carol later said.

Following this period of McCarthyism, the Army began to recognize the need to introduce modern business methods into its leadership and management practices, and Kowalski, who had an ego and "fought like hell to get a job worthy of himself," was subsequently assigned to help found the Command Management School located at Fort Belvoir, Virginia. Kowalski created, organized, and became the first commandant of the school, and he chose to model its pedagogy after the Harvard Business School Case Study method of learning. According to his son, this was "radical military thinking at the time." Another radical policy Kowalski implemented was preventing the "natural proclivity" of staff at the school to say "no" to requests. He told the staff that they could approve things without his concurrence, but if they wanted to disapprove something, they had to come to him. This policy "promoted action and progress."

The school regularly had guest speakers who were businessmen and elected officials, which Barry thinks created connections for his father and may have helped lead him to Congress. The idea of guest speakers seems to have come from a visit Kowalski made to Columbia University. When he returned home, Kowalski was infatuated with a speaker he had heard, Charles Percy, then president of Bell and Howell (and later a U.S. senator). Being commandant of the school gave him access not only to business leaders, but also to those in the highest levels of the Pentagon and political leaders in the executive branch and Congress. It was this latter group that Kowalski would join following his military career.

During his time in the Army, he had stayed in touch with his hometown friends, many of whom had entered local politics. Several of them had urged him to run for office when he returned from Japan. Kowalski eventually retired from the Army in 1958 to run for Congress from Connecticut, and he was elected to the Eighty-Sixth Congress that year. He had been strongly supported by a local political boss who needed a Polish candidate to run because of the heavy Polish constituency in the state. In 1960, he was re-elected to the Eighty-Seventh Congress, but had lost a bid in 1962 for a seat in the U.S. Senate from Connecticut when his political sponsor would not endorse him. He ran as an independent and lost, turning his sponsor into an enemy. He subsequently wrote an unpublished memoir about this experience titled "Worms in Charter Oak," a strong indictment of the influence of political bosses and the danger of vested interests in a democracy.

In January 1963, Kowalski was nominated by President John F. Kennedy to be a member of the Subversive Activities Control Board, or SACB, a body established in 1950 to examine communist influence in various organizations. Ironically, the hearings before the Internal Security Subcommittee were postponed several times owing to a "rumor that somewhere in the power structure there might be a suspicion that he was a peacemonger."[14] Eventually, Kowalski was confirmed in October of that year, and he served until September 1966.

According to his son, Kowalski

> did not want the appointment. But Dad needed a year of service at a presidential appointment level on top of his time in Congress for four years to achieve a substantial retirement. His battle to run as an independent for the Senate had left him out of favor. Consequently, his enemies in the administration offered that appointment for two reasons: (1) Dad did not want the job (it offended his liberal political views), and (2) it would be difficult for Dad, a liberal, to get confirmation votes in the Senate. And they only promised a nomination, not a job. Give him job he doesn't want and likely cannot get. And so Dad had to "campaign" to get it. To be confirmed, he spent time getting the votes of southern conservatives. Once on the board, however, Dad found a sympathetic soul, Governor Francis Cherry of Arkansas (who preceded the infamous Orval E. Faubus). They teamed up to defeat everything that was a threat to civil liberties. Cherry had been also nominated for the board in a begrudged fulfillment of a political obligation to him. The anticommunists regretted the day those two partnered up. The two of them could together prevent repressive board action and did. Under Kowalski/Cherry, the SACB became an irrelevance; although Dad and Cherry had only a couple of years to work together [Cherry died in 1965], they accomplished it. Maybe Lyndon B. Johnson shrewdly made those appointments to undermine the anticommunist movement? More likely, Dad always felt that he got the last laugh out of the matter.

President Johnson did not renominate him, and Kowalski reportedly made no effort to seek renomination. "It's not," he said later, "much of a job at all."[15] It was during the time he served on the board that he worked on this manuscript.

Kowalski's continuing an interest in Japan during this time was demonstrated by a letter he wrote in late June 1960 to President Eisenhower, whose visit to Japan had recently been canceled owing to riots over the Japanese government's handling of the ratification of the revised bilateral security treaty.[16] In his capacity as congressman-at-large representing Connecticut, Kowalski wrote to the president to propose dispatching General MacArthur to Japan again on a mission to improve relations with Japan:

The friendship of the Japanese people is of tremendous importance to the United States in the fight against Communism. Recent developments indicate clearly that the generally pro-American feelings which prevailed in Japan during the post-war years have deteriorated to an alarming degree.

During my four and a half years of military service in Japan, I found that the Japanese people had a warm regard for America. The American they admired above all others was General Douglas MacArthur, in whom they had complete trust.

In view of the increase of anti-American feeling in Japan and mindful of the esteem in which General MacArthur is held by all segments of the Japanese people, I respectfully suggest that you consider sending him to Japan on a friendship mission. Such an assignment could be made under terms and provisions deemed appropriate by you.

I am convinced that General MacArthur, by talking to the rival political groups and by meeting again with the Japanese people, could do much to restore the friendly feelings of the people of Japan toward our country.

We cannot afford the loss of Japan. I am sure that General MacArthur could help prevent such a tragedy for the free world.[17]

Another thing Kowalski worked on before and after his retirement was his inventions. It may have been his engineering background, or his open-mindedness, that allowed him to come up with practical and prescient solutions to problems. Frank conducted experiments at his home on Regent Drive in Alexandria, Virginia, on the way to Mount Vernon, the residence of George Washington. Because of the availability of military housing, Frank and Helene did not purchase a house until he became a member of Congress. "[Because they were] children of the depression, they bought a $40[,000 house] in 1958 with cash. In fact, my parents paid cash for everything: automobiles, furniture, appliances, etc. It rubbed off on us kids," son Barry recalled.

Frank's hardy, Polish immigrant mother-in-law, Sophie Bober, died in May 1974. At the funeral, his daughter urged him to see his doctor because "he looked wan and his cheeks sunken." He had been having heart trouble in the previous years, a leaky valve combined with arteriosclerosis, but he had stubbornly refused heart surgery. In August, he finally went in to Dewitt Army Community Hospital at Fort Belvoir for tests and treatment. The evening before his surgery, on October 10, a Thursday, he gathered his children and then four grandchildren, "held court and told us all he loved us, ending with the conclusion that, since the odds were then, seven out of ten in his favor, we'd likely be laughing about the tears the next day." "Pacu," the nickname granddaughter Kelly gave Kowalski, went in for open heart surgery, a new procedure at the time, at Walter Reed Army Medical Center on October 11, 1974. During surgery, he had an infarction and died while on the operating table.

He was survived by his wife, who grieved "enormously" and "depended on [her son] for emotional and other support." Helene, who continued to live in the house they bought in 1958, eventually passed away at the age of seventy-nine of two heart attacks on August 13, 1989. She had been hospitalized for symptoms of heart failure. "She was tired and perhaps ready to die," her son remembers. Barry's oldest daughter, Kelly, with whom Helene was very close, returned from Africa, where she had been teaching and doing documentary filming. The two had a great talk, and "as if [her grandmom] had been had been waiting for Kelly to return, she died of heart failure that night. Again, a chance for the desired goodbyes."

Barry, who after serving in the Marine Corps in Vietnam went on to a distinguished career in the U.S. Department of Justice, was a seasoned and experienced trial lawyer with the Criminal Section of the Civil Rights Division when his mother died. Fortunately, she had been able to make it to the Great Hall of the Department of Justice to see her son awarded the John Marshall Award for Excellence in Trial Advocacy in 1985 for the conviction of the white supremacists who had assassinated controversial radio host Alan Berg.

Carol, who had earned her master's degree in counseling psychology, taught high school English literature and served as a high school guidance counselor in Fairfax, Virginia, and later, after retirement, was a volunteer counseling abused women in Williamsburg, Virginia.

Kowalski would have certainly been proud of the family he helped raise, and probably of the military he helped create in Japan. It was neither attacked by an outside force nor used to attack another country.

After consulting with his sister, Barry donated his father's papers to the Library of Congress in 1990, and they were processed in 1992 and are open to researchers. It is in these papers that a very important story of an American's—and indeed America's—involvement with postwar Japan is found.

In ending this brief biography of Kowalski, I would like to dedicate this book to another fine, sincere, honest, and hardworking officer, Colonel Stephen J. Gabri, United States Marine Corps, who has been a mentor and friend, and whom I believe Kowalski would think very highly of had they been able to meet and work together. By chance, Steve's own family also came from the central part of Europe and had a successful life in the United States. In Okinawa, Japan, first on the staff of III Marine Expeditionary Force as the G-4 and now as the chief of staff of the Marine Logistics Group, he has worked hard to develop the Marine Corps' relationship with the Ground Self-Defense Force and with the militaries of other allies and friends in the region, all to maintain readiness to bring about a more peaceful and stable world.

CHAPTER ONE

GRACE OF HEAVEN

It is reported that when Shigeru Yoshida, the doughty prime minister of Japan, was informed on June 25, 1950, that the communists had struck across the 38th parallel into South Korea, he bowed to his ancestors and whispered, "It's the grace of heaven." History has since clearly recorded that on that day the sun goddess, Amaterasu, smiled upon her people as Japan once again began to resume her destined role as a great Asian nation.

Better than anyone else, Yoshida knew how thoroughly and completely Japan had lost the war. Shorn of her empire, deprived of her vast merchant fleet, denied access to the customary sources of raw materials and food, her island economy in shambles, Japan at the end of the war lay prostrate, her heroic people exhausted and her government in abject submission. As one of the resurrected leaders in those critical days, Yoshida bowed to the power of the conquerors as bamboo bows before a storm. Struggling valiantly against overwhelming odds, Yoshida sparked the titanic task of digging a nation out of the rubble of war, of reconstructing a government, of maintaining law and order, and of breathing into the soul of his people an uncompromising belief in the dignity of Japan. Only those who lived through those terrible days can know the total horror of a nation in defeat.

The devastation of Japan is a tragic testimony to the vulnerability of a modern nation to the horrendous destructive capability of massive air power. Hordes of American bombers had laid waste to the major cities of the country. Tōkyō, Ōsaka, Kōbe, Yokohama, and a score of other centers had been gutted. Hiroshima and Nagasaki were A-bombed. Under this pounding from the skies, the Japanese industrial machine collapsed, and production in the home islands came to a virtual halt. When the bombing stopped, one-quarter of the nation's industrial capacity had been destroyed and another third of her physical plants had suffered severe damage. Eighty percent of the cotton textile plants had to be scrapped. Coal production deteriorated to the point where not enough coal was mined to operate railroads. Chemical production, so essential for industry and protection of public health, dropped to 21 percent of prewar years. The great steel mills of the nation were silent in the rubble, while the shipyards stood still, their rusting cranes and girders entwined in the stillborn vessels on the water. By November 1945, total industrial production in Japan had dwindled to 9 percent of the wartime peak.

More critical than the destruction of Japan's industrial capacity was the chaotic dislocation of the food supply system. Historically a food-deficit country, producing only 85 percent of its requirements during the war, Japan for years had been importing about 3 million tons of food a year, mainly from Taiwan, Korea, and Manchuria. By 1946, the food distribution system was hopelessly snarled. Whereas during the war years, rice collection from farmers produced 36 million *koku*, only 19 million *koku* were collected from farmers in the crop year of 1946.[1] If it had not been for the timely shipment to Japan of nearly 900,000 tons of food donated by the United States, thousands of Japanese would have died of starvation. As it was, thousands still suffered from malnutrition. In the cities, hunger and misery were prevalent as people struggled to survive in the rubble in primitive shelters, in rags, without heat, and without food. Life was endurable only on farms, nearest to the source of food.

To compound this unrelenting misery, the population of Japan continued to explode. By 1949, 5 million of the 6,614,000 Japanese nationals, military and civilians, had been brought back from Southeast Asia, China, Manchuria, Korea, the Soviet Union, and islands of the Pacific. These teeming millions, joined by some 5 or 6 million newly born by 1950, brought the population of the country to approximately 83 million. Compressed into an area about the size of California, limited by topography to 15 million acres of cultivated land, with their industry and world trade disorganized, the people of Japan seemed indeed forsaken by their ancestors. For the family, naked survival became the sole purpose and objective of life.

The Japanese, however, know how to endure, and the struggle for existence took on the pattern of a giant anthill that had become cruelly disturbed. Farmers hardly left their fields, praying for rain and fertilizer. Fishermen made their delivery runs with torn nets and inadequate fuel for their engines. Workers reported to gutted mills and factories hungry, cold, and inadequately clothed. Those who were fortunate to have employment in an office slept on their desks for lack of better shelter. Hundreds of thousands were unemployed, while thousands of others shared the same job, doubling up. A driver of a motorcycle, for example, had to have an assistant driver, who was forced to perch perilously somewhere on the front wheel. Jobs meant survival.

As the demand for necessities grew, a vast black market was born to supply the needs of the people in cities. In this new venture, the farmer became the man of the hour. He manipulated his harvest to outwit the government rice-collecting agencies. An extra *koku* of rice that could be hidden from the collector brought the farmer riches and economic power. The city slickers who operated the black markets in the cities now journeyed daily into the country to pay homage to their sources of supply.

A key person in the black market operations was the "rice carrier." This was a specialist in some instances, in others the family provider. The specialist customarily made two or three trips into the country a day to load liberated rice into a knapsack or a bag and carry the white gold to his or her town or city. A seasoned rice carrier was especially adept at evading or buying off the police. Often the most successful rice carrier was the policeman's wife.

While on the one hand the black market stimulated a fantastic surge in raw capitalism, producing many powerful black-market millionaires, the suffering of the masses in the devastated cities encouraged the growth of radical and subversive elements. The beleaguered housewives, waiting in line for their rice rations, were particularly susceptible to the influence of the radicals. Too often the ration distribution centers would run out of staples. On such occasions, the operator of the center would try to induce the housewives to accept sweet potatoes or some other substitute for rice. Only a Japanese person can understand what it meant to the women to be offered sweet potatoes instead of rice, their main staple. The radical provocateur, waiting for precisely such a breakdown in the distribution system, would rush forward to lead the housewives in a banzai charge on the rice warehouse. The provocateur would then capture the rice and distribute it to his women warriors. Nothing won the appreciation of the housewives so much as a successful fight for their rice rations. It is reported that the heavy vote that the Japan Communist Party (Nihon Kyōsantō) delegate Yoshio Shiga received in his campaign for the Diet, or national parliament, representing the city of Ōsaka at that time, was owing in great measure to the success of his agents at the food distribution centers.

During these tragic years, most of the people existed through the exigency of what became known as "bamboo shoot living." In their struggle for survival, the Japanese literally peeled the very clothes off their backs, one layer after another, like peeling bamboo shoots, to buy food for themselves and their families. Clothes, valuables, and household goods were pawned, family treasures sold, even military medals were traded for a bowl of rice. Yet during all these trying times, I saw individual Japanese walking the streets with toothpicks prominently poised in their mouths as though they had just finished a satisfying meal. Most dramatic of all were the unmatched and unbent heroes who in the spirit of the ancient samurai hungered and suffered rather than do anything dishonorable or break the law. The nation was traumatically shaken one day when the distinguished judge in the Tōkyō District Court, Yoshitada Yamaguchi, died of starvation rather than dishonoring himself by going to the black market.

When Prime Minister Yoshida greeted the Korean War with his quiet "It's the grace of heaven," he was reacting only in part to the desperate economic situation that continued to face Japan in 1950. More important, Yoshida saw the Korean conflict as a God-given opportunity for an accelerated peace treaty and eventual independence for the nation. The "unconditional surrender" terms had brought to Japan American crusaders who tore the very fabric of the country, reorganizing the political, social, economic, and even religious patterns of the people. Japan trembled under the impact of these reforms and the consequences they ushered in.

The objectives of the occupation of Japan as formulated by the Allied powers and transmitted by the Far East Commission to the supreme commander for Allied powers (SCAP) were as follows:

1. To ensure that Japan will not again become a menace to the peace and security of the world.

2. To bring about the earliest possible establishment of a democratic and peaceful government that will carry out its international responsibilities, respect the rights of other states, and support the objectives of the United Nations. Such a government in Japan should be established in accordance with the freely expressed will of the Japanese people.

The Allied nations further agreed and directed SCAP that the above objectives should be achieved in the following manner:

1. Japan's sovereignty will be limited to the islands of Honshū, Hokkaidō, Kyūshū, Shikoku, and such minor outlying islands as may be determined.
2. Japan will be completely disarmed and demilitarized. The authority of the militarists and the influence of militarism will be totally eliminated. All institutions expressive of the spirit of militarism and aggression will be vigorously suppressed.
3. The Japanese people shall be encouraged to develop a desire for individual liberties and a respect for human rights, particularly the freedoms of religion, assembly and association, speech, and the press. They shall be encouraged to form democratic and representative organizations.
4. Japan shall be permitted to maintain such industries as will sustain its economy and permit the exaction of just reparations in kind, but not those that would enable it to rearm for war. To this end, access to, as distinguished from control of, raw materials should be permitted. Eventual Japanese participation in world trade will be permitted.

Under these directives and policies, some of which were unusually harsh and restrictive but all of which were aimed at establishing a progressive modern democracy, General Douglas MacArthur, the fabulous supreme commander for Allied powers, carried on the greatest peacetime revolution the world has ever seen. First, the nation was completely and totally disarmed. Anyone remotely responsible for the war or supporting it, except the emperor, was purged. The purge list included all professional military officers, top politicians, and the nation's most successful and influential industrialists, bankers, and businessmen. A new ultra-democratic constitution was forced upon the country, humanizing the emperor, giving women the right to vote, and forever prohibiting military forces and war potential in the nation.

A host of American Army officers, DACs (Department of the Army civilians), consultants, economists, scientists, and all manner of experts scrambled over the rubble of Japan. The Japanese government, national and local, was reorganized. Americans introduced the election of governors, mayors, and hundreds of other officials who previously had been appointed to their post from Tōkyō. We helped the Japanese to recodify their laws and change their judicial system. We assisted in organizing labor unions, women clubs, farm and fishing cooperatives, and parents and teachers associations. We stimulated the Japanese to build new hospitals, to reform their penal system, and to reorganize their police forces. Proudly we guided the reorganization of a democratic educational program, initiated private and public welfare programs, and helped to establish an extensive system of medical care centers. Most significant, we introduced a land reform program in which the Japanese government achieved what the communists had promised when they had turned land over to millions of families who for centuries had worked the soil daily but had not owned it.

The Americans and the Japanese who labored on these great programs can be proud of a job well done. Some of the tax reforms may have been imposed autocratically and by coercion, but the result was to bring a great nation more completely into a progressive world.

From the American point of view, it was a benevolent occupation. We labored for Japan as conscientiously as we had fought for America. If there were mistakes, they were sincere mistakes stemming from lack of understanding of Asian culture rather than from malice. Many Americans returned to the United States thoroughly Nipponized, singing the praises of the Japanese people. On their side, thousands of Japanese admiring power, especially foreign power, became astonishingly American, or so it seemed.

In commenting on the historical significance of the occupation on the occasion of the fourth anniversary of the Japanese surrender, General MacArthur said, "I dare say that no occupation in history has been subject to such an extraordinary divergence of opinion carried in the media of public expression than has the occupation of Japan. Some writers have been extravagant in their praise, others no less extravagant in their criticism. Simultaneous attacks have been leveled against occupation policy by the leftists as too revolutionary and by conservatives as too liberal. The truth, awaiting the judgement of history, will rest somewhere in between." He concluded his statement with the words, "Of the Japanese people I can pay no higher tribute than to repeat that they have fully and faithfully fulfilled their surrender commitments and have earned the freedom and dignity and opportunity which alone can come with the restoration of a formal peace."

With the crisis breaking in Korea, the Japanese people were to demonstrate a deep appreciation for their conquerors. They could have turned against us, as so many conquered people have done in history, but instead they not only remained friends but actually became allies. Thousands of young Japanese volunteered to serve in American military forces to help us in Korea. And when American wounded returned to hospitals in Japan and blood for our troops was not available from the United States, thousands of Japanese men and women, the common people, gave their blood. We were all grateful for their cooperation and support. I regret to say, however, that too many Americans have failed to understand that the Japanese have their own vital interests as a nation that sometimes coincide with our own but on occasion diverge.

A people's traditions, hopes, and aspirations are deeply rooted in a nation. No adversity can block them out. Nor will they be forgotten or forsaken. And so the Japanese people will always remember that before their unconditional surrender their country was one of two major powers that had never lost a war; the other was America. Nor can we ever expect the Japanese people to accept for their country the role of a neutral Switzerland in Asia, as the victorious Allies had directed. The Korean War accordingly, by "the grace of heaven," stirred anew a deep-seated yearning in the hearts of the Japanese. They saw America committed to a war on the Asian continent. They knew America would need Japan. Out of that need they hoped would come a new day: a treaty of peace, respectability, and national dignity. By the miracle of Korea, an emasculated Japan was about to regain its manhood. History since is replete with the marvelous achievements—political, economic, and social—of a revitalized democratic Japan.

For myself, I have chosen to touch upon only a small segment of that illustrious history: the story of the rearmament of Japan, a story of covert, surreptitious, illegal rearmament, forced by the accident of war and fashioned by the expediencies of a deteriorating military situation in Korea. And so I return to that war.

A short time after our radio carried the news of the Korean invasion, I met my old friend Bunzō Akama, governor of Ōsaka Prefecture, who was visiting Tōkyō.[2] Our conversation immediately turned to the war.

"It looks bad, Mr. Governor," I said.

"Really, Colonel?" answered the governor. "War is bad, but the Japanese are not too unhappy. America will need Japan and we will be your friend. The war will be over soon."

Many thought so, but reality belied our wishful thinking. As the communist invaders pushed relentlessly down the peninsula of Korea, it became increasingly evident that neither the supreme commander's "*ukase*," nor our air or naval forces, which performed quite effectively, could stop the aggressor.[3] The North Korean forces swept the disorganized South Korean units and our small American advisory group from the fields. The situation became so chaotic that only the strong will of SCAP prevented our ambassador and the American flag from fleeing Korea. If we were to halt the aggression, American ground troops would have to be sent to Korea.

After the hectic week of uncertainties, General MacArthur launched his tragic double offensive. The 24th Infantry Division, one of the American units on occupation duty in Japan, was alerted for battle. Almost immediately, to show our resolve to the world, a battalion of the 24th was rudely jerked from its comfortable Japanese barracks and catapulted into the war. Rapidly in succession, one battalion of the 24th after another was dumped piecemeal into the meat grinder of Korea, each battalion understrength, undertrained, and underequipped. The officers and men did their best with what they had. The courageous commander of the 24th Division, Major General William F. Dean, personally led his troops on the field of battle until he was captured in the struggle.[4] But neither courage, patriotism, nor outbursts of loud national propaganda are adequate substitutes in war for military power, for men teamed and trained with weapons and equipment.

We were now committed on the Asian continent, fighting in a whirlwind that would suck into its vortex the cream of our youth and billions of dollars in natural treasure. This sacrifice was to be made in a remote area of the world, an area that our Joint Chiefs of Staff in a secret memorandum of September 1947 had said was of "little strategic interest."

Some months before the North Korean attack, Secretary of State Dean G. Acheson, supported by our Joint Chiefs of Staff, drew a line of demarcation in the Far East between communism and the Western world. In effect, we said, "Communism this far and no farther." That line extended from Alaska to the Philippines and included on our side the Aleutian Islands, Japan, and Okinawa.

Taiwan and Korea were not within the "Acheson Line." Accordingly, in South Korea we maintained only a small military advisory and assistance group.

In Japan we had four understrength divisions. The 7th Infantry Division was stationed in the northern part of Honshū, the largest of the four Japanese islands, and on Hokkaidō, the sparsely populated northernmost island, near the Soviet Kuriles and Sakhalin. The 1st Cavalry Division was located in the Kantō Plain, with some of its units in the city of Tōkyō, where it assumed the character of palace guards for SCAP. The 25th Infantry Division was comfortably resting in the Kansai Plain with its headquarters in Ōsaka, at the time Japan's second largest city. The 24th Infantry Division, which was the first to become engaged, was scattered over the southernmost island of Kyūshū, lying directly south of Korea. These forces were deployed in Japan to defend the country. They were not intended to fight on the Asian mainland.

With the commitment of the 24th to Korea, the 25th Division was sideslipped south to defend Kyūshū. But it did not remain there long. By July 18, the 25th Infantry Division and the 1st Cavalry Division joined the 24th in the war, and Lt. Gen. Walton H. Walker rushed his Eighth Army Headquarters from Yokohama to Korea. Thus, three weeks after the Korean War began, only the 7th Division with some Army service troops and Air Force units remained in Japan, and even the 7th was alerted to go.

In those crucial days, the United States became rapidly aware that we did not have enough forces in Japan to stop the communist aggression. Moreover, anxious examination showed that we could expect no reinforcements from the United States for months. We had the atomic bomb, but we had no ground reserves.

When the 7th finally embarked for Korea, there would be no ground troops left on Japan to protect the Japanese government and our bases from internal insurrection, let alone an attack from without. A nation of 90 million people had been completely disarmed. Its warships, aircraft, tanks, military transport, artillery, machine guns, and rifles had been committed to junk heaps. Even its officers' samurai swords had been carted off as souvenirs in the baggage of our officers and enlisted personnel returning to the United States. The country was a military vacuum.

Japan and America were at a critical crossroads. The situation called for bold and creative action. It was of little value now to debate whether we should have gone into Korea. The decision had been made, despite inadequate military capabilities. But the United States has always in its history been blessed with having the right man in the right place at the right time. So it was in June 1950. At this critical moment in our history, America had the only man who could have done what was necessary in Japan. For it is indeed doubtful that there was another man in the service of the United States except General MacArthur with the self-assurance, the self-conceit, and the moral courage to order the rearmament of Japan. This he did, contrary to international agreements at Potsdam, in violation of instructions from the Far Eastern Commission, in contradiction of the noble aspirations of the Japanese constitution, and with little help from his own government.[5]

CHAPTER TWO

JAPAN BEFORE KOREA

International conflicts, like all violent human events, can result from conscious planning, provocative acts, or miscalculations. In 1950, it was probably that American miscalculations in the Cold War, which was then being waged between the United States and the Soviet Union, influenced a flow of events that precipitated the Korean War. Certainly the communists caught us completely by surprise. Yet if those responsible had been watching events as they unfolded in the world and hardened in Japan, we should not have been surprised.

The forces that had held communist Russia in alliance with the Western nations were always under severe stress and strain. When Germany surrendered, the alliance came apart. The Cold War in Europe began the day the fighting war with Germany ended. Soviet communism overran Eastern Europe and pushed menacingly toward Greece. For a time, the United States hesitated, then on March 12, 1947, President Harry S Truman, in a bold move, announced what became known as the Truman Doctrine, declaring the determination of the Unites States to block Soviet communist expansion. Three months later, the Marshall Plan gave substance to our declaration. As the months went by, the United States became increasingly committed to using military power to carry out its foreign policy in Europe. Twelve nations, headed by Britain and France, rallied to our support, and on April 4, 1949, the North Atlantic Treaty, pledging "collective security of the North Atlantic Area," was signed in Washington.

On October 1, 1949, less than six months after the formation of NATO, the Red Chinese drove Chiang Kai-shek's regime from the mainland of Asia, and Mao Tse-tung established a communist government in China. Herbert C. Hoover, former president of the United States, commenting on the situation in the Far East, posted the score in the Cold War as 400 million to zero, referring, of course, to the loss of 400 million Chinese to communism, a slight underestimation.

In the months that followed, the Big Three foreign ministers (of the United States, Britain, and France) met to examine and ponder the world situation. With the formation of NATO, Europe seemed secure. In the Far East, however, communism had overrun the heartland of Asia. If the Cold War was to be stabilized, the West had to face up to the enemy in that area. The Big Three foreign ministers talked about "total diplomacy" and hinted about demonstrations of power. There was vague speculation about actions to be taken in Japan, where the United States maintained an occupation force of substantial ground, sea, and air power. If a demonstration of power was needed in Asia, Japan was the place to make it.

It was not clear what the Big Three foreign ministers meant by "total diplomacy." Seemingly the concept proposed a containment of the Soviet Union on all fronts—economic, political, and military. One facet of the "total diplomacy" strategy seemed to contemplate a policy designed to destroy the prestige and influence of the Russians in the Japanese environment. In retrospect, one can now see that this strategy fashioned three blows that were struck at the Soviets during the later part of May and early June 1950, only weeks before the Korean War. The first of these blows knocked the Russians out of the negotiations on the Japanese peace treaty.

Exploratory talks on a peace treaty with Japan had been going on for some time. As early as March 19, 1947, General MacArthur, in an interview with the press, indicated that he thought Japan's sovereignty should be restored "as soon as possible." At that time, the supreme commander envisioned a special status for Japan, a kind of international protectorate under "mild" controls and guidance from the United Nations. It is significant that General MacArthur, back in 1947, pointed out that "if the UN is ever to succeed, this was the most favorable opportunity it had." He conceded that it might be advisable to reconsider Japan's pledge against maintaining "war potential," suggesting that a small military establishment for the nation might be desirable. Nothing ever came of General MacArthur's proposal, but who knows what course events might have taken in the Far

East had the occupation forces been removed and Japan placed under United Nations protection.[1]

In the spring of 1950, rumors began to circulate in Tōkyō about a separate peace treaty for Japan with each of the Allied nations, which immediately polarized Japanese politics. In the controversy that developed, Prime Minister Yoshida and his Liberal Party (Jiyūtō) were prepared to sign a peace treaty with any of the nation's former enemies willing to recognize Japan's sovereignty. The Japan Socialist Party (Nihon Shakaitō) protested loudly, wanting a multilateral agreement that would give Japan a single peace treaty with all the Allied nations, including the Soviet Union. The debate came to a head when Dr. Shigeru Nambara, president of Tōkyō University, dramatically declared that he stood for a "total peace treaty or none." Yoshida is alleged to have retorted privately, "He's crazy." Publicly, the prime minister replied on May 3 that Dr. Nambara "was playing to the galleries."

While the controversy raged in Japan, the Soviet Union continued to obstruct every effort to reach a multilateral agreement. Suddenly, the United States decided to give Japan a separate peace treaty whether Russians participated or not. On May 18, 1950, the United States accordingly announced that Defense Secretary Louis A. Johnson and General Omar N. Bradley, chairman of the Joint Chiefs of Staff, planned to discuss with General MacArthur in Tōkyō the military implications of a peace treaty with Japan. On the following day, May 19, President Truman told the press that he hoped a Japanese peace conference could be held soon, and he said he had appointed John Foster Dulles to negotiate the peace treaty. About two weeks later, the Japanese government, in an unprecedented statement for a vanquished state, bluntly declared that Japan was ready to sign a peace treaty with any nation. That opened the way for a separate peace treaty with the United States and shut the Soviet Union out of any negotiations. The first card in the game of "total diplomacy" had been played.

The next two power plays were more direct. In 1950, there were two viable aspects of communism in Japan: the Japan Communist Party and Soviet Union's representatives on the Allied Council of Japan in Tōkyō. These two elements of Soviet influence had to go.

The Japan Communist Party was a legal political organization, permitted by General Headquarters (GHQ) in November 1945 to exist as a political party. It subsequently had several delegates elected to the Japanese Diet. In the depressed city areas, the party had considerable influence among the unemployed and dispossessed. In Ōsaka, for example, the Communist Party leader, Shiga, had received overwhelming support from the electorate. By 1950, communists were aggressively organizing noisy cells in the universities.

The first blast offensive against communism was fired by General MacArthur. In an elegantly phrased press release, SCAP declared,

> [The Japan Communist Party] has cast off the mantle of pretended legitimacy and assumed instead the role of an avowed satellite of an international predatory force and a Japanese pawn of an alien power policy, imperialistic purpose, and subversive propaganda.
>
> That it has done so at once brings into question its right to the further benefits and protection of the country and laws it would subvert and raises doubt as to whether it should longer be regarded as a constitutionally recognized political movement.

The announcement was a pointed invitation to the Japanese government to outlaw the Communist Party. It was not an occupation forces directive, but it left no doubt in anyone's mind what SCAP wanted. The days of good feelings and friendly fellowship were at an end. The cautious prime minister, however, was not eager to stick his neck out. Though he gave General MacArthur's press release customary lip service, he made no overt move against the communists.

Impatient with Japanese reticence to act, SCAP moved directly against the Communist Party. It sent out Dr. Walter C. Eells, an employee of the Civil Information and Education Section, on a one-man campaign against communists in universities and colleges. This was a sudden, unprecedented departure from past occupation policy. Up until the Eells campaign, it had been the accepted procedure for SCAP officials to advise university administrators, professors, and students on educational matters, but Americans customarily avoided politics. Though many officials, of course, spoke out in private against communism, Dr. Eells was the first SCAP emissary to launch a public anticommunist crusade. The reaction at the universities was violent. When he appeared on the platform at Tōhoku University in northeastern Japan, communist-led students raised such a howl that his lecture had to be canceled. This was the first time that a Japanese audience demonstrated directly against someone from SCAP. In Tōkyō, we were shocked. Dr. Eells made additional attempts to address other university groups, but his appearances were greeted with increasing violence and disorder. Finally, when President Nambara of Tōkyō University joined the students protesting that "[Dr. Eells' views] do not, in some respects, harmonize with the national circumstances of Japan," the harassed doctor was sent home. The Japanese educators, it would appear, had imbibed so deeply the theory of American democracy that our effort to crush communism in the country was momentarily frustrated by their devotion to our teachings.

On May 30, 1950, events took a new turn. Thousands of Japanese gathered in what was announced as a "People's Rally" on the Imperial Palace Plaza, in full view of the Dai Ichi Building, General MacArthur's GHQ. The rally was called to protest alleged repression of people's rights by the Japanese government. Coming out of the Dai Ichi at noon, I was amazed at the mass of people milling about on the plaza. Enjoying the beautiful day, I crossed the street and walked among the throng. It was a typical Japanese gathering, packed with thousands of young people, mostly students, interspersed with working men and women and the idle curious who were always attracted by such an event. The people were friendly, and as far as I could see, the crowd was orderly. Here and there, small groups were assembled listening to individual speakers who seemed to be answering questions mostly. A few policemen stood quietly observing the crowd.

Suddenly, near some low trees, there was a violent movement in the mass of people. The group seemed to pack in upon itself, then burst like agitated ants. Stones began to fly. I saw the Japanese police rush in. I thought I saw an American captain and two enlisted men join the police as they moved into the mob, but I may have been wrong. It is possible that the Japanese police were trying to rescue the Americans from the mob.

I recall at that time asking my Japanese friend, "What the hell are all the Americans doing there?" He didn't bother to answer but was yelling and pulling at me. "This is bad, Colonel. Let's get out of here." I didn't have to be urged. This was the first time I had seen a Japanese crowd directly attack Americans. I later learned that the mob threw one of the soldiers into the palace moat and the other two were mauled.

This rough affair created great excitement at the Dai Ichi Building. I was later told that the "People's Rally" was communist-organized, and the sudden riot against the Japanese and the Americans was communist-inspired.

SCAP obviously could not tolerate this affront. Seven days after the gathering on the Imperial Palace Plaza, General MacArthur directed the Japanese government to purge the 221 executive members of the Communist Party Central Committee. The newspapers headlined the event, featuring General MacArthur as the man who knocked the "brains" out of the Communist Party.

Meanwhile the third major offensive of our "total diplomacy," which was directed at destroying Russian prestige and influence in Japan, was progressing rapidly toward a successful conclusion.

When the war in the Pacific ended, the powers that fought Japan established in Tōkyō an international body known as the Allied Council for Japan. Although the authority of the council was vague, its general purpose was to serve as an advisory council for the Allied supreme commander. It was intended that the council would consult with and help General MacArthur to administer the country, and the council met from time to time, but since SCAP was an American general commanding what essentially was an American occupation headquarters, the council had little influence or impact on the administration of Japan.

The Soviet Union was represented on the council by Lieutenant General Kuzma Derevyanko, who had about fifty Russians on his staff. The offensive to drive the Russians out of Tōkyō was undertaken at the highest level. General Derevyanko found himself under increasing attack from both American and Australian representatives. In every conceivable way, the Russian representatives were shown that they were not welcome in the country. Rumors began to circulate that since Japan was under American occupation anyway, there was no reason to have the Soviet Union tell us how to govern the country, and the Allied Council was to be discontinued. Council meetings became infrequent and finally ceased altogether. The Soviet Union's representatives, always isolated, now lost their reason for being in Japan. On May 28, 1950, without any previous warning, about a month before the North Korean invasion was launched, General Derevyanko and forty-six members of his staff sailed for Russia with their wives and children. The walkout was never explained. In the Western press, the departure was hailed as a great defeat in the Far East for the Russians.

Thus, by early June 1950, only a few weeks before the North Koreans drove south into Seoul, the United States, working closely with the Japanese government, struck three major blows against Soviet prestige in Japan. First, the Russians were rudely shut out of negotiations for an Allied peace treaty with Japan. Second, General MacArthur decapitated the Soviet-sponsored Japan Communist Party. And third, the Soviet representatives on the Allied Council for Japan were literally driven out of the country. American firmness and power had been clearly demonstrated.

No one can criticize the actions taken. What is bothersome, in retrospect, is that we failed to anticipate any reaction from the other side, or if we did, we failed to do anything about their capabilities. We seemed to be enthralled with our own huge successes. Actually, we should have recognized that the Soviet Union could not take these blows to its national prestige and influence in the Far East, no more than we could have weathered similar defeats. Our counterintelligence agencies should have been especially alert, for international power responds to the same laws of action and reaction as any other human behavior.

What is even more significant is that we failed to understand that international reaction is motivated by self-serving interests and is contained only by power adequate for the situation. Although our actions in Japan had been bold and decisive, we lacked the power needed to contain the Soviet capability for reaction in the Far East.

What were the capabilities of our military forces in Japan? The Pacific War had ended five years before. The Japanese people and government had turned out to be pliable, responsive, and remarkably friendly. For American officers and noncommissiond officers (NCOs), and particularly their families, life in Japan was comfortable. For the soldiers, most of whom were youngsters, entertainment and women were cheap. There was much emphasis on saluting, but military training was not exacting; the men and their officers enjoyed the name and life of *occupationnaires*, a kind of governmental tourists with extended visas in the pleasant clime of Japan.

There were good reasons for this softness. In occupied Japan, soldiering was not a premium. There were other very important tasks assigned to the Army. To begin with, many of our military personnel were helping the Japanese people recover from a devastating war and were carrying out the democratic reforms America was introducing. Our officers and soldiers were engaged in such governmental activities as surveillance of the land reform program, distribution of rice and fish from the farms and fishing villages to the large cities where food was in short supply, and surveillance of tax collection. All these programs were important not only to Japan but to the United States, for America had to supply Japan with about 15 percent of its food requirements, and delinquent Japanese taxes meant that the United States would have to balance the Japanese budget with American dollars.

As a consequence, our officers and soldiers became more government officials than military fighters. The organized Army units also found it difficult to train because Japan is a land of rugged mountains, and where the terrain permits military training, the land is intensely cultivated. What had been firing ranges and training areas before the war were now farmlands. In addition, because Japan was not suitable for classical armor operations, a decision had been made not to assign tanks to its defense. Accordingly, when Korea exploded, we had no armor in the Far East. All these factors tended to produce in Japan an American Army of barracks soldiers.

General MacArthur, as the supreme commander, was lord of all he surveyed. Only incidentally was he responsible for the supervision of the Far East military force as its overall commander. In the five years of the occupation, MacArthur had mellowed and now lived the life of a retired gentleman soldier, more interested in keeping Prime Minister Shigeru Yoshida in power than in maintaining the efficiency of his divisions. The great white conqueror had isolated himself completely, living in the spacious American Embassy Chancery and working in his Dai Ichi Building. For years prior to the Korean War, he had disassociated himself from his men. No one knew for sure whether General MacArthur had ever inspected the troops outside of his capital city.

For the Japanese, General MacArthur was the symbol of authority. He filled an emotional void that had been created when the emperor was put in mothballs by our forces. At a time when it was unlawful for the Japanese people to display their national flag, MacArthur was a good substitute. They petitioned him for their rice rations, gratefully accepted his benevolent constitution, marveled at his dignified utterances, paid homage to him each day as he entered and departed from the Dai Ichi Building, and honored him with presents of the most elegant grasshoppers in the land.[2]

The following story about General MacArthur may have more truth than humor. A new arrival from the United States was being oriented by one of the old Japan hands. They were in a village one day observing the operations of the newly organized agricultural cooperative. The recently arrived American, admiring the wonders of the occupation, asked his more experienced associate what the farmers thought of MacArthur. "Let's ask one of them," answered the old hand. Turning to a Japanese in the rice paddy, he asked the graybeard what he thought of the supreme commander for Allied powers. The man listened intently as the interpreter framed the question, then after a long, thoughtful silence he answered very seriously, "The emperor picked a good man to run Japan."

Our military weakness was especially transparent in Tōkyō. On June 19, I attended a military review held on the Imperial Palace Plaza in honor of Secretary of Defense Johnson. A special reviewing platform had been constructed for the secretary, military staff, and distinguished guests. I don't believe I have ever witnessed such a galaxy of stars as flashed on that day in the Tōkyō sun. In the place of honor was Mr. Johnson and next to him was General MacArthur, with General Bradley, chairman of the Joint Chiefs.

The Tōkyō newspapers called the affair a "gigantic military review." They must have been referring to the squads of generals on the reviewing stand. Personally, I was shocked by the stark reality of our military weakness in the Far East. For it was obvious that the GHQ had scraped the bottom of the military barrel from the environs of Tōkyō to assemble a conglomeration of 12,000 "troopers" from the Army, Navy, Marines, Air Force, and WACs, or Women's Army Corp. It was a pathetic picture, sadly demonstrating the depth to which our military position in the Far East had degenerated. If Johnson, as a civilian secretary, could not recognize our inadequacy on that day, surely General MacArthur and General Bradley, both distinguished soldiers, knew that we were playing world power politics with inadequate military capabilities.

Socially, the review was a huge success. American ladies sitting in the stands on the left of the secretary's platform sighed with deep emotion as they admired the elegance of General MacArthur. And he looked magnificent, head high, chin up, blanketing a huge shadow over Secretary Johnson, General Bradley, and the lesser generals who crowded the reviewing stand.

It is doubtful, however, that the "gigantic military review" impressed the Russians. If they could have been as blinded by our military elegance as were our ladies and national leaders, everyone would have been much better off. But on the eve of the Korean aggression, we had been fooling ourselves so long and so effectively that we believed our own propaganda. The dollar had become so much of a symbol of power in the United States that we believed it could buy anything in the world, even the defeat of international communism. Glibly, we talked of loans and military aid to Taiwan, Korea, and Japan. At the same time at home, we were cutting our own military forces. Like the Romans, we were going to buy mercenaries to fight for us, or so we thought.

In June 1950, the newspapers were proclaiming that in the forthcoming meeting with Secretary Johnson and General Bradley, General MacArthur would unfold his program for securing Japan, Taiwan, South Korea, and all of Southeast Asia. According to the press, MacArthur's plan was a great bargain. He had found a way for the whole of Southeast Asia to be "bolstered by US aid at low cost." The American public and the free world were also pleased to learn, one week before the communists' attack, that MacArthur was reassuring his distinguished visitors in Tōkyō that "South Korea is being effectively buttressed against Communist assault and subversion by American support of the Syngman Rhee regime."

Everything was rosy. No one questioned reality. Our great public figures guaranteed our security. It was a small wonder then that only a few days before the communists marched into South Korea, peacemaker Dulles should glare defiantly across the 38th parallel, while Chairman Bradley should relax in the Tōkyō Army Exchange Store examining a fishing pole.

To all outward appearances, by the middle of June, our "total diplomacy" in Japan had been a resounding success. The Communist Party had been decapitated. Russians had been driven out of the country. And a decision had been made to sign a unilateral peace treaty with the Western Allies. We had been tough, and the Soviet position in the Far East had been sorely rocked. Yet the situation was loaded with danger because our hard line rested on a pathetically soft military capability. Although no one seemed to be concerned, reaction from the communist world was inevitable and only a question of time. The counterattack in Korea caught us unbalanced and unprepared. It will be the same every time we act from our emotions rather than reason and when our commitments are beyond our military capability.

CHAPTER THREE
BASIC PLAN

At the time the Korean tragedy exploded upon the world, I had completed two and a half years' duty in Japan, serving in various military government assignments throughout the country. Two months before the communist attack, I had come to Tōkyō as executive officer to Major General Whitfield P. Shepard, then chief of the Civil Affairs Section, at General MacArthur's headquarters. It was a pleasant assignment, especially desirable as my wife and two children were comfortably located in a Western-style Japanese house on the outskirts of beautiful Meiji Park, a fifteen-minute drive from the office.

By early July, however, as the first understrength battalions of the 24th Infantry Division were flown from southern Japan onto the Korean Peninsula, the tempo at the Dai Ichi Building, MacArthur's GHQ in Tōkyō, reached fever pitch. The war struck hard and furiously. Each day more and more of my friends disappeared from their usual jobs, without a word of good-bye. A few days later, I would read about them in the official reports, making history in Korea, or filling a space on the casualty list.

The Korean War caught MacArthur's headquarters completely by surprise. A makeshift staff, known as Republic of Korea (ROK) Headquarters, was hurriedly thrown together at the Dai Ichi Building to direct the war against the communists. Officers for this small command headquarters came from various sections in GHQ. Many continued to work in their primary assignments, running the war on a part-time basis in addition to their other duties. It was fortunate that this stopgap arrangement continued only for a few weeks because for some of the officers the dual responsibilities became a nightmare.

General Shepard, my boss during this hectic period, became deputy chief of staff of ROK Headquarters and worked round the clock. He was on the job sixteen hours a day, seven days a week, without the benefit of time-and-a-half pay. Meanwhile, General MacArthur was making headlines in all the newspapers. His majestic, "We go!" as he climbed on board his plane and set out for Korea bordered on comic opera except for the tragic seriousness that gripped those of us who wondered how many would have to follow.

Conferences at the Big House, as the Dai Ichi Building was called, were practically continuous, with General Shepard assuming a more and more secretive role. This was unusually disconcerting as he habitually discussed his problems with me.

On July 9, the telephone rang and when I answered, Major General W. A. Biedelinder, the G-1 (Personnel) GHQ, wanted to talk to Shepard. I buzzed the general and in accordance with our operating procedure remained on the phone listening.

"Say, Shep," General Biedelinder began, "we want your exec [executive officer] to command a regiment in Korea. Will you make him available?"

I could hardly believe my ears. Command a regiment in Korea! I had been hoping for such an assignment for days. There was a long silence, so characteristic of a Shepard reaction, and then he finally answered, "I'll be over to talk with you in a little while."

I hung up the phone and waited. I knew that General Shepard was aware that I had been listening, but he hardly stirred in his office; the place remained quiet as a tomb. After fifteen minutes of this cat-and-mouse game, I could stand the suspense no longer. I walked into his office and said, "General, I want to go to Korea."

No answer.

"General," I began again. "I don't want to seem ungrateful, but this is my chance to command a regiment."

He cocked his head to one side, as was his habit, then, fixing me with a cold gray stare, he said, "You're not going. I need you here."

His reaction made no sense to me. Anyone could do my job, but to command a regiment—that was a job for a soldier. But my arguments were as effective as ramming one's head against a concrete wall. I have never worked for a more stubborn man. Finally, as he got up to leave, he gave me slight hope. "I will talk to you after I see Biedelinder."

In about an hour, he returned from his talk with G-1, and as he walked past my desk, he motioned for me to follow him into his office. "Close the door and sit down," he ordered.

I obeyed, my pulse beating wildly. As I sat down in a chair facing him, the general clasped his hands and with great seriousness began. "Frank, I know how much you want to command a regiment, but you are not going to Korea. I cannot let you go because you and I have a big job to do here in Japan. I have been designated by General MacArthur to organize the National Police Reserve [NPR], a Japanese security force of 75,000 men with four divisions. This is the beginning of the Japanese army. You are going to be my chief of staff, so forget Korea."

While my head wheeled as I tried to assimilate the implications of what General Shepard had just said, he reached into his briefcase and pulled out a top secret document. "This," he said, handing the document over to me, "is the Basic Plan. I want you to read it over and over until you know every sentence by heart."

Then, while I thumbed through the Basic Plan that was to be the bible for the new Japanese military force, General Shepard continued, "The situation not only in Korea but here in Japan is serious. Our four divisions now stationed on these islands are all going to Korea. In a few weeks, except for the Air Force and a few Army Service troops, there will be no Americans left in Japan. We have a job to organize and train four Japanese divisions to take the place of the Americans. As you know," he went on, "there are a quarter of a million American dependents, women, and children in Japan."

I don't know rightly what I answered. My whole attention was concentrated on the Basic Plan, and I began to read hurriedly, trying impatiently to grasp the whole picture. When I finished reading, there were a million questions racing through my mind. As I looked up, General Shepard smiled and asked, "And now, what do you think?"

"This is tremendous, General," I answered. Then, realizing the honor that my boss had extended by selecting me as his chief of staff, I mumbled inadequately, "General, I'm honored with the assignment."

As quitting time approached that afternoon, there was consternation and confusion in the Civil Affairs Section, to which I belonged. We had our first top secret paper to secure overnight, and we had no adequate safe for the purpose. I consulted my assistant, Lieutenant Colonel Wellington Glover, but when I showed him the "Top Secret" label on the Basic Plan his eyes popped. His assistance at that moment consisted of helping me to worry, which he did sympathetically. Finally, our administrative officer, Chief Warrant Officer John W. A. O'Brien, a calm, solid soldier, came to our rescue, suggesting we deposit the document in the security room of the chief of staff at the Dai Ichi Building. Relieved by this suggestion, Colonel Glover and I strapped pistols on and, viewing everyone we passed with suspicious stares, walked hurriedly the several blocks to the Dai Ichi with the Basic Plan securely locked in a briefcase, and the briefcase in my left hand, closely watched by my assistant.

At the Dai Ichi, I handed the document to the security sergeant, who glanced at it with such a complete lack of reverence that I hesitated to leave it in his care.

"Oh, it's the Basic Plan," he said disdainfully.

"Yes," I answered, almost adding, "shh, not so loud."

As we left the Dai Ichi, Colonel Glover finally gathered sufficient courage to ask, "Say, Boss, what's in that paper anyway?"

"Sorry," I answered very seriously, "can't tell ya, but it's hot."

Months later, when Glover and I handled thousands of top secret papers in the front office of the Advisory Group, we enjoyed many laughs as we recalled that hectic day when the Civil Affairs Section received its first top secret paper. I've often noted how deeply concerned everyone behaves when initially given classified information or documents and how blasé many become when security is an everyday matter.

Under usual circumstances, organizing a military force in the face of a raging war would have demanded most stringent security measures, but in Japan we were faced with the requirements of not only keeping the enemy in the dark but keeping our friends from knowing what we were doing. The Japanese constitution prohibited maintenance of any kind of military force. The nation had renounced war and war potential forever. Accordingly, we could not initially even tell the Japanese officers that the NPR (or Kokka Keisatsu Yobitai) was to be the army of Japan.

Because Japan was prohibited by the constitution from establishing an army, General MacArthur undertook the rearmament of Japan under the pretext of international authority. It had been agreed at Potsdam by the Allies that Japan could have a maximum of 200,000 police officers to maintain law and order. These, of course, were intended to be police and in no sense Army, Navy, or Air

Force troops. Under this agreement, SCAP had authorized the Japanese to organize municipal police forces and National Rural Police (Kokka Chihō Keisatsu). MacArthur restricted the strength of these organizations to a total of 95,000 municipal police officers, serving in Tōkyō, Ōsaka, and other major cities and towns of Japan, and 30,000 police officers in the National Rural Police. The latter were organized and administered on a national basis and served throughout the country in villages and rural areas in units varying from four or five officers to several squads in locality. This gave Japan a total of 125,000 police officers, leaving 75,000 vacancies authorized under Potsdam.

As the supreme commander for Allied powers, General MacArthur accordingly had the authority to expand the police force of Japan by 75,000. This he did in a letter he dispatched on July 8, 1950, to Prime Minister Yoshida directing the Japanese government "to establish a national police reserve of 75,000 men." Note the rhetorical reasoning and the esoteric justification for augmenting police forces in a democratic society:

TOKYO, JAPAN
8 JULY 1950

Dear Mr. Prime Minister:

In my keeping with my established policy to re-invest autonomous authority in the Japanese Government as rapidly as the situation permits, I have visualized the progressive development of law enforcing agencies adequate to the maintenance of internal security and order and the safeguard of Japan's coastline against unlawful immigration and smuggling.

By letter of September 16, 1947, I approved the recommendation of the Japanese Government for an increase in the overall strength of Japan's police force to 125,000 men, making provisions for a new national rural police force of 30,000 men. It was then the view of the government, in which I fully concurred, that the strength recommended and authorized was not an arbitrary determination of future police requirements but designated to provide an adequate force around which might be built a modern and democratic police system oriented to an effective decentralization of the police responsibility in harmony with the constitutional principle of local autonomy.

Subsequent action in the recruitment, equipping and training of the police force then authorized has proceeded with commendable efficiency. The concept of autonomous responsibility has been faithfully observed, essential coordination has been carefully developed and the proper relationship between the police and private citizenry has been progressively forged. As a consequence, the Japanese people today may take justifiable pride in this agency for the enforcement of law at all levels of government. Indeed, it may be credited to both organizational police efficiency and the law-abiding character of the Japanese people that, despite a much lower police strength in relation to population here than is to be found in most of the other democratic states and the general post-war impoverishment and other adverse conditions usually conductive to lawlessness, Japan stands out with a calmness and serenity which lends emphasis to violence, confusion and disorder which exist in other nearby lands.

To insure that this favorable condition will continue unchallenged by lawless minorities, here as elsewhere committed to the subversion of the due process of law and assaults of opportunity against the peace and public welfare, I believe that the police system has reached that degree of efficiency in organization and training which will permit its augmentation to a strength which will bring it within the limits experience has shown to be essential to the safeguard of public welfare in a democratic society.

Insofar as maritime safety in the harbors and coastal waters of Japan is concerned, the Maritime Safety Board has achieved highly satisfactory results, but events disclose that safeguards of the long Japanese coastal line against unlawful immigration and smuggling activity requires employment of a larger force under this agency than is presently provided for by law.

Accordingly, I authorize your government to take the necessary measures to establish a national police reserve of 75,000 men and expand the existing authorized strength of the personnel serving under the Maritime Safety Board by an additional 8,000. The current year's operating cost of these increments to existing agencies may be made available from funds previously allocated in the General Account of the National Budget toward retirement of the public debt. The appropriate sections of the Headquarters will be available, heretofore, to advise and assist in the technical aspects of these measures.

Very Sincerely,
DOUGLAS MACARTHUR

MR. SHIGERU YOSHIDA
PRIME MINISTER OF JAPAN,
TOKYO

It is indeed an anomaly that General MacArthur, the man who liquidated the Japanese militarists and wrote the constitution prohibiting the nation forever from maintaining military forces, should, in this fashion, order the rearmament of Japan.

Years later, the Japanese would argue about the inadequacies of the NPR as a military organization. Their military personnel, especially, would take great delight in blaming their politicians and civilian officials who initially staffed the headquarters of the force for failing to understand the basic requirements for a military establishment. What they all forgot is that the Japanese did not initiate the rearmament of their nation and that the constitution even today prohibits military force. Japan has an Army, Navy, and Air Force now only because General MacArthur, assuming international authority, expanded the police forces of the nation.

MacArthur's plan for the National Police Reserve initially envisioned a paramilitary force that could be later expanded into an army of four infantry divisions. In the surreptitious approach that had to be adopted, it was essential that in the beginning this force operate within the apparent limits of Allied agreements and the pseudo-legality of the new Japanese constitution. Proceeding with great caution, the planners decided the new force would be progressively equipped. The character of the organization, the caliber of the weapons, and the nature of the equipment were to be dependent on the receptivity of the Japanese people and the international situation. Obviously, it was to be a calculated, creeping rearmament tuned to the will of the Japanese public and the Allied reaction. Thus, from its inception, the NPR existed in the extremely uncomfortable twilight zone of questionable legality. As a result, during the initial phases of the organization, American military advisers with the NPR had to talk from both sides of their mouths, and the Japanese leaders of the force, except for a few who were in the know, were bewildered. One division commander, a former police chief, was genuinely disappointed when his units received M-1 rifles instead of police billy clubs.

The original plan provided for a national headquarters, two corps or intermediate headquarters, a service force, and four regions or divisions. Each region was to be patterned after a U.S. infantry division. But because the original planners had to provide a maximum number of divisions out of the 75,000 total, the strength of an NPR region was pared to 15,200, about 3,000 fewer soldiers than a United States division at that time, which required ruthless emasculation of some of the divisional units. The NPR infantry, with four rifle companies and a strength of 1,000 soldiers, was a compromise between the U.S. infantry battalion and the extinct Imperial Japanese battalion. Everyone in the force was to be armed initially with a carbine as rapidly as possible (the Japanese public and Allied opinion permitting), with individual and organic weapons and equipment added as they became available.

Significantly, the new security force was to serve as the direct instrument under the immediate control of the prime minister. As a national force, it was to be organized, equipped, and trained in such a way as to ensure immediate commitment in the event of an emergency. To enhance its character as a reserve, the force was to be independent of the National Rural Police force and municipal police, maintaining a separate and distinct entity.

Initially there was considerable discussion at GHQ as to which American agency should organize, train, and control the NPR. Customarily, in organizing a foreign military force, we utilized military advisory groups. Faced with an illegal rearmament, though, we could not do this in Japan. Three agencies were nevertheless considered: the G-2 (Intelligence) Section GHQ, the G-3 (Operations) Section GHQ, and the Civil Affairs Section. The Intelligence Section, under its forceful and melodramatic chief, Major General Charles A. Willoughby, who was MacArthur's principal historian and special confidant, exercised control over all Japanese police forces and wanted the NPR in its special domain. General Willoughby had been uniquely successful in organizing these forces and was prepared, as I shall discuss later, to rearm Japan rapidly and efficiently. Precisely for this eventuality, he had gathered under his control in the Japanese Demobilization Bureau an outstanding staff of former Japanese generals, admirals, and colonels. But General Willoughby had two powerful antagonists in GHQ, the G-3 Section, which was professionally opposed to Willoughby's empire building, and Brigadier General Courtney S. Whitney, MacArthur's chief of the Government Section, ghostwriter, aide extraordinaire, and bosom luncheon companion. Moreover, for reasons of military cover, it was highly desirable to place the new organization in what might be considered a government-oriented agency. The supervision of the NPR, accordingly, fell to Major General Shepard as chief of the Civil Affairs Section. Willoughby retained control of the initial recruiting for the force and shared with Whitney the power of screening and approving the top Japanese leaders.

In a directive issued July 14, 1950, Major General Shepard was designated the general officer responsible for the development and control of the National

Police Reserve and was authorized to communicate directly with agencies of the Japanese government on all matters pertaining to the NPR. In American channels, under the cover of Civil Affairs, he was directed to establish a military advisory and control staff to provide guidance to the Japanese government concerning the organization, equipment, training, and control of the force. In this same directive, the G-2, through its Public Safety Division, was given responsibility for furnishing guidance on matters related to recruitment, and the G-3 was responsible for providing guidance on initial deployment and subsequent utilization of the force.

One of the most difficult problems that had to be faced was the question of who would be eligible to serve in the force. This immediately raised the issue of whether career military officers and others that had been purged should be excluded from the NPR. The advantages of using experienced military leaders in the NPR were apparent to all concerned. The former military leaders of Japan, however, had been purged in accordance with Allied international agreements, and their use in the NPR not only would have been a flagrant violation of the announced policy of the supreme commander for Allied powers, but would have caused serious repercussions in the Western world at a time when the United States was making every effort to lead the United Nations against aggression in Korea. Furthermore, though many of the former militarists and their supporters favored inclusion of career officers and those purged in the NPR, the Japanese people as a whole were deeply concerned about the clause in the constitution outlawing war. Moreover, they generally opposed rearmament and feared the use of ex-career officers in the NPR. The Japanese government, of course, recognized the practical handicap of organizing a paramilitary force without qualified leaders, but it was deeply concerned about the views of the Philippines, Australia, and other nations. Under the circumstances, it preferred to wait for reactions to the steps it was taking. Accordingly, in the initial plan it was decided that all those purged and all career officers of the Japanese Imperial Army, Navy, and Air Force would be excluded from the NPR. Nevertheless, despite the decision, the problem plagued all of us who worked with the force, and as I will show in a succeeding chapter, it caused a serious strain within the GHQ staff and created a fissure that spread to the Japanese.

While General Shepard rushed from one conference room to another, my special mission as the chief of staff was to find and select the key American personnel for the organization. As Korea had a top priority for personnel, my initial reaction was to seize all the best officers then assigned to the Civil Affairs Section, but Major General Shepard, retaining responsibility for both organizations, would not permit me to rob the parent unit. I managed, after much pleading, to obtain his concurrence to the assignment of Lieutenant Colonel William M. Albergotti, a field artillery officer, as G-3 of the new advisory and control group. The selection of Albergotti was a happy choice that neither Shepard nor I ever regretted. Albergotti was at that time serving as chief of the Education Division of the Civil Affairs Section. A solid citizen, mature, painstaking, tactful with determination, Lieutenant Colonel Albergotti turned in an outstanding performance in a critical assignment, accomplishing his mission with a minimum of fanfare. Cooperative and sincere in his operations with the Japanese, he laid the foundation for an understanding and mutual trust that remained for years. Master Sergeant Clifton E. Ratcliff was the second individual I succeeded in wrangling from the Civil Affairs Section. He became the top soldier of our organization. As my personal assistant, Sergeant Ratcliff played a varied role in the Advisory Group, exerting an influence on Major General Shepard, the staff, and the Japanese headquarters that far extended his rank. Working twelve and fourteen hours a day, seven days a week, Shepard, Ratcliff, and I became close personal friends. We argued with one another, even yelled at each other at times, but we were all loyal to the job, and Ratcliff and I had a high regard for our commander.

The other key individuals of the initial staff were assigned to the group by the Far East G-1 and included Colonel Charles E. Knowlton, Adjutant General, who became our G-1; Lieutenant Colonel Harold R. Weetman, our G-4; and Lieutenant Colonel Paul A. Freyereisen, the comptroller. These were the men who initiated the rearmament of the nation. Other officers and noncommissioned officers were added to the staff as they became available.

In addition to selecting the key members of our staff, our major task was to find a suitable office space for the national headquarters of the new force and for the American staff that would be required as advisers. After considering several possible locations in Tōkyō, G-1 GHQ resolved our worries by making available for our use the buildings of the former Japanese Tōkyō Maritime Training School.[1] The U.S. 7th Cavalry Regiment, part of the 1st Cavalry Division, moved into these facilities after the surrender and had since then enjoyed a most desirable location and home away from home. Now they were moving. When Major General Shepard and I visited the installation on July 15, the troops were loading into trucks and jeeps, preparing to embark for Korea. They were tired, unhappy-looking soldiers, loaded with packs and equipment, bidding good-bye to their friends and families. It was difficult to realize at that time that these "Tōkyō Commandos" of the 1st Infantry Division were to become heroes of Korea.

On July 21, we took over the barracks vacated by the 7th Cavalry Regiment, and Sergeant Ratcliff announced that the Civil Affairs Section Annex (CASA), the cover name for our Advisory Group, was operational.

Meanwhile, on July 18, a joint American-Japanese conference was held in Tōkyō to determine several basic operational policies. The conference was attended by Mr. Katsuo Okazaki, cabinet secretary of the Japanese government who was later to become the first foreign minister of an independent, democratic Japan; Mr. Takeo Ōhashi, the attorney general of Japan; Major General Shepard; and Colonel Howard E. Pulliam, chief of the Public Safety Division, SCAP. The conference attendees discussed and reached working agreements regarding the administrative and operational control of the force, recruiting responsibilities of the various agencies involved, and arrangements for financing the NPR. Although General MacArthur had directed the prime minister to establish the NPR, no action could be taken until the Japanese government promulgated a national ordinance. Until such an ordinance was issued, there could be no legal basis for the organization. We, of course, were eager to get moving, and both General Shepard and Colonel Pulliam pressed for an immediate governmental program. Mr. Okazaki, however, objected strenuously, pointing out that the Diet was in session and that even though the prime minister's party would support the government, the Socialists in the Diet were strong enough to raise a violent rumpus. Accordingly, he urged that the ordinance be delayed until after August 3, the date on which the Diet planned to adjourn. Though our forces were hard-pressed in Korea, and Japan remained unprotected against communist attack and subversion, Prime Minister Yoshida refused to be rushed. He resisted all American urgings until the Diet adjourned. Finally, on August 10, 1950, with the Diet adjourned, Yoshida's cabinet promulgated Cabinet Order No. 260, establishing the National Police Reserve.

The cabinet order, when issued, was a masterpiece of evasion and chicanery. No one could begin to suspect that the innocent words of Article I were intended to initiate the rearmament of Japan. This article states, "The purpose of this Cabinet Order is to establish the National Police Reserve and to provide for the organization thereof . . . for the purpose of supplementing the strength of the National Rural Police and Local Autonomous Police Force to the extent necessary to maintain peace and order within the country and to guarantee the public welfare."

Given the conditions as they were in the summer of 1950, one can excuse the cabinet order as the only method the Japanese government had to comply with a SCAP directive. Japan was, after all, still an occupied country; sovereignty rested in the supreme commander for the Allied powers. Until Japan could secure a peace treaty, it could be argued that the authority of the occupying powers superseded the constitution of Japan, but that argument is sophistry.

Traditionally the constitution of a nation is a sacred document. Where it may be expedient to sidestep unpopular laws, the constitution is self-correcting through the process of amendments. Accordingly, the rearmament of Japan, undertaken as it was in the face of constitutional prohibitions, raises some awkward legal questions and stirs fundamental queries.

CHAPTER FOUR
CONSTITUTION BANS WAR

Why did Japan adopt a constitution banning war, military forces, and war potential? And faced with such a constitution, why did those in power not amend the constitution to permit legal rearmament of the nation? The answers to these questions are rooted in history.

Article 9 of the Japanese constitution, which was ratified in 1946 and went into effect in 1947, renounces war, bans war potential, and prohibits the maintenance of land, sea, and air forces. Its purpose could not have been clearer if it had been one of the Ten Commandments. But because its provisions have created formidable obstacles to rearmament and have raised difficulties for U.S.-Japan security arrangements, the article has been a source of continual embarrassment to American policy makers and Japanese government leaders.

In later years, both governments tried to disavow responsibility for the disarmament clause. On the American side, documents were released to support the argument that no one in the United States really intended that Japan should be permanently disarmed. Successive conservative governments in Japan, on the other hand, maintained that the no-war, no-arms clause did not mean at all what it said, and in any case a nation has an inherent right to self-defense. But, as we shall see, if the constitution does not mean what Article 9 says, then its framers were careless or they went to a lot of trouble to create stumbling blocks in other unrelated articles of the constitution to make it difficult to maintain viable military forces under its provisions.

Those who argue that it is a mystery how the provisions of Article 9 got into the constitution cite two American documents issued within a few months of the surrender of Japan. In the first of these, Secretary of State James F. Byrnes, on October 17, 1945, in secret instructions to Mr. George C. Atcheson Jr.,[1] General MacArthur's political adviser, directed in part that the future Japanese constitution may or may not provide for an emperor, but if the emperor was retained, the constitution should include a safeguard that "any ministers for armed forces which may be permitted in the future should be civilians and all special privileges of direct access to the throne by the military shall be eliminated."

The second of these two documents, a subsequent fourteen-page policy paper titled "Reform of the Japanese Governmental System," adopted on January 7, 1946, by the State-War-Navy Coordination Committee (SWNCC),[2] contained views similar to the instructions Secretary Byrnes sent to Atcheson. The SWNCC policy paper was sent to General MacArthur for his information. It provided the following:

> Although "The Ultimate Reform of the Government of Japan" is to be determined by the "freely expressed will of the Japanese people," the Allies . . . as a part of their overall program for the demilitarization of Japan, are fully empowered to insist that Japanese basic law be so altered as to provide that in practice the government is responsible to the people, and that the civil is supreme over the military branch of the government.

SWNCC further elaborated:

> Although the authority and influence of the military in Japan's governmental structure will presumably disappear with the abolition of the Japanese Armed Forces, formal action permanently subordinating the Military Services to the Civil Government by requiring that the Minister of State of the members of the Cabinet must, in all cases, be civilians would be advisable.

From the above two cited documents, it would appear that neither Secretary Byrnes nor the SWNCC contemplated any need for a disarmament provision in the Japanese constitution. If this was the intention of the U.S. government, then why was the controversial provision inserted in the constitution? The answer is that there were at the same time other directives and other forces at play in the United States and Japan.

On August 29, 1945, the U.S. government issued its Initial Postsurrender Policy for Japan. In this document, the supreme commander for the Allied powers was given clear and specific guidance on the basic program for the occupation and subsequent rehabilitation of the country. The policy directive in part declared,

> Japan will be completely disarmed and demilitarized. The authority of the militarists and the influence of militarism will be totally eliminated from her political, economic and social life. Institutions expressing the spirit of militarism and aggression will be vigorously suppressed. Japan is not to have any Army, Navy, Air Force, Secret Police organization or any Civil Aviation.

The instructions were specific and clear and formed the basis for an unrelenting program designed to uproot every vestige of militarism in Japan. All regular career officers of the Imperial Army and Navy were purged. The highest military policy makers were executed as war criminals, and most significant, all propaganda agencies of the occupation forces and the Japanese government were concentrated on an inspired peace campaign within the country. The national slogan became "peace based on justice and order."

In October 1945, General MacArthur directed Prince Naruhiko Higashikuni, an uncle of the emperor who served as prime minister immediately following the surrender, to revise the constitution of the nation in line with occupation forces' policy announcements. Prince Higashikuni selected Prince Fumimaro Konoe, a former prime minister, to take the lead in democratizing the constitution. Prince Konoe and his advisers held several conferences with Mr. Atcheson and other State Department officials in Japan. Before Konoe could reduce his views to writing, though, the Higashikuni government fell and General MacArthur directed Mr. Atcheson to cease negotiations with Konoe. The Konoe recommendations, which were reported to the throne, contemplated eventual rearmament and subordination of the military to the civil elements of the government. SCAP announced that it was not sponsoring Prince Konoe's recommendations and his proposals had no impact on the constitution.

About the middle of October 1945, after Baron Kijurō Shidehara became prime minister, General MacArthur again issued instructions to the Japanese government to reform the constitution. Baron Shidehara promptly appointed state minister Jōji Matsumoto to head a group known as the Constitutional Problem Investigation Committee to determine whether or not the constitution needed to be revised and if so to what extent.[3]

After several months' delay, during which time it became evident that the Japanese were making little progress on their new constitution, General MacArthur called Prime Minister Shidehara into a conference on January 21, 1946. The men talked privately for two hours. General MacArthur, in the following account of the meeting reported in the May 8, 1951, edition of *U.S. News and World Report*, endeavors to show how the idea of Article 9 was born at this conference:

> The Japanese people, more than any other people in the world, understand what an atomic warfare means. It wasn't academic with them. They counted their dead and buried them. They, of their own volition, wrote into their Constitution a provision outlawing war. When their Prime Minister came to me, Mr. Shidehara, and said, "I have long contemplated and believed," and he was a very wise man—he died recently—"long contemplated and believed that the only solution to this problem is to do away with war." He said, "with great reluctance I advance the subject to you, as a military man, because I am convinced that you would not accept it, but," he said, "I would like to endeavor in the constitution we are drawing up, to put in such a provision." And I couldn't help getting up and shaking hands with the old man, and telling him that I thought it was one of the most constructive steps that could possibly have been taken. I told him that it was quite possible that the world would mock him—this is a debunking age, as you would know—that they would not accept it. That it would take great moral stamina to go through with it, and in the end they might not be able to hold the line, but I encouraged him and they wrote that provision in. And if there was any one provision in that Constitution which appealed to the popular sentiment of the people of Japan, it was that provision.

Baron Shidehara was later quoted on numerous occasions to have said that he originated the constitutional ban on war. Dr. Matsumoto, however, has maintained that Baron Shidehara claimed he originated the "no war" provision as a fiction and that the Japanese constitution was actually written by his cabinet. In a letter to Dr. Kenzō Takayanagi, chairman of the Japanese Commission on the Constitution,[4] on December 15, 1958, General MacArthur confirmed that the prime minister proposed inserting a provision in the constitution banning war, but he left in doubt the question of who was responsible for including the provision outlawing military forces.

After his conversation with General MacArthur, Baron Shidehara called a series of cabinet meetings to discuss Dr. Matsumoto's proposals for a new constitution. During these deliberations, it seems that the prime minister failed to acquaint the cabinet with the substance of his conference with the supreme commander. In any case, though Baron Shidehara may have favored a disarmament clause for the constitution, he did not suggest such a provision to his colleagues. Matsumoto's draft, which later was presented to SCAP and was leaked to the *Mainichi Shimbun*, did exactly the opposite. It clung tenaciously to the past and tried to preserve as much as possible of the traditional views. Interpreting his instruction broadly, Dr. Matsumoto essentially produced simply a revision of the Meiji constitution and not in any sense a drastic one. The draft contained, among other proposals, a provision that the emperor should retain "supreme command of the Armed Forces." The draft was accompanied by an "explanation" that included a statement hopefully leaving the door open for eventual rearmament. This statement in part suggested that "Even if the time should arrive, when, upon the completion of the Allied Occupation, Japan is permitted to rearm, the Armed Forces would be of very limited scope such as one necessary for the maintenance of peace and order in the country. However, the nation on its own part should have no intention of having any Army or Navy such as it had before."

Though the emperor in the Matsumoto draft retained supreme command of the military, the constitutional revisions incorporated adequate controls so that the military could not in the future establish independence or precedence over civilian authority. It would seem, then, that the Matsumoto draft satisfied the requirements of the secret instructions the secretary of state had sent to General MacArthur's political adviser and the views of the SWNCC policy paper sent to the supreme commander for his information. If the United States did not desire the Japanese government to outlaw war and renounce having armed forces, but only to ensure that in the future the military was controlled by civilian authority, the Matsumoto draft was a satisfactory basic document.

Events that followed the publication of the Matsumoto proposals in the *Mainichi Shimbun* clearly demonstrate that the occupation forces were thoroughly dissatisfied with the Japanese revision effort. Following strong press criticism, on February 1 SCAP Headquarters requested early action from the cabinet on its proposals. It was February 8, however, before Dr. Matsumoto presented his draft to the SCAP Government Section. Impatient with the Japanese maneuvers and acting apparently on the newspaper version, General MacArthur decided that the cabinet had failed to meet the requirements of the Potsdam Declaration. He ordered Brigadier General Courtney Whitney, head of his Government Section, to write a new constitution as a guide for the Shidehara cabinet. Emphasizing his views on total Japanese disarmament, General MacArthur, in a short note on February 3, five days before the Matsumoto draft arrived at SCAP, directed General Whitney that the constitution include a provision as follows:

> War as a sovereign right of the nation is abolished. Japan renounces it as an instrument for settling its disputes and even for preserving its own security. It relies on the higher ideals which are now stirring the world for its defense and protection. No Japanese Army, Navy, or Air Force will ever be authorized and no rights of belligerency will ever be conferred upon any Japanese Force.

There certainly was no question what the supreme commander wanted in the new Japanese constitution. If the views of the U.S. government were different from those of its commander in Japan, those views never modified General MacArthur's instructions. His personal note was changed somewhat by his staff so that when the draft of the new constitution was completed by the Government Section, Chapter 11 read,

> RENUNCIATION OF WAR
> Article VIII. War as a sovereign right of the nation is abolished. The threat or use of force is forever renounced as a means of settling disputes with any other nation.
> No Army, Navy, Air Force, or other war potential will ever be authorized and no rights of belligerency will ever be conferred upon the State.

On February 13, General Whitney carried the American-drafted constitution to the members of the cabinet. He advised the Japanese government that Dr. Matsumoto's proposals were completely and totally unacceptable. Moreover, he made it clear that the supreme commander wanted the Japanese to use the American draft as a guide in writing the new constitution. The Japanese were shocked. They fought the American document article by article.

The opposition rallied around the leadership of Shigeru Yoshida, who at the time was foreign minister in the Shidehara cabinet. Yoshida was determined to salvage as much as possible of the Meiji constitution, arguing that it should be revised rather than discarded in favor of a completely new document. As the debate on the Japanese side continued, Baron Shidehara apparently was convinced that there was no hope for compromise. Yoshida disagreed. Finally, Shidehara and Yoshida approached SCAP trying to revive the Matsumoto draft. General MacArthur was adamant. The stalemate on the Japanese side is said to have been finally cracked by Emperor Hirohito, who personally urged Shidehara and Yoshida to accept the principles laid down by the occupation forces.

On March 6, 1946, a slightly revised version of the American draft was adopted by the Shidehara cabinet and presented to the Japanese people. General MacArthur gave the document his "full approval," lauding Article 9 (previously Article 8 in the American draft) with the statement, "By this undertaking and commitment Japan surrenders rights inherent in her own sovereignty and renders her future security and very survival subject to the good faith and justice of the peace loving peoples of the world."

During the discussion in the Diet, there was deep concern regarding the meaning of Article 9. Members wanted to know whether Japan by this provision was, in fact, renouncing the inherent right to self-defense and was banning armed forces even for self-defense. Yoshida, who in the meantime had become prime minister, responded on June 26, 1946, to these questions in the Diet as follows:

> The provision of this draft concerning the renunciation of war does not directly deny the right of self-defense. However, since Paragraph 2 of Article 9 does not recognize any military force whatsoever or the rights of belligerency of the state, both wars arising from the right of self-defense and the rights of belligerence have been renounced. The recent war was largely fought in the name of self-defense . . . one of the serious

suspicions or misunderstandings about Japan today is that Japan may endanger world peace by rearming and fighting a war of revenge at any moment. I believe that the first thing that we must do today is to correct this misunderstanding before anything else.

In this statement, Prime Minister Yoshida made it clear that the official position of the Japanese government was that Article 9 prohibited rearmament even for self-defense. Nevertheless, Hitoshi Ashida, chairman of the House of Representatives Committee on Constitutional Reform (Shūgiin Kenpō Kaisei Iinkai), proposed two amendments (shown in italics below) to the clause renouncing war, changing Article 9 to read:

Aspiring sincerely to an international peace based on justice and order, the Japanese people, forever, renounce war as a sovereign right of the nation, or the threat or use of force, as a means of settling disputes with other nations.

In order to accomplish the aim of the preceding paragraph, land, sea, and air forces, as well as other war potential, will never be maintained. The right of belligerency of the state will not be recognized.

It is interesting to note that the amendments were taken to SCAP for clearance. General Whitney discussed the implications of Ashida's changes with his staff and was aware that the new phrase might be interpreted to mean that in the future Japan could establish a self-defense force. He nevertheless approved the amendment. Five years later, Ashida claimed that it was his intent precisely to modify Article 9 so as to permit self-defense forces in the future. If that in fact was his intent, he never publicized his views during the six-month debate that went on in the Diet. Moreover, Prime Minister Yoshida consistently held the position that the maintenance of armed forces, even for self-defense, was denied by Article 9.

After the most searching deliberations in the Diet and extensive discussions in the press, the House of Representatives passed the new constitution on October 7, 1946, and the House of Councillors (Upper House) passed it on October 29, 1946. The constitution was promulgated on Emperor Meiji's birthday, November 3, to go into effect six months later on May 3, 1947.

There is no doubt that the Japanese resisted their constitution. They did not want it. It was forced upon them by the supreme commander over their most serious objections. When Dr. Matsumoto tried to include a loophole that would permit limited rearmament at a future date, presumably after a peace treaty, General MacArthur personally stepped in to direct that "no Japanese Army, Navy, or Air Force will ever be authorized." The idealism engendered by this forced feeding crumbled when Japan regained a measure of its independence.

For several years after the constitution was adopted, it was the well-publicized view of the United States and the Japanese government that Japan could not rearm. Article 9 was uniformly accepted as a prohibition against rearmament. This view of course was shattered in 1950 when American occupation forces moved from Japan to Korea. Faced with a completely disarmed Japan, General MacArthur ordered Prime Minister Yoshida to organize, equip, and train a so-called National Police Reserve. Through American channels he directed our military to organize, train, and deploy a Japanese military force of four infantry divisions. This force would in time be armed with rifles, machine guns, mortars, tanks, artillery, rockets, and aircraft.

The attempt to justify such an organization and such armament in the face of the legal prohibitions of the constitution and the legislative record made during the 1946 debates in the Diet was pure sophistry. I had a difficult time trying to keep up with the sleight of hand that the Japanese judges, officials, and people employed to make Article 9 disappear, but as far as the Americans were concerned, no one gave the Japanese constitution a moment's thought. General MacArthur's noble experiment of 1946 went up in a puff of smoke in the war environment of 1950.

While the successive conservative governments passed through several deplorable stages trying to justify the legality of the new military forces, initially contending that the NPR was not an army, later arguing that in the modern world a nation that did not have nuclear weapons did not possess armed forces, and finally maintaining that Japan possessed the inherent right to defend itself, the opposition political parties insisted nonetheless that the constitution was being violated. Following the establishment of the NPR and the stationing of American military forces in Japan after the peace treaty, numerous attempts were made to bring the constitutional questions to courts. In March of 1959, at the height of controversy over the revision of the security treaty, the Tōkyō District Court ruled that the establishment of American bases in Japan was unconstitutional. Our forces nevertheless remained in Japan and in December the Japanese Supreme Court reversed the decision of the Tōkyō District Court, ruling that having American military forces stationed in Japan did not violate the constitution. On the question of the constitutionality of the Japanese military forces, there were no definitive findings until 1961, when the Japanese Supreme Court ruled that a nation possesses the inherent right to defend itself against attack. These decisions, however, have been unacceptable to a large segment of people, and the opposition parties continue to resist expansion of the armed forces and the stationing of American troops in Japan.

In addition to Article 9, there are two other articles in the constitution that posed and still present serious legal obstacles to any rearmament program. These are:

> Article 18. No person shall be held in bondage of any kind. Involuntary servitude except for punishment of crimes is prohibited.
>
> Article 76. The whole Judiciary power is vested in a Supreme Court and in such inferior courts as are established by law.
>
> No extraordinary tribunal shall be established, nor shall any organ or agency of the Executive be given judicial powers.
>
> All judges shall be independent in the exercise of their conscience and shall be bound by this Constitution and the laws.

Article 18 prohibits involuntary servitude. This is interpreted to mean that there can be no compulsory service in the armed forces. There can be no draft or universal military service. Even in an emergency or war, no one can be drafted into the military forces. Up until recent times, though there have been some problems, the Japanese have experienced no critical difficulties in recruiting for the limited forces the country maintains. What will happen if there are not enough volunteers to fill the future military requirements is anyone's guess. It is difficult to believe, however, that a nation of 100 million people can indefinitely continue under a constitutional restriction that prohibits a draft in time of war.

Even more important is Article 76. This article is interpreted to mean that the Japanese military establishment cannot have a court-martial system. At the time we organized the NPR and up to the present, armed forces personnel were subject only to civil courts. In the days of the NPR, the most serious action that could be taken against a man for a military offense was to give him administrative discharge. Yet I was amazed to find the NPR soldiers, in the performance of the most demanding tasks, to be efficient, effective, and as disciplined as any troops I served with. Nevertheless, the Japanese army, navy, and air force, today known as the Ground Self-Defense Force, Maritime Self-Defense Force, and Air Self-Defense Force respectively, are the only military forces that I know of in the world to exist without court-martial authority. It is inconceivable that this situation would be tolerated in the event of a national emergency.

Why then wasn't something done during all these years to amend the constitution? The answer is simple arithmetic. The successive governments of Japan have not had the votes in the Diet to change the constitution.

To amend the constitution of Japan requires, as a first step, a two-thirds vote in both houses of the Diet. The revision must then face a referendum. In 1950, and since that time, the government party on various occasions has had sufficient strength in the House of Representatives to muster a two-thirds vote. In the House of Councillors, however, the Socialist Party, together with various splinter parties, have maintained enough strength to block any government effort to change the constitution. And so, in recent years, a balance has been struck in the Diet that permits the nation to maintain military forces despite constitutional obstacles while the opposition prevents all attempts to correct the conditions that engender the obstacles.

Human behavior, however, adjusts rapidly to strange twists and turns. Initially, when we began equipping the NPR in 1950, everyone cautiously tried to limit the nature and caliber of weapons, anxious to avoid accusations of rearmament. Today, the Japanese forces are equipped with the most modern conventional weapons and munitions available in a bristling world. In the future, unless the people, fearing retaliation, object at the ballot boxes, the government can be expected to accept American nuclear and even biological weapons. Article 9 has been so completely disregarded that the Japanese governments have behaved as though the no-war, no-arms clause never existed.

On the other hand, Articles 18 and 76, which have had a most critical impact on the composition and discipline of the military forces, are obeyed as though they were hewed in stone. And so while Article 9 was relegated to the ash can, the other two articles have remained sacrosanct from the time the NPR was organized.

The three articles examined above have had a traumatic impact on Japan, its people, and the military forces we initiated with the establishment of the NPR. Article 9 stifled our initial organization and training efforts, while Articles 18 and 76 have warped and crippled these military forces in their development. But who knows how damaging has been the hurt to the inner soul of a people who have been forced to trample upon national idealism, grinding their constitution underfoot? And who knows how severely justice has been twisted by a nation's judges floundering to find a way to give their army, navy, and air force constitutional validity?

Japan has moved through history in strange and erratic ways. It may again in time find its rightful place in the sun. In the recent past, it has gone through critical extremes. Rising from an idyllic slumber in the middle of the nineteenth century, it burst upon the world three decades ago in full-blown militarism. Defeated in the Pacific War, the people accepted, indifferently at first, then with conviction, an idealistic constitution, dedicated to world peace, forsaking war and renouncing armed forces and military potential forever. Then, once again under our prodding, the nation turned its back on its noble aspirations, marching over its constitution into an uncertain and confused future. In retrospect one wonders, why did we have to play God with these people?

CHAPTER FIVE

YOSHIDA'S VIEWS

After the cabinet order establishing the NPR had been duly promulgated, Major General Shepard and the key members of our staff were invited to a dinner given by Prime Minister Yoshida at his official residence in Tōkyō.

As I rode in the Army sedan that afternoon with the general, I was acutely conscious of the historical significance of the occasion. Japan was being rearmed. We were to be artisans, or, more correctly, the midwives at the birth of a new military force in the world. The prime minister of a great nation had invited us to meet him and get acquainted with the top leaders of his government. As the men of two nations whom fate had selected to build the new military forces of Japan, we would be looking each other over very carefully. The talk would be subdued, but what was said then by the Japanese I knew would become the fundamental policy of Japan on rearmament. I wondered what Yoshida would have to say.

The descendants of the immortal *tennō* were helplessly caught in the furious crosscurrents of history. After a tragic and catastrophic war, Japan was being reshaped politically, socially, and economically by a foreign power. And now, with the eruption in Korea, destiny dictated that Japan should once again have a military force. As though playing a huge joke, though, destiny arranged that this force was to be organized, trained, and deployed by a Yankee general, a colonel whose parents had been born in Poland, an operations officer of Italian blood, a comptroller of German ancestry, and others who only a few days before had seen Japan for the first time. The samurai in their ancient graves must be whirling, I thought, at this turn of events.

The prime minister and the leaders of this proud and dignified people could only hope that these conquerors possessed the ability and the skill to build something worthwhile. If we did not, then the Japanese people could only pray that the holy spirit of sun goddess Amaterasu visited upon the ancestors of these sacred islands could not be destroyed. After we had left, the future leaders of Japan could correct everything else if American military tutelage did not corrupt the flame of patriotism and devotion to country that burned in the hearts of the people of Japan.

For my part, I was a little sad that Japan was to be rearmed. Whatever were the forces that motivated America to write a Japanese constitution banning war forever, I viewed the effort as a noble human goal. A nation of 90 million people had renounced war and all war potential. Humanity, or at least a considerable segment of it, seemed to have taken a crucial turn away from violence as a way of settling international controversy. Man, here in the East, appeared to be genuinely trying to fashion himself in the Christian image of God. Now that noble human aspiration was to be crushed. A "Great Lie" was unfolding in which America would join and in which I would personally join. A "Great Lie" that would declare to the world that the Japanese constitution did not mean what it said. A "Great Lie" that soldiers, guns, tanks, cannon, rockets, and airplanes were not war potential. The written constitution of a nation, perhaps the greatest political achievement of mankind, was to be dishonored and trampled upon by the United States and Japan. For the constitution of Japan, which America inspired, clearly prohibits a military establishment and outlaws war and all war potential forever.

As I rode along that day, I wondered what might have been the situation in the world if the North Koreans had not marched south, if Japan had remained, say for a decade, a living nation without a military force. Could it have remained without armaments for as long as ten years? I don't know. Who can tell what might have happened had America accepted General MacArthur's recommendation in 1946 to place Japan under a United Nations mandate?

As the situation developed in 1950, with the United States committed to a ground war on the Asian mainland, national self-interest necessitated the rearmament of Japan and excused, in our minds at least, any violence that we contemplated to the constitution of another nation.

The die is cast, I said to myself. If Japan was destined to be rearmed, it was perhaps best that we should be the ones to control the rearmament. If we tried hard enough, we might at least be able to build a democratic military force, dedicated to the people and subject to the control of the representatives of the people. One thing was certain: it was important that we carefully tend this new military sprout to make sure that the roots got a good start. Someone once said, "As the twig is planted, so grows the tree."

"I wonder," I said aloud to myself.

"What did you say?" asked General Shepard, roused from his own inner thoughts.

"Nothing, General. I was just wondering what kind of an army we're going to build."

"That's a good question," he answered.

We had arrived at the prime minister's residence, and I followed General Shepard into the reception room. Prime Minister Yoshida, his round little body clad in a black kimono and his feet relaxing in white *tabi*, came forward a few steps to greet us with a warm, gracious smile.[1] I studied Yoshida for a moment. I found that I liked him. Even in his quaint traditional Japanese attire, he seemed to be a regular fellow. As I bent forward in the low bow, I noted that he had a pleasant, roundish face and that his eyes twinkled with a friendly alertness. I had the feeling that I was seeing a man poured in a dual mold—a jolly little Japanese Santa Claus, sans whiskers, and a stubborn, efficient business executive. I muttered something about being honored to meet him, and his eyes gave me their full air of attention for a moment. He clasped my hand in his and turned to meet Colonel Albergotti, who was following me. I moved on to be introduced to four members of Yoshida's cabinet, each minister dressed in a dark, Western-style business suit and each looking efficiently pleasant.

Presently, I found myself with an interpreter and the minister of justice, Takeo Ōhashi, in the prime minister's beautiful little garden. As I openly admired the inspiring handiwork of the skillful Japanese partnership with nature, Mr. Ōhashi was telling the exciting story of the historic assassination of a previous prime minister in this quiet garden.[2] I knew that tragic story of how the militarist cut down a prime minister for the glory of Japan, but hearing it from the justice minister here in the cool shadows of the prime minister's garden, I fully expected at any moment to see the historic characters once again live through their roles.

Then, for some stupid reason, probably self-conscious of my Army uniform, I laughed and nervously blurted out, "Well, anyway, Yoshida-san has nothing to fear from us; we're not Japanese militarists."

Mr. Ōhashi looked at me quite awkwardly, and I didn't blame him. I heard the interpreter translating. "No, that's right, but there are still many militarists in Japan," replied the justice minister, and he appeared deeply concerned.

Shortly we sat down to an excellent American-style dinner, reinforced with some fine wine. I was seated across and one chair over from the prime minister. Although it's always difficult to talk through an interpreter, conversation in two languages at the dinner table, by its very nature, makes one feel especially inadequate and uncomfortable at times. As I talked to the prime minister, for example, he nonchalantly carried on with his soup. When I finished my comments, I would turn to my soup. Then, while the interpreter translated in my place, Mr. Yoshida, the other guests, and I would continue with our meals. Finally, the prime minister would say, "Ah, so," and he would look up to smile at me. If he was more inclined to talk than to suck at his soup, he would push his bowl aside and deliver himself of his views. At such time, I didn't see how I could stroke soup while the prime minister talked, so I would courteously and attentively sit at ease. When the prime minister stopped talking and the interpreter took over, I felt that I could return to my meal. Maybe I was wrong. As the maneuvers went on, I had an opportunity to look around the table. I noted that Major General Shepard and our staff members would stop all operations while the prime minister talked. This slowed the dinner considerably and was especially difficult for the interpreter. By the time the main course arrived, the comments by all were short and punctuated with long intervals of silence. Blessed by this learning process, the dinner went much faster.

In my military assignments throughout Japan, I had become too keenly aware of Yoshida to have any illusions about the prime minister. Fundamentally a bureaucrat, Yoshida, in most respects, was a conservative. Now sitting near the prime minister, I reflected on the man and his emergence to power.[3]

He was the product of the occupation of Japan. Under our policy of indirect rule in which Americans administered the nation and promulgated our revolutionary changes through the Japanese government, the bureaucracy of the country became indispensable. Moreover, with the military and the presurrender politicians purged by the occupation forces, the bureaucrats had an open field in politics and in the administration of the nation. A purge had precipitated Yoshida into the prime minister's chair. Most of the new leaders of Japan, like Kijurō Shidehara, Hitoshi Ashida, and Mamoru Shigemitsu, had been former government officials and not politicians. Astute and ingratiating, these men and hundreds of other bureaucrats had formed strong personal links in the controlling sections of SCAP Headquarters. The Americans, for their part, dependent on the government and its bureaucracy, supported their "opposite numbers" not only in their official duties but in their personal ambitions. Yoshida did not suffer from the embrace of the supreme commander.

I had been privileged, however, to observe the attitudes of too many layers of the Japanese bureaucracy at the city, prefectural, and national levels to entertain any ideas that the governmental structure of Japan was giving most of our reform programs more than a polite acquiescence. I sensed the farmers, labor leaders, teachers, students, and intellectuals generally appreciated our efforts, but precisely because these segments of Japanese society were motivated to action by American ideas, the bureaucrats were fearful of our innovations. Certainly no one would accuse Yoshida of any enthusiasm for SCAP directives that decentralized control of the police forces, emasculated the powerful Ministry of Education, encouraged the formation of democratic school boards, and stimulated, guided, and protected the development of a strong trade union movement. I make these observations not particularly to be critical of the Japanese bureaucracy and the politicians it projected into power, for there was normal opposition in Japan to our programs and the bureaucracy was only especially adroit in its surreptitious resistance. What I am suggesting is that it was much easier for Americans to show the Japanese people how their misguided and badly informed leadership led them into a disastrous war than to design corrective methods and new institutions acceptable to the aspirations of a foreign culture. That which fitted and worked satisfactorily in America did not necessarily fit and produce desirable results in Japan. One would have to be blind to not have recognized that many of the American-conceived programs were an anathema to the prime minister and the former government of officials who dominated the conservatives in 1950.

Yoshida was a son of a wealthy family named Takeuchi, whose influence and power was deeply rooted in the politics of the Meiji revival. He was a devout royalist, totally committed to the throne. The emperor may have been used for evil in the past by militarists, but the imperial institution remained for Yoshida the central core on which the destiny of Japan rested. In common with the custom of many Japanese, Shigeru became the adoptive son of Kenzō Yoshida, an influential businessman and silk manufacturer. Yoshida's future career was even more enhanced when he married in 1909 the daughter of Count Nobuaki Makino, who became foreign minister in 1913 and imperial Houshold Minister in 1921.

Having attended Tōkyō Imperial University, the training school for all future government officials, Yoshida advanced steadily through the imperial diplomatic ranks. He served in China and Rome, and finally became ambassador to the Court of St. James. Essentially a diplomat with strong connections in political and business circles, Yoshida in the presurrender period was concerned chiefly with international affairs. Nevertheless, in 1936, when Prime Minister Kōki Hirota, who incidentally was a prominent member of the Black Dragon Society, was forming a new cabinet, he offered the foreign minister post to Yoshida, who at the time was considered a liberal. Yoshida accepted and was in the process of helping the prime minister select members for his cabinet when the army protested his appointment so furiously that Hirota was forced to drop him. The "Sakan," or field grade of officers of the Army General Staff, had not forgiven Yoshida for his 1932 report estimating that the staffs of the foreign and naval ministries were unanimously agreed that "the Army should be restrained." Moreover in the eyes of the militarists, Yoshida was too enamored with the British to be considered a safe risk for high imperial office.

Serving as president of the Japan-British Society at the time of the outbreak of war in Europe, Yoshida felt compelled to go into virtual retirement. He was not so immobilized as to be completely inactive, however, for after the attack on Pearl Harbor, he managed to do himself inestimable good by smuggling to the interned American ambassador, Joseph C. Grew, his regrets over the war. He further qualified himself for acceptance by the occupation forces by being imprisoned for the last three months of the Pacific War for advocating peace negotiations through British channels.

In the early days of the Japanese rearmament, Yoshida remained a firm antimilitarist. He personally supervised the screening of all officer candidates for the new military forces. It is extremely doubtful that many militarists of the former Imperial Army and Navy slipped into the NPR and the organization into which it evolved.

When the supreme commander for Allied powers occupied Japan, Yoshida was brought into the government as head of the Foreign Ministry, and as previously discussed, he played an important role in the writing and final acceptance of the constitution in Japan. His opportunity fell upon him by accident. Ichirō Hatoyama, former minister and politician, having formed a successful party of conservatives, was elected to the Diet and was virtually assured of being named prime minister. But in a sudden switch of events, Hatoyama was purged by the occupation forces, and Yoshida was propelled into the prime minister's office.

The 1949 elections, however, which I observed closely, were no accident. The Japanese electorate, which in previous elections had voted for the middle parties, in 1949 became polarized, with large segments of the population attracted to the extremes on the right and left. While the Japan Communist Party gained strong support throughout the country, Yoshida was re-elected with a heavy conservative vote. He continued in power, promising to take a strong hand, in cooperation with the United States, against internal subversion and foreign communist pressure.

With the dinner over, Yoshida sat back and began to puff on his cigar. Presently he got up, and we all moved away from the table to sit down in some comfortable chairs in another room. I was fortunate to find a chair near the prime minister. He began talking quietly. He was obviously eager to impress all of us with the importance of the great program upon which we were jointly embarking. He was warm in his appreciation of General MacArthur for authorizing and directing the establishment of the NPR. He said that now that the American forces had departed Japan for Korea, Japan was a military vacuum. As prime minister, he was deeply concerned about the security of his country. He was glad that America permitted his nation to organize a police reserve, which he could use to support the police forces of the country. No government, he said, is worthy of the name if it does not have the means to maintain law and order. The NPR would give his government that power.

I was favorably impressed by the prime minister and listened intently. The Korean War was going badly for us in those early months, and I wondered what the head of the Japanese government thought of the military action on the mainland. Waiting for a break, I interjected, "Mr. Prime Minister, how do you judge the Korean War to be going?"

His response was direct and forceful. "It is a police action," he said disdainfully. "The North Korean armies are coolie armies. They will be smashed by General MacArthur. As soon as you get some troops, tanks, and airplanes over there, the North Koreans will run like sheep."

I had only that day talked with one of our infantry battalion commanders who had been wounded and evacuated from Korea a few weeks before. The battalion commander was not as enthusiastic about our capabilities as was the Japanese prime minister, and I could not help but wonder who was right. I thought I sensed too much disdain for the Koreans in the prime minister's voice, and later, as the Koreans continued to push our forces more tightly into the Pusan perimeter, I wondered whether Yoshida had not been unduly biased by his past experiences in Korea, Manchuria, and China. The Japanese army must have regarded the armies they fought on the Asian continent as "gooks" or coolies, very much as our own people tended to think of all Asians as "gooks."

My attention was drawn to the prime minister again as he continued to talk: "I am very happy that Japan can now show the United States that we are your friends. The Japanese people will show you their gratitude for your fine work in Japan. You will see. We will be your good friends."

"Will you send the NPR, Mr. Prime Minister, to help us in Korea?" I asked with a mischievous smile. I glanced at General Shepard. He was furious.

"The NPR will never go to Korea," answered the prime minister without a moment's hesitation. The finality with which he answered my deliberate query rang with such positive conviction and sincerity that in the months ahead I never built up false hopes, as did other Americans, about the employment of Japanese forces in Korea. Then, very quietly, the prime minister began to unfold his basic views about the NPR and Japanese rearmament. "You must understand," he said,

> my government is in a very difficult situation. We cannot rearm Japan at this time. The obstacles to rearmament are most difficult. We certainly cannot send the NPR to fight in Korea. To begin with, Japan has a constitution which bans all war potential. If you read your recent history, you have found that I did not want to go so far in the constitution. I was overruled by the Allied powers, and so we have a constitution that prohibits rearmament. It will not be easy to amend the constitution because that requires a two-thirds vote in both houses of the Diet. The opposition, mainly the Socialists, as you may know, holds more than one-third of the seats in the House of Councillors. They will not support my government on rearmament. I think it is also important to recognize that the people of Japan are not ready for rearmament. The occupation has done its job well. You have disarmed us actually and spiritually. You have turned the people not only against militarists but against everything military. You will recall that for a while you even took the pistols away from our police. Moreover, you have given the women the right to vote. They

are more than 50 percent of the population, and they are against war and rearmament. You have read of our women marching into our stores and destroying our war toys. It will take a lot of hard work to re-educate the Japanese people. It is also a fact that Japan is a poor country. Our economy is just beginning to revive. We cannot finance rearmament. No, gentlemen, Japan cannot rearm. I am grateful, however, that the occupation forces have permitted Japan to organize and deploy a police reserve. This will provide a force for our international security. We will be able to defend Japan against subversion from within, and, if you do your job well and my people do theirs well, we may in time develop a force which will be able to defend Japan from attack from without. This must be a slow, gradual process, moving step by step. But most important we must educate our people on the need for such a force.

Basically, in 1950 Yoshida was convinced that what he considered to be agrarian Russians were no match for the technologically advanced, highly industrialized Americans. He further regarded Red Chinese military power as composed of primitive coolie armies. Under these circumstances, he concluded that neither the Soviet Union nor Red Chinese nor a combination of both would dare to confront the United States in direct combat. Under the protective American umbrella, therefore, there was no need for any hurried rearmament in Japan.

Moreover, Yoshida was very much aware of the deep-rooted suspicions with which Japan was regarded in Australia, New Zealand, the Philippines, and other Southeast Asian countries at that time. He preferred to adopt the helpless behavior of an aggrieved Mahatma Gandhi. At the same time, he knew that if he publicly showed a reluctance to rearm, he would tend to quiet any fears that Red China or the Soviet Union might entertain about Japanese military resurgence. The friendship of a politically neutral India, with whom a profitable trade was just opening, also had to be cautiously cultivated.

On the other hand, there was severe opposition to the caution and reticence of the prime minister. Many of our people were laboring under the illusion of American omnipotence. Many thought that all we had to do was to order the Japanese to fight in Korea. In part this view of omnipotence stemmed from the conqueror concept that some of our military leaders assumed on occupying the Japanese islands. This was a natural pose that fighting troops assume upon crushing an enemy, but in the pleasant, agreeable occupation environment among an acquiescent, yielding population, even our American ladies and dependent children regarded themselves as great conquerors. The Japanese were always treated courteously by Americans, of course, but from a superior position. We were the Great Occupying Power.

I remember an American Corps commander in his farewell speech at a large social gathering on the eve of his departure from Japan for the United States. He was haranguing the officers of his command and their ladies gathered to bid him good-bye that they should never forget that "we are the conquerors." He concluded, "We're too soft on these damn gooks anyway."

A few days earlier, I had seen this man give a most revolting exhibition of the "conqueror concept." I was in an automobile following his sedan through a "downtown" street of a large city packed with Japanese vehicles, handcarts, streetcars, and pedestrians. I watched in horror as his car plowed through the mass of humanity, equipment, and animals. Then the inevitable happened: the sedan rammed into the rear of a stalled Japanese streetcar. I stopped my automobile as the general jumped out, followed by two aides. His face was livid red; he rushed forward to the front of the streetcar. As Japanese scattered in all directions, the American general caught the diminutive Japanese streetcar motorman by the neck and shoulders and began to shake him as a terrier might shake a small animal. Then, with a flood of obscenity, he threw the little fellow to the street. This was American omnipotence at its naked worst, but there were many smaller barons in the occupation forces who were convinced that all we had to do was command or lash out and 90 million Japanese would jump.

The Japanese militarists, who considered the Korean War as a grand opportunity for their own ambitions, similarly found Yoshida's views inadequate. Although they were unable to come out publicly because they had been purged, they nevertheless conducted an aggressive underground campaign trying to stir those in government to launch an all-out rearmament. One of their most potent arguments was raising the specter of communist takeover. With the Americans committed to leave Japan for Korea, the militarists and their allies cried for immediate rearmament of Japan with troops who had not so long ago served in the Imperial forces.

Prime Minister Yoshida, however, had a genuine horror of the military. During the war, he had been arrested and kept under close surveillance by the militarists and their thought police, and he had not forgotten the experience. He was not eager to take them into partnership now that he was head of the government.

The Korean War might have been sent "by the grace of heaven" for Japan, but Yoshida knew he had to move slowly, carefully, and intelligently. When he received General MacArthur's letter directing the initial rearmament of the nation, he made his decision. No matter how much pressure our commanders or diplomats tried to exert on him, Yoshida never wavered from his decision. He neither expanded the NPR nor accepted a single weapon for the force until he was satisfied that it was politically and diplomatically safe for Japan to take the next step forward on a gradual, quiet, unruffled, and deliberate march back to her appointed place in the sun. It is not without reason that his political colleagues had named him "One Man" Yoshida, as he called the shots and made his own decisions.

Yoshida's views together with the Basic Plan became the guiding policy for our Advisory Group in rearming Japan.

CHAPTER SIX

STRUGGLE FOR CONTROL

The decision to exclude former military officers from the NPR was not an easy one to make. The new forces needed men with military experience, and there were thousands of former officers of the Imperial Army and Navy who were eager to serve in the new organization. Many Americans and Japanese thought that under the conditions of national emergency, it was stupid not to use them. But the world had not yet recovered from the terror of Nazi and Japanese militarism, and only a few of the most rabid American militarists dared to embrace the recently disgraced military men of Japan.

One of the first acts of the occupation forces in Japan was to demobilize the military forces of that nation. Having crushed and disbanded the Japanese military, SCAP then directed that no career military officer would be permitted in any position in the public life of the nation. This action was taken in accordance with the terms of surrender for Japan agreed upon at Potsdam and announced by the heads of the governments of the United States, Great Britain, and China. In part, these terms demanded that "there must be eliminated for all time the authority and the influence of those who have deceived and misled the people of Japan into embarking on world conquest, for we insist that a new order of peace, security and justice will be impossible until irresponsible militarism is driven from the world."

Our government firmly supported this worldview, and in August 1945 in the Initial Postsurrender Policy for Japan, General MacArthur was instructed as follows:

> High officials of the Japanese Imperial General Headquarters and General Staff, other high military and naval officials of the Japanese Government, leaders of ultranationalist and militarist organizations and other important exponents of militarism and aggression will be taken into custody and held for future disposition. . . . Former career military and naval officers, both commissioned and non-commissioned, and all other exponents of militarism and ultranationalism shall be excluded from supervisory and teaching positions.

Though Potsdam inspired the purge, the policy was a revolutionary blessing to the Japanese people. Without the purge, there could have been no reforms. It was the purge that enabled the people of Japan to get rid of the entrenched leadership that had carried the nation into war and destruction. It was the purge that permitted the country to take its first steps on the road to democracy. Unshackled from the stifling control of the parochial militarists, Japan responded enthusiastically to the social, political, economic, and governmental changes that the American occupation introduced. Swept up in this revolutionary spirit, there were few in Japan pressing for the return of the leaders of the old order. Neither the people nor the government wanted the military back. Prime Minister Yoshida and his cabinet were, of course, fully aware of the desirability of using experienced former officers in the NPR, but they were not prepared to precipitate a public debate on the issue.

Since the prime concern of GHQ was to organize and deploy a Japanese force as soon as practical to fill the military void created by the departure of American divisions for Korea, those in the Dai Ichi Building were not eager to get into a hassle with the Joint Chiefs or the State Department about changing the purge directives. General MacArthur and his chiefs accordingly accepted the purge policy as an inconvenience, but not a block to building a Japanese force. It was generally agreed that by using Americans in top leadership positions, a satisfactory initial organization could be established. With one notable exception, General MacArthur's staff recognized the advisability of putting off to the future inclusion of former military leaders in the National Police Reserve.

The uncompromising exception was the irrepressible Major General Willoughby, MacArthur's intelligence chief. Completely out of sympathy with announced policy, Willoughby was determined from the beginning to bring former

Imperial career officers into the NPR—purge or no purge. Neither opposition from the staff nor hints from General MacArthur himself seemed to deter Willoughby. Initially the elements of his G-2 Section worked in the open, trying to convince everyone concerned that the new force could not be organized without the purged Imperial officers. When these efforts failed, pressure operations went underground. As the resistance continued, I was amazed to find to what extremes a group of influential, determined, thoroughly dedicated staff officers in an American military headquarters were capable of going to circumvent their government's directives and even international agreements. Prewar Japan was not the only example of self-righteous military officers demonstrating that they knew better than anyone what was good for their country.

It cannot be denied that from a military point of view, General Willoughby's position was unassailable. It was logical. An effective military force, he contended, could not be organized, trained, deployed, and commanded by civilians. A military establishment required professionals, people with military training, and experienced career officers.

General Willoughby argued that since the purge eliminated practically all former officers of the Imperial services, except a few lieutenants and captains, the purge had to go. If we limited the leadership of the NPR to these inexperienced and untried junior officers and inducted civilians, we could hope for nothing better for months to come than a conglomerate of ineffective small units. In the face of the deteriorating situation in Korea and the need for an immediate force able to defend Japan, he considered the decision to continue the purge a fatal mistake. In his opinion, the situation called for drastic action. There was no time to wait for a gradual buildup. The situation demanded the recall to the service of Japan the best-qualified military leaders in the nation. There were thousands of them, courageous, dedicated men eager and ready to serve in the new force. General Willoughby knew exactly where to find them because he had carefully planned and prepared for such an eventuality as the one that now faced the Far East Command in Japan.

There are those in this country today who look upon General Willoughby as a rightist and extremist. General MacArthur is quoted as having called him "my lovable fascist," and indeed after his retirement from the army, General Willoughby became the adviser to Franco of Spain. My generation of army officers, however, knew General Willoughby best as an instructor of military history at the infantry school. We enjoyed his flamboyant, exciting personality. His conferences were not only interesting, but they were packed with original thinking and sparked with challenging analyses. He was a realist in those days at Fort Benning. Later, after ten years in service on the staff of the Great Man, he may have imbibed too heavily of the heady wine of infallibility that flowed so freely in the General Headquarters of SCAP. But he was a top soldier and a meticulous planner. One could expect him to be prepared for history as it unfolded in Japan. When the war in the Pacific came to an end, G-2 GHQ SCAP had a major responsibility in connection with the disarmament and demobilization of the Japanese war machine. General Willoughby, however, had fought the Imperial forces too many years not to appreciate the tremendous military asset that the demobilized officers represented. He was too alert an intelligence officer to permit this asset to slip through his fingers.

Under the guise of surveillance, he conceived and organized the Japanese Demobilization Bureau (Nihon Fukuinkyoku). Ostensibly the purpose of the bureau was to assist the Far East Command to demobilize the Japanese military establishment and to maintain records of all former Imperial officers. But long after the Japanese had been demobilized, General Willoughby continued to operate his Demobilization Bureau. Six years after the surrender, the bureau had become his personal agency for the eventual reconstruction of the Japanese military establishment.

During the intervening years, Willoughby had gathered together in the Demobilization Bureau some of the most capable generals, admirals, and colonels who remained in Japan after those charged with war crimes had been tried and executed. In addition to maintaining records of those demobilized, the bureau made these former Imperial officers an adjunct of General Willoughby's G-2 Section. Under the guise of performing surveillance of Japanese communists, they attended political and labor meetings, labeling those they distrusted or considered undesirable as "inimical" to the interests of the occupation. Backed by General Willoughby, the reports of the Demobilization Bureau officers were read by the highest American echelons. The militarists had been purged, but as General Willoughby's special agents, the Demobilization Bureau exercised an important influence on the thinking of the occupation forces.

As an agency of records, the bureau had complete information on some 70,000 career officers who had been serving in the Imperial forces at the time of surrender. The officers of the bureau became the national representatives of those on the purge list. They maintained close liaison with all these officers throughout the land and could reach with equal facility the lowest-ranking demobilized lieutenant or the highest-ranking general or admiral. The officers of the bureau lived in the hope that someday the United States, faced with an emergency like Korea, would be forced to turn to the military brotherhood of Japan for help. On July 8, 1950, when General MacArthur dispatched his historic letter to the prime minister directing the establishment of a four-division force of 75,000 troops, the Demobilization Bureau knew that its day had arrived.

Under the basic directive of establishing the National Police Reserve, General Willoughby, as chief of the G-2 Section, was given responsibility with General Courtney Whitney, chief of the Government Section, for clearing all nominees for leadership in the organization. The Japanese National Rural Police, a national police organization serving in the rural areas of Japan, was given responsibilities by the Japanese government for recruiting for the NPR. Significantly the Public Safety Division of G-2 SCAP was responsible for surveillance and supervision of the National Rural Police. Accordingly, General Willoughby, as the chief of intelligence and the boss of the Public Safety Division, exercised a two-way control over the selection, clearance, and approval of the rank and file of the NPR. He had direct control through American channels and indirect control through the Public Safety Division.

Under the directives, it was natural that the Public Safety Division of SCAP should work closely with our Advisory Group on the NPR recruiting program, but it became rapidly evident to me that Colonel Pulliam, head of the Public Safety Division, had one objective: to install the Imperial officers of the Demobilization Bureau in the NPR. When we spoke to him about the purge directive, he waved his hand disdainfully. We were building a Japanese army and to hell with international directives.

One day, about the end of July, General Shepard asked me to come into his office. When I walked in I found a neat, soldierly, and forceful-looking Japanese talking to the general through our interpreter, Nicky Endō.

"Colonel Kowalski," General Shepard began, "I would like to present Colonel Hattori of the Japanese Imperial Army."

I extended my hand, perking my ears up sharply. Colonel Hattori, I mused. Who the hell is he? We exchanged pleasantries through Nicky, and shortly Colonel Hattori bowed to General Shepard and me and left the office.

"That's a good-looking soldier," I said, turning to the general. "Who is he?"

"You're going to see a lot of him," General Shepard answered. "That's your opposite number."

"You mean, General, he's going to be the chief of staff of the NPR?"

"Well let's say he's General Willoughby's nominee. Colonel Pulliam advises me that Hattori was a member of the Imperial General Staff. He is credited with having planned the Japanese invasion of Southeast Asia. I am told he's a top soldier. He's General Willoughby's number one man in the Demobilization Bureau. Yes, Willoughby wants him to be chief of staff."

"But what about the prohibition of the use of purgees in the NPR?" I asked with deep concern. "Is the purge directive to be revoked?"

"That's not our responsibility," responded Shepard. "We organize and train them. I'm not responsible for recruiting them."

"But, General," I persisted, "does General Whitney know about this fellow?"

"I don't know, and I don't care," answered General Shepard. "That's a matter for Willoughby and Whitney. You and I, mostly you, have your work cut out for you. I am advised that the Japanese Demobilization Bureau is prepared to furnish us not only Colonel Hattori but a complete cadre of qualified former military officers for the NPR. I want you personally, without any member of the staff knowing it, to prepare a cadre list for a four-division force. Try to keep the list under a thousand. Show the rank and position of each cadre officer you think we'll need. Try to have something for me tomorrow."

My orders were clear.

That night, I hurriedly studied the tentative tables of organization that Colonel Albergotti was developing for the NPR and concluded that an effective force of 75,000 troops could be organized with a cadre of 917 qualified Japanese officers. The next day, I submitted my suggested list of positions to General Shepard, who after a short discussion approved my recommendations. That afternoon, the Japanese Demobilization Bureau was put to work searching their files to find 917 individuals with the qualifications and rank necessary to fill our requirements.

General Willoughby now disregarded all directives. Two days after I had met him, Colonel Hattori was back in our headquarters with Colonel Pulliam and six former officers of the Imperial Japanese Army. Pulliam told us the Japanese had been selected to command the six NPR induction centers that were to be established. In the brief conversation I had with the members of the Japanese cadre, I learned that they had been assembled from all over Japan. It was obvious that these officers had been chosen long ago for the roles they were now to play in the recruitment program. Each had already been assigned to a specific station and was at our headquarters for his final orientation before taking command of his post. Willoughby had done a tremendous planning job and now Pulliam and Hattori were executing his plan with perfection.

The situation was moving so rapidly that I hardly had time to think about the change in policy we had undergone. Obviously, as far as the NPR was concerned, the purge was off. I was deeply disturbed by this turn of events and decided that I should know more about Colonel Hattori and those of his colleagues who would assume high posts in the new military establishment. Some very interesting information was uncovered for me.

Colonel Takushirō Hattori was born in 1901. At the outbreak of the Pacific War, he headed the Strategic Section of the Imperial General Staff (Daihonei Rikugun Sakusenka). Later he served as one of the military secretaries to the prime minister, General Hideki Tōjō.

In 1936, Colonel Hattori was alleged to have been a member of the notorious "Manchuria Clique" within the army. This was a group of military officers who had become convinced that the civilian government was either corrupt or incompetent. Foreign policy, they contended, especially for Manchuria and North China, should be determined by "those on the spot" in Manchuria, meaning of course the military clique. They further argued that such policy should conform to what they described as "absolute military necessity" in the field and that it was up to the civilian government to adjust itself to these necessities. "A very interesting person, this Colonel Hattori," I thought.

In 1944, Colonel Hattori became a member of a special group of influential staff officers of the Imperial General Staff who were responsible for coordinating the overall policy of the conduct of war. The regular group included four army colonels and four navy captains and was joined from time to time by aides to the prime minister and the war and navy ministers. Colonel Hattori obviously was one of the key officers of the Imperial General Staff.

After the surrender of Japan, officers who had held posts such as these were purged or worse, but Colonel Hattori, probably because of his special qualifications, was singled out for service with SCAP and assigned to the Demobilization Bureau. He and his colleagues escaped the purge because it became obvious to the occupation authorities that if the staggering task of demobilizing and repatriating the Japanese Imperial forces was to succeed, SCAP had to utilize knowledgeable former military officers of the Imperial Army and Navy. Accordingly, an executive directive was issued providing that "a person (otherwise qualifying as a purgee) who cannot be replaced by others may be appointed to public office by the authority of the Prime Minister." This enabled the G-2 to organize the Demobilization Bureau and staff it with former Imperial officers.

Colonel Hattori, in the five years since the end of the war, had surrounded himself with many distinguished officers, including at least two aides of General Tōjō: Colonel Susumu Nishiura, who had been chief of the Military Affairs Section of the War Ministry (Rikugunshō Gunmuka), and Colonel Kumao Imoto, former member of the Strategic Section of General Staff. There were others of equivalent stature, I was told, who would surely join Colonel Hattori in the NPR. I thought, "It's not for me to ask why, but to do or die."

In preparing the initial weekly report, which was to be submitted to the chief of staff of GHQ from our Advisory Group, General Shepard asked me to include a statement that he had conferred with Mr. Mori concerning the organization of the NPR. I was puzzled because I could not remember any visitor by that name. I also noted to my surprise that he had not asked me to report on the meetings we had with Colonel Pulliam, Colonel Hattori, and the former Imperial colonels. When the report was typed, I walked in with it to General Shepard's office. As he reached for his pen to sign it, I asked, "General, who is Mr. Mori? I don't remember him visiting us."

His hand stopped as though he had been shot, and when he looked up, his face was flushed. "That's Colonel Hattori," he answered.

"I don't understand," I began "This report goes to the Chief of Staff of GHQ."

"Mori is a G-2 cover name for Colonel Hattori," explained General Shepard. "Colonel Pulliam asked me to use it. He said that General Willoughby didn't want G-3 and the Governmental Section to jump him about using purgees in the NPR. He wanted me to give him time to discuss the matter with General MacArthur personally."

"But you can't be a party to this maneuver," I interjected. "After all, this is an official report on our activities. The deputy chief of staff, the chief of staff and very likely General MacArthur will read it. Personally, I don't like what General Willoughby is trying to do to you. You're right in the middle with this report."

When General Shepard didn't answer I decided that I had said enough. I'm sure he thought my comments over very carefully, though, because the next day he came into my office and said, "Get your cap, Frank. I want you to accompany me to GHQ. You haven't met General Fox, the deputy chief of staff, and I'd like to have him know you."

After introducing me to Major General Alonzo P. Fox, General Shepard brought out our weekly report and turned it over to the deputy chief. Then, to my surprise, he proceeded to explain in detail the Mori situation and his meetings with Colonel Hattori and the other officers of the Japanese Imperial forces. I was very proud of my boss at that moment and genuinely relieved to have CASA disentangled from this affair. Nevertheless, I was deeply disturbed by what appeared to me to be an underhanded maneuver by the G-2 Section to bring purgees into the NPR against written directives and obviously in a way that would circumvent opposition from other GHQ staffs.

Later that day, it was necessary for me to visit Colonel Laurence E. Bunker, aide to General MacArthur. After completing my business, Colonel Bunker asked me, "Frank, how's the organizing of the NPR going?"

"Well, as you can understand we've had our problems," I said. "We have no experienced Japanese in the NPR because of the purge policy, and most of the work has to be done by our American staff. But I understand, with the acceptance of General Willoughby's plan to use former career officers, things will go much better."

Colonel Bunker whirled around in his chair, his eyes blazing. "What do you mean?" he asked.

"I have the impression that the purge policy is to be revoked, or at least we'll be permitted to use some former officers of the Japanese Imperial forces in the NPR."

"The general hasn't approved that," snapped Colonel Bunker. "He will never agree to the use of purgees in the NPR. General Willoughby better stop this one-man resistance before someone's head comes off."

Leaving Colonel Bunker's office, I was satisfied that no purgees would be authorized in the NPR for some time. Even if Colonel Bunker did not go to General MacArthur directly, I knew he was friendly with General Whitney and his message would reach its destination.

As I had anticipated, on August 9, 1950, General Shepard, on instructions from GHQ, called in ex-Colonel Hattori and the six former Imperial officers who were to command the induction centers and informed them that for the present they and the other career officers were ineligible for the NPR.

The G-2 Section, however, was not prepared to give up yet. General Shepard was visited by an intelligence officer whose mission was to induce the chief of CASA to incorporate Colonel Hattori and his Imperial Army associates into the Advisory Group. He explained that the occupation forces purge directive provided certain categories for exceptions. Under these exceptions, Colonel Hattori and other distinguished Imperial officers were authorized to work for SCAP. G-2 would make these officers available to CASA. He pointed out that the Japanese police officials and civilians who were being assigned to the NPR were not qualified to organize, train, and develop a military force. Colonel Hattori and his staff would provide liaison and guidance. He cautioned, however, that the assignment of the Demobilization Bureau officers would have to be handled in the strictest secrecy to avoid criticism from the other sections of the GHQ staff. He assured General Shepard there would be no problem; G-2 would make sure no one found out about the operation. Colonel Hattori and his specially selected staff, he said, were exceptionally qualified for the task, and they were organized to assume a major part of the organizational load. CASA in fact would have little to do except supervise. Then he tipped his hand.

"We think it's very important that we do this," he said. "The arrangement will enable the Hattori team to keep abreast of developments in the NPR, and in this way prepare them for taking over command of the force when the misfits they are now sending you are thrown out."

By this time, General Shepard had had enough of the G-2 Section's intrigues to outwit the supreme commander. Supported by General Fox, he decided to make a clean break. I was genuinely pleased when finally one day he instructed me, "From now on I want you to give G-2 nothing to do with the NPR. If they ask for information or progress reports, refer them to the office of the deputy chief of staff, General Fox."

We may have closed the official channels between CASA and G-2, but I am sure this in no way hampered Willoughby from knowing anything he wanted to know about the NPR. He did, however, have to intensify his covert operations and change his tactics.

With the rejection of the Hattori team by CASA, Willoughby turned his wrath on the Japanese who were being appointed by the government to the top positions in the NPR. The struggle for control of the new force was finally focused on the appointment of the chief of the General Group. This post was similar to that of our chief of staff of the Army, and as such, the chief of the General Group was to be the top man in uniform.

Early in September 1950, Prime Minister Yoshida submitted the name of Keizō Hayashi, former official of the Imperial Household Agency (Kunaichō), governor of Tottori Prefecture, to fill the post of chief of the General Group. Under instructions contained in our basic directive, General Shepard forwarded the Hayashi nomination for clearance to General Whitney of the Government Section and to General Willoughby.

I think it is interesting to note that there was more to the appointment of Hayashi to this post than initially met the eye. He was, of course, a civilian with absolutely no military experience. But as the assistant steward of the Imperial household, Hayashi was as intimately associated with Emperor Hirohito as tradition would permit any person to associate with the son of heaven. After the war, Hayashi was one of a very limited circle of Japanese to see and talk with the emperor. In light of my close work with Mr. Hayashi for more than a year and a half, I became convinced that Emperor Hirohito named Hayashi to be the emperor's personal representative in the new Japanese military force. I might add that we were very fortunate to have General Hayashi as the chief of the General Group. He was a sincere, intelligent person who, as a dedicated and patriotic Japanese interested in the welfare of his country, understood power and valued the friendship of the United States.

We anticipated no problems on Hayashi's clearance with the Government Section. General Whitney had a consistent record of permitting the Japanese government maximum latitude in selecting their key government officials. In this case, considering the importance of cooperation between our military and the new forces of Japan, General Whitney swiftly found Hayashi qualified under the law and cleared him for immediate appointment.

General Willoughby, however, egged on by Colonel Pulliam and loyal to the Hattori team, decided on a waiting game, blocking the appointment of Hayashi for more than a month. For weeks, he calmly sat on the nomination, neither clearing nor disqualifying Hayashi. The delay created serious difficulties for our staff and the Japanese because we had to proceed with the organization of a headquarters without a chief. In the meantime, on the American side a vicious dogfight developed in the GHQ staff. CASA, G-3, and the Government Section joined forces to fight Willoughby. But I must say that he was not one to give up easily.

As the delay continued, one could feel the anxiety in the Japanese government. Mr. Keikichi Masuhara, the civilian head of the NPR, began to query General Shepard practically every day regarding the status of the Hayashi nomination. Under this pressure, General Shepard finally reported the situation to the chief of staff. But after ten years as MacArthur's intelligence chief, Willoughby had little concern or respect for the chief of staff. When the chief pressed him unduly, Willoughby settled the matter in his customary manner. On October 2, Mr. Masuhara, in a highly excited state of mind, rushed into General Shepard's office with a letter from G-2 GHQ SCAP. The letter was signed by Colonel Rufus S. Bratton, Willoughby's deputy, and informed the Japanese government that the nomination of Hayashi to be chief of the General Group was disapproved.

"What do I do now?" asked Mr. Masuhara. "General Willoughby does not like Mr. Hayashi. I know he wants Colonel Hattori to be chief. But the Japanese government has confidence in Mr. Hayashi."

General Shepard studied the letter carefully for some time, absorbed in deep thought. Then he looked up at the director general.

"Tell me, Mr. Masuhara, does the prime minister want Mr. Hayashi?"

"Sure," answered the director general.

"Then there is only one thing you can do. Go to Mr. Yoshida and ask him to take the matter up personally with General MacArthur."

"I see," answered Mr. Masuhara. And off he went on the double.

A few days later, General Whitney called Shepard to inquire whether he still wanted Mr. Hayashi for the post of chief of the General Group. When Shepard answered in the affirmative, General Whitney said, "You can have him." With that, the controversy ended, and Mr. Hayashi became the first chief of staff of the new military establishment of Japan.

On the day that General Hayashi completed his first year of service as chief of the General Group, I went over to congratulate him and to thank him for his fine cooperation. We sat around sipping tea and reminiscing.

"Do you remember, Colonel," asked Hayashi, "the first day I came into your office?"

Did I remember? How could I forget the new chief of staff of the NPR reporting for duty in that long-tail cutaway? I smiled, "Oh, I remember that day very well, General."

"I was all excited that day," went on General Hayashi. "It was a great triumph for me. You recall my nomination had been held up for over a month. G-2, as you know, did not want me to be chief of staff. They had someone else in mind for the post." And he laughed.

"But what you don't know," he explained,

is that there were personal objections to me. Colonel Pulliam opposed me. We had a personal disagreement several years ago. He was very angry at me. In 1945, at the time of the surrender, I was an official in the Home Ministry [Naimushō]. I remained there until October when I was appointed governor of Tottori Prefecture. After fourteen months, I returned to the Home Ministry as chief of the Local Administrations Bureau. About that time, 1947, the police forces were reorganized in Japan, and the National Rural Police was established. Our government decided to appoint Mr. Noboru Saitō director general of the National Rural Police. As the chief of the Bureau of Local Administration, I had to "carry the ball," as you say, for Mr. Saitō. Colonel Pulliam, as the chief of the Public Safety Division of SCAP, demanded we designate Chief Suzuki of the City of Ōsaka director general of the Rural Police. You know Suzuki-san well, Colonel. He was your chief of police in Ōsaka.

I nodded and General Hayashi continued his story.

Well, we agreed that Suzuki was a fine man, but there were many in the Japanese government who didn't like him. You know, Colonel, the people of Japan thought that he was too close to the Americans. We have all tried to cooperate with the occupation forces, but our people want their leaders to be Japanese in spirit. I am sorry, but Suzuki-san earned the displeasure of many Japanese. I tried to explain to Colonel Pulliam why we opposed the Suzuki appointment. He became very angry, jumped up and down, and pounded the table. He yelled at me. "God damn it," he said, "you want a saint to be a chief of police? If you appoint a saint, I will get rid of him the next day."

"I was not especially against Chief Suzuki," General Hayashi went on. "It was a matter of principle. He had earned the displeasure of many Japanese, and we wanted the right to appoint the director general without interference from Americans. And so Mr. Saitō was appointed, and that made Colonel Pulliam very angry at me. When I was nominated for my post, Colonel Pulliam did everything to stop me. I am sorry he did not like me."

"Are you saying, General Hayashi," I asked, "that the delay in your appointment resulted from a personal disagreement with Colonel Pulliam?"

"It was more that G-2 wanted a former Imperial officer in as chief of the General Group," answered General Hayashi. "General Willoughby had chosen Colonel Hattori for the post, and he had the whole Demobilization Bureau waiting to take over the NPR." And he laughed, obviously enjoying the events of that struggle.

I laughed with General Hayashi, assuring him that all Americans were now happy that he was the chief of the General Group. I was sincere in what I said because I had learned to respect General Hayashi and considered him a staunch friend of the United States. In fact, in my experience in Japan, I found that those who could really be counted among our friends were those who were the most patriotic Japanese—those most devoted to Japan. On the contrary, I always shied away from those Japanese who tied to impress me with their devotion to America.

The appointment of General Hayashi having been confirmed, the principle was firmly established that if a Japanese nominee qualified under the law for appointment in the NPR, there would be no interference from Americans. Furthermore, it was clearly established that the leadership for the new force would have to come from others than career officers. Until they were depurged at some future date, former Imperial officers would be ineligible for the NPR.

Though General Willoughby had received a severe setback, he was still in an excellent position, as head of the intelligence-gathering agencies, to paint a black picture of the NPR. His intelligence summaries and specially provided studies stressed the capability of the Japanese Communist Party to penetrate the NPR. The organization was a natural target for the communists, he contended, and he uncovered diabolic plots by the comrades to take over the new army. His reports varied as to the time that the communists would seize control of the new organization, but he intimated that the takeover would be facilitated if the force continued to be officered by incompetent and inexperienced civilians. The remedy of course was to end the purge and induct former officers of the Imperial Japanese forces.

When the communist scare tactics seemed to have no impact on GHQ, reports began to appear alleging corruption in the procurement sections of the NPR and inefficiencies in training, organization, and logistics. These reports found their way to the desks of the top staff officers in GHQ, generating inquiries to CASA and difficulties for our staff and the Japanese. By the end of 1950, however, Colonel Pulliam returned to the United States for retirement and General Willoughby began to fade away quietly, showing less and less interest in the NPR as his own time for retirement approached.

On the Japanese side, the struggle for control intensified. New maneuvers were now undertaken. The Hattori clique joined forces with various splinter groups of former Imperial Army and Navy officers and politicians. Their efforts centered on discrediting the new force.

Critical articles began to appear in the Japanese press blowing up management difficulties into corruption and inefficiencies. Some of these articles unfortunately contained a measure of truth; the initial costs of organizing the NPR were very high. When the alleged procurement irregularities were finally investigated, it was found that most of them were nothing more than human mistakes made by inexperienced personnel working under the severe pressure of trying to organize a new military force in the face of emergency in Korea and the vacuum that existed in Japan. Nevertheless, certain sensational newspapers were highly successful in inflaming an easily outraged public against Japan's new military establishment. The Japanese editorial below was typical of the criticism unleashed by self-serving former militarists:

> In the light of the low morale and numerous scandals in the National Police Reserve, preparations are steadily progressing for conversion of the NPR into a new Japanese Army. . . . However, capable former military officers and civilian experts in national defense maintain that it will be difficult to foster a strong guiding principle and united spirit in the NPR, since it has become overridden with corruption worse than that exposed in government administration offices, and its personnel is composed of all sorts of people gathered together from various government offices. They, therefore, insist that an entirely new army should be created

instead of converting the NPR into a military force.... Qualified former military leaders are reluctant to join the NPR. Only a very limited number of former military men of dubious character are willing to sell themselves to the NPR.

The effort, of course, in these editorials was to undermine confidence in the new organization with a view of eliminating it completely and organizing in its place something more responsive and acceptable to military men such as Colonel Hattori and his colleagues in the Japanese Demobilization Bureau.

In addition to the propaganda line about inefficiency and corruption, a campaign was launched to disdain the NPR because it was too American. The salvation for Japan, according to these experts, was to make a clean break with what had been imposed. These men argued that Japan should build a new Japanese-oriented army, divorced from American military concepts. Former Japanese military officers and so-called military experts began to question whether the American army system was the best for Japan. Wasn't it too expensive in concept? Wasn't the American discipline too fragile for the Japanese? How could Japan, a poor country, get the money that was needed to buy ammunition that Americans fired up in practice? Articles were published to show that the *yobitai*, or NPR soldier, under American training and discipline had no fighting spirit. He was pictured as a hired mercenary lacking patriotism. When some of the younger officers of the NPR who accepted and admired the American training methods spoke out for the new concepts, they were derided as young, inexperienced upstarts.

Throughout this difficult period, Mr. Masuhara and General Hayashi bore the brunt of these attacks. It was distressing enough for the director general to carry his heavy responsibilities, but he at least was a civilian official performing a political task. General Hayashi, on the other hand, was a civilian converted overnight into a general officer with the title, position, duties, and prerogatives of a military commander. Though he better than anyone else in those formative days appreciated his limitations, he was in fact the top soldier in uniform directly responsible for the command of all the troops. Under those circumstances, most of the senior officers of the Imperial Japanese Army and Navy who had lost the war for Japan were now panting on the sidelines waiting to pounce upon him.

I had come to respect the chief of the General Group as an exceptionally competent man, an outstanding executive, and a fine soldier. He was learning his new trade rapidly, adapting comfortably to the new military organization, and winning the confidence of the American officers of the Advisory Group.

Rumors began to circulate that Mr. Masuhara and General Hayashi were considering resigning their posts. Deeply disturbed, I spent several days talking to General Hayashi, urging him to reconsider. He was unhappy about not only the public criticism of the NPR, but the fact that a severe disagreement had developed between Mr. Masuhara and himself over the question of whether men in uniform would be permitted to appear before committees in the Diet. General Hayashi felt strongly that men in uniform had an obligation to report in person to the Diet. I could not agree with his position, pointing out that the director general or whoever might be the civilian head of a future military establishment must be the responsive official. I agreed that it was desirable for men in uniform, under some circumstances, to appear before the Diet, but that such appearances should be made only with the authority of the director general or the civilian minister of the future defense power. I'm not sure that I convinced General Hayashi, but a very important principle of civilian control over the military was hammered out in the crucible forming the NPR.

Both Mr. Masuhara and General Hayashi were too deeply dedicated to their country to permit personal differences or official disagreements to stand in the way of duty. It was obvious to both that neither could quit his post; nevertheless we were all relieved when both remained at the helm of the NPR.

The fight to disband the NPR nevertheless continued on throughout 1950. It festered in the disappointed breasts of a host of former Imperial officers. It embarrassed friends of the United States and spilled over in debate on the floor of the Diet. The struggle involved the top leaders in the Yoshida cabinet.

The controversy came to an end when Prime Minister Yoshida, in October 1952, ordered the 75,000-man NPR to be expanded to 110,000 troops and changed its name to the National Safety Force (NSF). The first phase of Yoshida's policy of "gradual rearmament" was completed, and the nation moved on to the intermediate step in the quiet amorphism of the Japanese army.

CHAPTER SEVEN
ADVISERS AND OPERATIONS

NPR Headquarters was established in the Japanese Maritime School (Kōtō Shōsen Gakkoō) buildings in Tōkyō in the latter part of July 1950. Actually, at that time only General Shepard and I moved into the building to open the Civil Affairs Section Annex, the cover name by which the U.S. Military Advisory Group was to be known for the next two years. The Japanese director of the NPR was not selected until a fortnight later, and several weeks elapsed before Japanese headquarters personnel began to assemble. In the meantime, General Shepard assumed actual command of both Americans and Japanese. American Army officers were assembled to operate the new NPR in the field. The advisers became operators.

Except for my slight acquaintance at that time with Colonel Albergotti, the key members of the CASA staff were all complete strangers to one another and to me. In order that we might become better acquainted and to coordinate our initial projects, I decided to hold daily staff meetings. I soon found, however, that everyone had so much work to do that the conferences were interfering with the accomplishment of our mission. Daily conferences were accordingly discontinued, and the section chiefs concentrated their attention on the organization and development of their respective offices and operational procedures.

Our early days were especially difficult as none of the initial members of the CASA staff had ever had any experience on a military advisory group. And of course none of us had ever organized an army from ground zero. We proceeded cautiously, feeling our way along. Several weeks elapsed before I was prepared to publish firm staff procedures. As so much of the organizational work was accomplished in oral discussions with Japanese governmental agencies and individuals, we kept the general and each other informed through brief written summaries covering the major actions taken each day.

Like all chiefs of staff, I had my troubles harmonizing individual members into an effective working team, as freewheelers are occupational hazards of any organization. By virtue of his official proximity and personal relationship with the commanding general, however, the chief is in a powerful position, and the members of the staff are usually quick to cooperate with him. Occasionally, however, there are those members who strive to establish a direct line to the general. I had two such individuals on my staff. At every opportunity, these two tried to bypass me. By riding close herd on them in the formative period, I pulled them under my control and, I am certain, avoided some serious difficulties for all concerned later.

In observing many headquarters, I have noted that all chiefs of staff have their troubles with the special characters on the staff. MacArthur's headquarters was loaded with wheelers and dealers. It was a well-known fact, for example, that Major General Willoughby, the intelligence officer, reported through General Edward M. Almond, MacArthur's chief of staff, when that suited the interests of General Willoughby. Similarly, Brigadier General Courtney Whitney, chief of the SCAP Government Section, as MacArthur's constant luncheon companion, enjoyed a direct line to the commander in chief, which of course he used daily. Even Major General William F. Marquat, chief of the SCAP Economic and Scientific Section, was in the habit of avoiding the chief of staff by slipping into MacArthur's office on Sunday mornings. All military headquarters suffer in varying degrees from these prima donnas. It is indeed some kind of miracle General Almond succeeded as well as he did in coordinating the military and governmental activities of these unique headquarters. General Almond himself was no pushover. A star performer, he was not an easy chief of staff to approach.

The most inaccessible person, however, was the great SCAP himself. He had become so insulated in his ivory tower that except for the three generals mentioned above, he talked only to his chief of staff, conferred occasionally with the Japanese prime minister, and only annually accepted the homage of Emperor Hirohito. He, of course, had no telephone. It is reported that during staff meetings, MacArthur monitored the discussion from an adjoining room. When a decision was necessary or MacArthur disapproved of staff proceedings, he would surreptitiously signal to the chief of staff, who would jump up from the conference table to receive instructions from the supreme commander. Major generals, such as Major General Shepard, who was MacArthur's chief of the Civil Affairs Section, deputy chief of staff of ROK Headquarters, and the man designated to organize the Japanese army, considered themselves highly honored to be permitted a private audience with the general once during a two- or three-year tour in Japan.

In CASA, the situation was pleasantly different from the rarefied atmosphere of GHQ SCAP. Here General Shepard was so accessible to everyone that my difficulty was to keep people out of his office so that he would have time to handle urgent business. The little people, particularly the coffee *sukoshis* and the stubborn little old Japanese man who delivered ice, must have been especially delivered to plague me.

When Sergeant Ratcliff and I made our office floor plan for the CASA headquarters, naturally we selected a large impressive room for the commanding general. But Shepard was a simple, humble man. Paying no attention to the floor plan, he established himself in what we considered an insignificant room adjacent to the entrance of the building. No arguments or pleading by Sergeant Ratcliff or myself had any influence on the old man. He remained to the last day of his tour with CASA in his little room, watching everyone who entered the building. His door was always open. Shepard was a rare exception among generals.

An embarrassing situation developed when Sergeant Ratcliff liberated a water cooler from an unsuspecting organization and had it moved to CASA. Some days after the installation of the water cooler, I heard a noisy commotion in the hall with the unmistakable voice of Ratcliff shouting, "No go in! No! General busy. I sign. I sign." I walked out and found the forceful sergeant trying to take some kind of paper away from a wizened little old Japanese man who had delivered ice for the cooler. The little man was holding his own, fending the sergeant off with one hand while he edged himself with determination toward the general's office. When I walked up to the struggling pair, the sergeant had secured a firm grip on the collar of the little ice man. Ratcliff was beaming triumphantly.

"Get a load of this nip, Colonel. He wants the general to sign his ice receipt. He made the general sign the damn poop sheet every day this week, but I caught him today, before he could get in."

At that moment, General Shepard came out of his office. The iceman darted forward before Ratcliff could stop him and handed the ice receipt to the general, who dutifully signed it and went back into his room without a word to either of us. Beaming happily, the little fellow bowed politely first to me, then to Ratcliff, and sucking in a loud hiss of air through his toothy mouth, he left the building. In typical Japanese fashion, having his ice receipt signed by General Shepard on the first day he delivered the ice, the old fellow would accept the signature of no one else that summer. On several occasions, when General Shepard was in conference with top Japanese government officials, the ragged little old man would force his way into the general's office, stop the conference, thrust his ice receipt in front of Shepard, get it signed, and then, backing out politely, he would bow and hiss while the Japanese officials looked on in amazement.

As our staff grew, we gave more and more attention to our personal comforts. Everybody liked coffee, so Sergeant Ratcliff hired some Japanese girls to make and serve coffee for the headquarters. The girls were tiny things whom someone promptly christened "coffee *sukoshis*" (literally, coffee "little," or little coffee girls). The five of them, holding hands, would serve General Shepard coffee in his office amid giggles and embarrassed wigglings. What a pack of trouble they were for me! Every Wednesday, the general gave them a box of Hershey bars. The other days of the week except Sundays, when they did not work, the general listened to their personal troubles. He would call me in to solve the problems. Saturday was my worst day with the little coffee girls. On this day, the medical officer and the administration officer would together inspect the kitchen and coffee. Regularly every Saturday, the medical officer would "skin" the administration officer to bawl out the coffee *sukoshis*, who would promptly start crying, and then all five, holding hands, would run for sympathy to the general. Invariably, the old man would side with the *sukoshis*, and on those days, the administration officer would find himself uncomfortably facing the sarcasm of the medical officer and the unrelenting glare of General Shepard.

Always the general would call me in and ask, "What are you and that dumb administration officer trying to do to the coffee *sukoshis*?" I would shake my head hopelessly, mumble something, and go out. On occasion, if the administration officer was successful in the footrace to the front office and got to me in time, I could run in and explain to General Shepard the administration officer's side of the story before the coffee *sukoshis* arrived in tandem at his door. On these fortunate occasions, the general would listen as usual to the girls' complaints, but at least the harassed administration officer and I would win a moral victory over the *sukoshis*.

Every time I saved face for the administration officer, I earned the wrath of the coffee *sukoshis*. After these pyrrhic victories, it usually cost me several bars of candy before I found my coffee good enough to drink.

In addition to being an excellent cover for organizing the NPR, the Civil Affairs Section Annex was well suited to assist in the initial development of the Japanese military force. Besides our headquarters in Tōkyō, there were eight civil affairs regional headquarters located in the key geographical subdivisions of Japan. The staffs at these regional headquarters were not large, but all the military and civilian personnel had had considerable experience working with local Japanese officials and community leaders. The regions knew their areas, were in direct communication with our office, and maintained close liaison with all Japanese institutions and activities under their surveillance. Most important, at a time when every officer and person that could be spared went to Korea, civil affairs was a going concern in Japan. In July, August, and September, while our troops departed Japan and fought in Korea, the civil affairs regions located camps for the NPR, processed supplies and weapons, and organized the first raw Japanese recruits who reported into their regions. The military and civilians of those field organizations performed magnificently and deserved the lion's share of credit for helping to secure our military bases in Japan while our divisions struggled to retain a toehold on the Korean peninsula.

CASA's overriding mission in those hectic early days was to put a Japanese military force in the field immediately to take the place of the American divisions that had gone or were on the way to Korea. Our plan called for recruiting, inducting, and deploying in camps 75,000 recruits in a period of two months. Since we wanted maximum distribution of the force, this meant that in that period we had to locate and prepare for occupation about fifty camp facilities. Fortunately, we were able to house about 40,000 of the 75,000 troops in camps previously occupied by American forces. The remainder of the units had to be located in various factories, schools, workers' dormitories, and any facility that had some kind of roof. We pushed the Japanese contractors unmercifully to prepare these camps for our first inductees.

As I was responsible for the final approval of the camp facilities, my office was always crowded with Japanese governors, mayors, and lesser politicians promoting their particular locations. Even months after the entire force had been established in its camps, the politicians continued to visit me to give glowing reports on the facilities they had available for camps in their areas.

On the day after President Truman relieved General MacArthur from his command (April 11, 1951), three Japanese governors came in to pay their customary courtesy call. While we exchanged greetings and drank coffee, I thought it would be interesting to see what the Japanese thought of General MacArthur's departure. So I asked, "What do you think, gentlemen, of what President Truman did to General MacArthur?"

"Ahh!" responded one of the governors. "Truman-san does not beat around the bush." I am sure his was the most poignant evaluation of the MacArthur affair.

A second governor, evidently deeply concerned about "face" for Japan, said with real disappointment in his voice: "General MacArthur has five stars. General Ridgway only three." At the time General Matthew B. Ridgway replaced General MacArthur, Ridgway was a lieutenant general, whereas MacArthur, of course, was a five-star commander.

While we rushed frantically all over Japan searching for camps, initial directives went out through Japanese rural police channels to recruit the men. To our great relief, 400,000 Japanese volunteered for the force of 75,000. There would be no problem recruiting people. But who would command this mob when it assembled in the various camps, and who was going to train them? Even as the recruits began to report to the rural police induction centers, there were only a handful of Japanese officials at the desks in the director's civilian office, and the top Japanese to wear a uniform had not yet been selected.

As the time approached for opening, our first camps were faced with two impossible obstacles: the lack of American personnel and the total inexperience of the Japanese staff. With Korea crying for American personnel, GHQ had absolutely no one to give us. On the Japanese side, with purgees eliminated from the force there was no one with any military experience in the NPR Headquarters, and no one in the field to command a camp. This was a bootstrap operation in every sense of the expression.

Americans, accordingly, had to assume command of the NPR at the national level and at the camp level in the field. At the national level, CASA became a Japanese headquarters. At the camp level, we decided to assign one American officer, preferably a major, to each one thousand Japanese inductees and a maximum of two to each camp. Most of the NPR camps were staffed by one American officer and two enlisted personnel. These Americans brought their Japanese inductees into camp, housed them, fed them, organized them into battalions, selected leaders from among the recruits, and gave them their initial training as soldiers.

To paraphrase from the past, "Never have so few controlled and trained so many." I shall never forget the hectic experience we had with the initial one thousand inductees we moved into an abandoned American camp. I had been frantically calling GHQ for a week begging for an American officer to command our first Japanese camp. Even on the day the recruits for this camp were being processed by the National Rural Police at their induction centers (a two-day affair), we had no American to assign to command them. I was seriously considering sending my deputy, Lieutenant Colonel Glover, when an American major stuck his head into my office. He wore the cross rifles of an infantryman. My hopes soared. "Who are you?" I asked, my excitement growing.

"Major Kenneth Stevens," he answered, saluting. "I was told at GHQ to report to Colonel Kowalski."

"You're in the right place," I rejoiced to myself. "Sit down, Major Stevens, I'm Colonel Kowalski."

"Is this where I get lined up for Korea?" he asked hopefully.

"No, Major," I answered. "Here you get lined up for the NPR."

"What's that?" he asked with a frightened look.

"Relax, Major, you'll find out soon," I offered. After verifying his assignment with GHQ, I beamed with pleasure at the realization that my prayer had been answered with a real, live, and somewhat sleepy infantry major.

I learned from Major Stevens that he had just arrived by plane from the West Coast. He said he had been on the move for about three days. He was exhausted. He had been told in the United States that he was going to Korea and now he wanted to know if there was anything he could do to get out of the NPR assignment. I did a superb sales job on him, if I say so myself, and as I began to unfold a small part of the plan for the new Japanese force, his eyes grew in excitement. I knew I had him.

"Now, Major Stevens," I continued. "You are going to take over one of the most challenging and exciting jobs you have ever had in the Army. You are going to be daddy to a new Japanese military force. You will organize, house, administer, equip, and train a Japanese infantry battalion, the first in the new Japanese army. And you're going to do that without letting a single Japanese know that they are anything but part of a police force.

"The Japanese National Rural Police, that's like our state police, are assembling your new recruits at five of their police stations, in two-hundred-man groups. They are coming to your camp tomorrow, one thousand of them. They have no officers and no noncommissioned officers. You will get no Japanese officers or noncoms. They are raw recruits. If you are lucky some of the inductees may have been noncommissioned officers in the Imperial forces. They have no weapons and no equipment. When they arrive, they will not even have their mess kits, but they will be damn hungry and you better find some rice to feed them. The first thing you will have to do is set up some kind of organization to move them about. Select and appoint your own leaders. Get what help you can from the rural police, and God help you.

"By the way, Major Stevens, have you ever been to Japan before?" I asked.

"No, Colonel," he smiled. "I have never seen a live Japanese until I got off the plane this morning."

"Well, OK then, you have no problems," I said, smiling.

"Your camp is here." I pointed on the map. "It's about a ten-hour train ride. Sergeant Ratcliff, my assistant, has shipped one thousand beds, mattresses, and pillows to your camp. They should be there tomorrow about the same time your men arrive. We are also shipping you a thousand carbines. Two American noncoms will report to you tomorrow. You're practically a plutocrat," I laughed. "Now, as soon as you house them and feed them, I want you to organize them into an infantry battalion. Colonel Albergotti, our G-3, will give you a table of organization. Most important, Major Stevens," I emphasized, looking at him severely, "as soon as you receive your carbines, I want you to teach those men how to shoot. I mean load and shoot in a hurry. You can watch them hit something at a later time when you have time to do that. Right now teach them how to load and shoot. Do you understand?" I asked for further emphasis.

"Yes, sir," he answered.

"Colonel Albergotti, our G-3," I continued to instruct him, "will call the civil affairs officer in the area. He will meet your train and will be instructed to help you in every way possible. I will call the Japanese governor of the prefecture in which your camp is located. He will also meet you at the train. He's a fine fellow and will take good care of you."

"And now, Major Stevens," I said, looking at him sharply again, "never forget what I am going to tell you now. You will be the only one in your camp, the only one in your area for that matter, who will know that you are organizing an infantry battalion. Others, of course, will suspect it, but only you will know. As far as the Japanese are concerned, and that applies to all Japanese, the governor, the police, and the NPR, you are organizing a police reserve. The constitution of Japan prohibits an army. You will not call the men soldiers, and you will not call the officers by any military rank. If you ever see a tank, it isn't a tank, it's a special vehicle. You can call a truck a truck. Do you get what I'm saying?" I finally stopped.

"Yes, sir," he answered.

"A lot of luck to you, Major. You will need it. Call me direct anytime." I stuck out my hand and shook his warmly, congratulating myself that our first camp was on the way.

"Sergeant Ratcliff," I added, "will arrange your train transportation and will take you up to Colonel Albergotti."

When Sergeant Ratcliff took over, I couldn't resist calling out after Major Stevens, "Get moving, Major, your train leaves in two hours."

Major Stevens did a splendid job. Most of the other Americans who followed him took over their respective camps with little more orientation than I was able to give him. Everyone sensed the urgency of the situation and appreciated the historical significance of the occasion and their own involvement, and they did their best.

As we struggled with the recruiting program and plans for the reception and training of the new force, word must have gone out through logistical channels to give us immediate support. Suddenly one day CASA was shipped 75,000 U.S. M-1 carbines and a like number of U.S. Marine combat boots for distribution to our Japanese volunteers. We experienced no difficulty in fitting the wiry Japanese troopers to the carbines, but it was a considerable problem to fit the Marine combat boots to the small feet of our Japanese defenders. Undaunted, our new allies proceeded to cut down the boots to the feet of their new owners as unconcerned as an American soldier might be in altering his trousers. Whoever thought of sending us the combat boots was a genius, for footwear for the new soldiers was every bit as important as weapons. Many of the inductees that summer came sans shoes or in sneakers.

During the months that the inductees were being processed and moved into camps, all planning and operational tasks had to be performed by Americans. For all practical purposes, the NPR became our creation and our creature. There was only a minimal Japanese staff assembled at headquarters, and the Japanese officials who were initially selected for the new army had little or no military experience.

We were fortunate that the prime minister had assigned some fine executives of the National Rural Police to help the new force get started. These men performed Herculean tasks, but they thought and functioned naturally in terms of their police experiences.

I don't suppose there was ever an army organized quite in the manner we organized the NPR, and certainly there was never an American advisory group that functioned as we did in Tōkyō. In the United States, in the building up for World War II in Europe and Asia, we expanded our force by the cadre method. We would withdraw from a trained or semitrained organization a cadre of officers and men, 10 or 15 percent of the unit. This cadre then became the skeleton upon which we built and trained a new unit similar to the parent organization from which we took the cadre. The expansion was accomplished simply by bringing in recruits from civilian life. In Japan, we had no cadres. We had no headquarters, no cooks, mechanics, or supply personnel. We brought in raw civilian recruits, formed them into companies, and then gradually integrated the companies into battalions. It was a "do-it-yourself" job, with inductees organizing themselves. Six months later, we began to organize regimental and division headquarters. General Headquarters evolved as Japanese officers became available.

In the meantime, CASA staff wrote the initial directives for recruiting, deployment, procurement, and training. American officers bargained with Japanese industry for uniforms, tents, mess equipment, and trucks. We even played an influential role in selecting and promoting officers and noncommissioned officers of the initial force. CASA in actuality, if not officially, commanded all NPR operations. Control over new equipment and camp facilities was completely in our hands. It was only after many months had elapsed that command and control was gradually turned over to Japanese commanders and governmental officials.

While the initial NPR camps were being established, American forces were rapidly departing from Japan. After July 1950, only the 7th U.S. Division remained, and it, too, was badly needed in Korea. It could not be sent over, however, until we could organize and deploy the NPR. As the Korean situation deteriorated, the demands for the 7th increased, and it was finally committed to depart Japan on September 10. This became a critical date for the NPR and a nightmare for CASA. When the 7th departed for Korea, a quarter million American dependents, women, and children, would be left behind in Japan.

What was even more disturbing were frightening rumors that the Russians had deployed two Red Japanese divisions on Soviet-occupied Sakhalin, which lies only a few miles north of Hokkaidō. These rumors were never clearly verified, but reports persisted that the Russians had manned several divisions with Japanese prisoners of war taken during World War II on the Asian mainland. The Sakhalin troops were reported to be well-equipped and bursting with communist indoctrination. Their alleged mission was to invade Hokkaidō as soon as the 7th Division departed for Korea. Though these rumors were discounted by some, the communist capability to do damage was so real that they could not be entirely dismissed.

In any case, CASA received instructions from GHQ to deploy ten thousand NPR personnel to Hokkaidō by September 10, the date scheduled for the 7th to embark for Korea. This was a formidable task. Hokkaidō is lightly populated and most of the ten thousand men had to be recruited in distant parts of Japan. Moreover, uniforms had to be fabricated, Marine boots cut down, and supplies and weapons channeled to meet the inductees. The most critical problem was housing for the troops. Hokkaidō, like Montana, is not very hospitable country in the fall and winter. The Japanese preferred the warmer climate in the south and moved to Hokkaidō only under pressure. Except for the camps occupied by the 7th Division, barrack facilities were extremely limited on Hokkaidō. We had no choice but to wait for the 7th to clear before we could move in the NPR.

Under these difficult circumstances, we scheduled the induction and movement so closely that our NPR trains actually closed in on the American camps in Hokkaidō as the trains loaded with the 7th Division troops and equipment departed their stations for Korea. We viewed the situation so critical that we assigned teams of American instructors on the NPR trains going north to teach the Japanese inductees en route how to load and fire their carbines. Many of the NPR members were recruited off the streets in Tōkyō, processed through their induction centers in two days, loaded into trains, and taught to shoot before they arrived at their destinations. The moves were executed with precision and great skill. Colonel John Drinkent, who was given responsibility for all NPR units in Hokkaidō, and his staff deserve major credit for the operation. On September 10, 1950, ten thousand Japanese assembled on Hokkaidō ready and eager to thwart any ambitions that the communists may have had in the area.

We never had to employ the NPR in a fight against the Red Japanese divisions rumored to be assembled in Sakhalin, but I wondered what kind of performance our Japanese, armed with our brand-new carbines and shod in cut-down Marine combat boots, would have turned in.

CHAPTER EIGHT
ORGANIZATIONAL PROBLEMS

On July 18, 1950, Chief Cabinet Secretary Katsuo Okazaki announced at a press conference in Tōkyō that the prime minister had selected the man to head the National Police Reserve. We were all excited by the announcement, eager to have a Japanese official assume responsibility for the force. As it was, we were making important basic decisions on the NPR with which the Japanese government and the nation would have to live. Moreover, it was extremely awkward for an American staff to commit Japanese funds that under the circumstances were required for immediate supplies for the organization.

We were very pleased when on July 23, Mr. Keikichi Masuhara, a career government official and the governor of Kagawa Prefecture at the time of his appointment, resigned his prefectural office and presented himself to General Shepard as the director general designee of the NPR. For three weeks, while the prime minister delayed promulgation of the Potsdam Ordinance that was to establish the NPR, the director general valiantly struggled to learn his new job. On August 14, 1950, the Diet having recessed, Mr. Masuhara, standing in the presence of the emperor and Prime Minister Yoshida in the Imperial villa at Hayama, was sworn in as the first director general of the National Police Reserve. On the same day, Mitoru Eguchi, a Labor Ministry (Rōdōshō) official, was formally appointed assistant director general. For all intents and purposes, Mr. Masuhara became the first minister of defense of postwar Japan.

Though I have never succeeded in evaluating and understanding Mr. Masuhara, reserving in my mind an unexplained uncertainty about him, I was favorably impressed when I met him for the first time in General Shepard's office. A handsome Japanese with a strong, expressionless Asian face, his loud voice drew my attention at our first meeting and many times subsequently. He had a tendency to boom out his queries and answers unlike most Japanese, who in conversations with Americans talked in subdued tones, sometimes in an almost whisper. During the two years I worked with the director general, I learned to respect his straightforward answers and inflexible will. On occasion, he was a veritable mule, and he showed signs of intentionally misunderstanding questions. He was, nevertheless, always dignified, displaying a warm sense of humor.

Though formally Japan was still an occupied country, General Shepard received the new director general as a dignified representative of a foreign government, setting thereby a pattern of behavior for the Advisory Group that differed distinctly from the conqueror complex practiced by so many of the SCAP officials. From the first visit, Mr. Masuhara was made to feel that he was the head of a Japanese agency with the American staff organized to assist him. An alert, patriotic Japanese, he accepted his position gracefully, in return setting a pattern of intelligent cooperation for the members of the NPR, which from those early days formed the basis for coordinated U.S.-Japanese operations.

In the initial conferences between General Shepard and Mr. Masuhara, I sat quietly in the office taking copious notes, interjecting an occasional suggestion. It was during these conferences that the fundamental policies regarding organization, procurement, supply, training, and operations were painstakingly developed. These policies reached after slow, deliberate consideration by one of Japan's most practical politicians were truly historic, laying a solid foundation for the future army of Japan. In these talks, the initial spirit of military cooperation between the two countries was born and the basic procedures for the joint employment of our forces carefully developed.

As Mr. Masuhara initially spoke English with difficulty (he learned rapidly) and General Shepard did not speak Japanese, these historic conversations were laboriously conducted through a female interpreter, Nicky Endō. Having served for approximately two and a half years in military government and civil affairs throughout Japan, I had a wide experience in conducting business with the Japanese. I found from this experience that my conversations and negotiations were most effective when I made use of interpreters who were Japanese nationals. I had been disappointed early in Nisei (Japanese-American second-generation) interpreters because they invariably tried to dominate the Japanese. They did not as a rule know the Japanese language well, and some of them, I regret to say, had their own special axes to grind.

From the very first, Nicky and I became friends, and I had to agree with the general that Nicky was smart and an outstanding interpreter for the chief of the Advisory Group. On several occasions, top Japanese officials purporting to be speaking for Mr. Masuhara urged me to ask the general himself to get another interpreter, but though I used my most persuasive arguments, General Shepard remained loyal to Nicky. I mention this problem with Nicky because interpreters serving as communication mediums play a tremendously important role in discussion between nations.

Because Mr. Masuhara had very little military experience, limited to a short tour as a lieutenant in the Service Corps of the Japanese Imperial Army during the war, he naturally relied on the advice and listened intently to the views of the CASA chief. Recognizing his limitation, Mr. Masuhara asked questions about everything. The discussions accordingly developed into educational seminars, with General Shepard a patient, courteous teacher and the director general an enthusiastic student, eagerly imbibing the words of the master.

Early in the discussions, it became apparent that there was a fundamental difference in what Mr. Masuhara thought the NPR Headquarters should be and our traditional American view of a military department. For a long time, the director general and his assistants did not understand what we were talking about, and we in turn, so accustomed to our own concepts, couldn't comprehend what he proposed.

In the traditional Western view, we envisioned NPR Headquarters in Tōkyō as a defense ministry, with a civilian element and a military staff. The civilian element, as in our own Department of Defense, was to be responsible for the political, budgetary, and overall policy direction of the establishment. The military echelon we viewed as a national headquarters staff responsible for operations of the force. We equated the director general of the NPR with our secretary of defense and considered him the civilian head of the military establishment.

As the discussions went on, it became evident that Mr. Masuhara had either been briefed inadequately or else he did not understand the mission and purpose of the new organization. He viewed himself as the head of a police force and liked to compare himself with Chief Noboru Saitō of the National Rural Police.

Under the circumstances, he saw no purpose for organizing two elements—separate civilian and military echelons—in the NPR. He wanted one large staff under his command to operate the NPR as any police force in the world is operated. We wanted a separate civilian policy staff that would control an operating military headquarters. The distinction was vitally important to us because we wanted to establish in the beginning the principle of civilian control over the military. If we permitted the director general to organize a single control group under his direct command, we were afraid that at some later date, a military man, on becoming head of the force, would be in a position to re-establish the notorious power of the militarists.

Having been indoctrinated for generations in this principle of civilian control of the military, we never considered any other kind of organization for the future army of Japan. More significant, we knew the history of Japanese militarism and wanted to provide legal and policy blocks within the structure of the force to prevent any possible resurgence of that militarism. I was especially aware that from 1936 to the end of World War II, no cabinet could be formed in Japan without an active army officer as minister of war and an active naval officer as a minister of the navy. Mr. Masuhara and the Japanese officials who gradually began to assemble at NPR Headquarters listened politely to our arguments, but we seemed unable to communicate with each other. Moreover, as the Japanese logically argued, since the NPR had no former Imperial officers and its bureaus were being staffed by civilians, why worry about a civilian control element?

For days, General Shepard labored with Mr. Masuhara, and the CASA staff worked with Japanese officials explaining the mysteries of civilian control. A year and a half later, when I served for two month as acting chief of the Advisory Group, I was still faced with the same problem. At that time, I had a detailed study prepared of the U.S. Department of Defense for the further orientation of the top Japanese officials who were then preparing the basic law for the National Safety Agency (Kokka Hoanchō, which was to succeed the NPR). It is amazing how difficult it was for the most democratic elements in Japan to understand and accept the inviolate Western principle of civilian control of a nation's military forces.

By the time Cabinet Order No. 260 establishing the NPR had been promulgated, Mr. Masuhara had been sufficiently indoctrinated to include in Article 4 of the order a covert provision for a civilian headquarters staff. Accordingly, Article 4 stated, "The fixed number of personnel of the National Police Reserve shall be seventy-five thousand, one hundred (75,100) including policemen of the National Police Reserve of seventy-five thousand (75,000)." Article 4 is deliberately silent about the remaining one hundred. They were added on the recommendation of General Shepard to provide the nucleus for the director general's office.

Having finally accepted the idea of a civilian headquarters and motivated by the age-old drive of the empire builders, Mr. Masuhara asked for five hundred people in his office. General Shepard, however, having a long-standing aversion to large numbers of civilians in a military organization, objected strenuously, suggesting that a small policy group of fifty civilians would be sufficient. Gradually, Mr. Masuhara lowered his sights to two hundred, and General Shepard finally compromised for a staff of one hundred. I was present when the agreement was reached and can still remember Mr. Masuhara's loud voice: "I see one hundred *stuffs*," he boomed, mispronouncing the English word "staff," as the "a" and the "u" sounds are sometimes hard for Japanese to enunciate.

From then on, the civilians in the director's office were known to American advisers as the "hundred *stuffs*." For purposes of identification, the director general issued a lapel button to each of the one hundred civilians of his headquarters. I considered myself especially honored when Mr. Masuhara personally gave me an NPR button with the number 101.

Except for the provision of these one hundred spaces above the National Police Reserve of 75,000, Cabinet Order No. 260 failed to give any hint of the civilian control principle we were urging so forcefully upon the NPR. The basic articles establishing the headquarters of the force and defining the responsibilities of the director general provide for a straight-line police type of organization, with the director general as the chief of the force.

Article 5 of the Cabinet Order simply stated, "The National Police Reserve shall have a headquarters, troops, and other necessary agencies." Article 7 briefly elaborated, "The headquarters shall have a Director General and Assistant Director General. The Director General shall be appointed by the Prime Minister. The appointment of the Director General shall be attested by the Emperor. The Director General shall direct [command] the functions of the National Police Reserve as its chief under the direction and supervision of the Prime Minister."

Though General Shepard calmly dismissed the question of civilian control and told me to be patient, I continued to be deeply disturbed by a sense of history. Lieutenant Colonel Albergotti, our operations officer, and Lieutenant Colonel

Freyereisen, our comptroller, were equally concerned about the principle involved, and the three of us took every opportunity to educate and indoctrinate the Japanese staff members with whom we worked. Where the situation permitted, we would incorporate in the NPR policies and procedures as much of our American concepts as we could.

About this time, I became deeply concerned about the appointment of NPR officers and senior civilians. In the United States, original appointment and subsequent promotions of all officers in our military force are made by the president with the advice and consent of the U.S. Senate. This procedure ensures all that appointments and promotions in the military are made by joint action of our political representatives in the Senate. Actually, this has meant that the Republicans as well as the Democrats in the Senate have a voice in the appointment and promotion of our military.

When the NPR was being organized, the Japanese proposed that both the civilian officials and the military officers should be appointed by the cabinet. I objected most strenuously to this proposal, arguing that the cabinet was composed of a particular party and as such did not represent all the people in the nation. Disregarding any possibility of political corruption, appointments and promotions of military officers under this arrangement would be made at the pleasure of a particular party. The minority political party or parties would have no voice in determining who would be appointed or promoted. I held that all original appointments and subsequent promotions of the NPR military officers should be submitted by the prime minister to the House of Councillors (Sangiin) for approval as is done in our country. I was at first surprised at the severity of the Japanese objections until I realized that the prime minister feared a battle royal with the Socialists in the House of Councillors on the question of initial appointments. And he didn't want to renew the battle every time he had to promote any NPR officer or appoint new ones.

I could not accept this argument of expediency in a matter so vital. Moreover, as I pointed out, it was possible under the proposal that after the cabinet approved the initial appointments in the NPR, the Socialist Party could win the elections. What would happen then? Would a Socialist cabinet dismiss all the NPR officers previously appointed and appoint new ones? Or would they do something less drastic like appointing their own followers or promoting their own people. The arrangement to my mind was fraught with extreme danger for the NPR and the future military forces of Japan.

I was convinced that if the occupation forces insisted, Prime Minister Yoshida would have receded from political expediency and accepted "advice and consent" control by the House of Councillors over military appointments and promotions. But there are not a few military officers in our forces who are above playing politics. I am sure principle was not pressed because there were those in the Far East Command who despised all socialists and the Japanese socialists especially as "reds." These men agreed with Yoshida that Socialist Party members of the House of Councillors should be given no opportunity to criticize our American handiwork or the appointments of our conservative friends in the Japanese government.

My arguments did not prevail, and Prime Minister Yoshida's cabinet appointed all the officers of the NPR. I believe the appointments were fair; certainly I could detect no political chicanery, but a vital principle of democratic government was violated. I disagreed so strongly with General Shepard on this issue that I contemplated asking being relieved from my assignment. I suppose the practical political considerations were overriding.

As the NPR proceeded to organize itself in some fifty camps scattered throughout the country, acquiring men and resources from the surrounding communities, the situation at the national level continued in a nebulous state. CASA provided the central impetus and guidance while Japanese officials slowly trickled into the Maritime School buildings. Finally the director general reluctantly agreed to subdivide his headquarters into two elements, a small civilian policy office and a military operational staff.

There was now established an NPR Headquarters with an allocation of one hundred civilians whose responsibilities were parallel with those of the office of the secretary of the Army and a General Group Headquarters. Initially assigned seven hundred spaces, equivalent in mission and functions to the Army Headquarters in the Pentagon, the chief of the General Group was assigned the same responsibilities as our Army chief of staff.

A large percentage of the civilians who joined Mr. Masuhara transferred from the National Rural Police, and although they took off their police uniforms and worked for the director general in civilian clothes, they thought and behaved like police officers. Those who were not police officers were mossback bureaucrats from the Communications Ministry (Denki Tsushinshō), the Finance Ministry (Ōkurashō), Transportation Ministry (Unyushō), and other central government agencies. The police chiefs particularly regarded NPR Headquarters as a kind of central police station.

The officers who were slowly recruited for General Group were equally ignorant in their duties. As mentioned previously, all professional officers of the Imperial Army and Navy had been purged by General MacArthur and were ineligible for the NPR. The top people in uniform in this embryonic Japanese army accordingly had no previous military experience. Most of them, as in the civilian NPR Headquarters, were career police officials. The administrators, engineers, finance personnel, and supply officials from the various national ministries were organized rapidly and their sections functioned effectively. The general staff sections, however, staffed with inexperienced police officers and some low-ranking former officers and noncommissioned officers of the Imperial Army and Navy who had not been purged, were hopelessly ineffectual. The only difference between the personnel in the NPR Headquarters and General Group was that those in the General Group wore uniforms.

The new chief of their headquarters, Senior Superintendent General Hayashi, likewise had no military experience, having served, as previously mentioned, as governor of a prefecture, Home Ministry official, and assistant steward of the Imperial household. Although in time I became very fond of General Hayashi and respected him for the fine executive he was, I must confess that I had my misgivings when he first reported for duty in striped trousers and frock coat. He certainly was the most unusual chief of staff that commanded an army.

As in the United States Army, there were many amusing incidents that occurred in those formative days with the officers commissioned directly from civilian life. Like all doctors, the chief medical officer, for example, had his own views about wearing the uniform. A nationally famous surgeon, he was induced to join the NPR only after much coaxing by the national government. Accordingly, Colonel Shellenberger, our chief medical adviser, treated him with considerable respect and finesse. Nevertheless, after having observed Major General Honna in various combinations of uniform and civilian clothes, I called Colonel Shellenberger into my office one day to straighten out the good surgeon.

"Doc," I began, "you've got to do something about your Surgeon General Fuminori Honna. He is a disgrace to the NPR uniform. Get him properly dressed, will you?"

"I'll try," laughed Shellenberger, "but I promise you no miracles."

In the next few days, I observed a perceptible improvement in Lieutenant General Honna's uniform, except he persisted in wearing a dilapidated civilian brown fedora. Once again I asked Colonel Shellenberger to come into my office. As he sat down, I saw a flashing twinkle in Shellenberger's eye. "I know it's about Honna and his fedora," he began laughingly. "This will get you. I took my fine friend personally to the supply office. There the old man tried on four or five uniform caps for size. He eyed himself with disgust in the mirror and then, with a determined finality he placed his brown fedora on his head and walked out muttering, 'I like this one best.' Since that time, he refuses to put on an NPR hat. If you think you can get General Honna into a uniform hat I urge you to try it."

I didn't have the courage to joust with the doctor, and General Honna continued wearing an NPR uniform with a civilian fedora.

One of the decisions that had to be made in those early days was whether the new force should be organized in the image of the Imperial Japanese Army or in accordance with the tables of organization of the United States Army. The Basic Plan was mute on this question. There were many good reasons to support both views.

Though we had crushed Japan in the Pacific War, the Imperial Japanese Army, as our own Army and Marines could attest, had proven itself to be a formidable fighting machine. The Japanese *heitai*, as an Imperial soldier, was second to none in the world. Inspired by a fanatical devotion to the god-emperor, he had been spiritually prepared to destroy the enemy or perish himself. The basic Japanese fighting force depended on manpower. It had little mechanized equipment and few supporting weapons. It was an army designed and trained to fight primarily with rifles, machine guns, and mortars. Japanese logistics were simple. Each soldier was trained to endure with minimum food and little ammunition. If we patterned the new armed force after the liquidated Imperial Japanese Army, we would achieve maximum manpower at minimum cost. The NPR would be cheap to organize, simple to maintain, and easy to train. Furthermore, despite the prohibition on the use of career officers, there were many former noncommissioned officers who were eager and well-qualified to build the new force in the image of the old.

We were also reasonably certain that there were those in Japan who would have no difficulty resurrecting the "liquidated" Imperial Army regulations, training manuals, and the literature that might be necessary to establish an effective organization. In addition, there were considerable stocks of old Japanese weapons still available to arm a substantial force. Most significant, those who favored modeling the new army on the old argued that if we imposed a new military system on Japan, we would build a force that would accept the privileges of American soldiers with none of the virtues of the Imperial Japanese fighters.

On the other hand, there were compelling reasons favoring the establishment of a new Japanese force organized on the American pattern. Japan had been systematically demilitarized, and munitions makers had been purged and their factories destroyed or converted to civilian manufacture. Weapons and much of the equipment for the new Japanese force for years would necessarily have to be supplied by the United States. As these would be of American design, the combat, supply, and maintenance units of the new forces would have to be organized in a way similar to American Army units. Furthermore and most significant, in the event of joint U.S.-Japanese military operations, the advantages of having two forces identically organized and similarly equipped were obvious. The two command and staff structures, communications systems and procedures, and logistical systems could be integrated and superimposed one upon the other with minimum disarrangement. This obviously was an overriding consideration. The NPR became a little American Army.

This decision, however, created a host of new and complicated problems. One of the most difficult was the requirement for Japanese manuals, both training and technical. Much of the early instruction in the use of carbines, M-1 rifles, and machine guns was accomplished without Japanese manuals through interpreters. Since many of the interpreters knew little about firearms, their interpretation of American instructions and especially nomenclature was something marvelous to hear on retranslation. But it's impossible for a modern army to train without manuals. Individual American camp commanders accordingly did their best to provide temporary mimeographed Japanese instructions locally produced. As General Group Headquarters began to recruit officers, we were finally able to publish a few Japanese manuals at the national level.

We encountered our most serious difficulties when we began to translate American manuals on tactics into Japanese. One must keep in mind that officially we were organizing a police force. Under the circumstances, there could be no talk about soldiers, fire and movement, entrenchments, and tactical maneuvers. Police group tactics are limited to riot control. What complicated the translations was our insistence that the Japanese use no military terms in the manuals.

One day General Hayashi came to me in complete frustration. "What are we doing," he asked, "organizing an army or police force?"

"You know the answer to that," I said.

"Yes, I know," he said. "We are organizing an army. You and I know that, but we can't tell our policemen that or the people. It is most difficult to describe a police attack on a bunker with artillery and flame throwers, especially when we have to disguise the words 'bunker,' 'artillery,' and 'flame throwers.' That's bad enough in any language, but I've got to invent characters for the phony names we have given some of these." Continuing with pencil and paper, he said, "Look, Colonel, this is a Chinese character for vehicle. You know we Japanese use Chinese characters. But I am supposed to call a tank a special vehicle. Tell me, Colonel, how do I change this Chinese character you see here for vehicle into a special vehicle and expect my *yobitai* to recognize it as a tank?"

"That's what they made you a general for," I gibed, and then we both sat down and laughed until tears came to our eyes.

Language is always a difficult barrier between people, but in Japan that year it sometimes gave birth to comedy, and on occasions almost brought on tragedy. We had adequate interpreters and many of the Japanese could speak some English, so we were always able to communicate, but it was the miscommunication that caused mischief.

One day, while examining a Japanese budget that had been translated into English and which itemized costs for rehabilitation of one of the new camps, I was amazed at the unusually large sum, almost 10 percent of the entire amount, that had been set aside under the term "roofing." Suspecting chicanery, possibly a separate deal for a roofing contractor, I called in our comptroller. When I showed him the item, he howled.

"That's a good one," he began. "The budget was prepared by one of the 'hundred *stuffs*' at the NPR Headquarters and was translated into English by one of their interpreters. You notice here that the item 'roofing' is roughly 10 percent. It was added to the Japanese budget as 'overhead.' Japanese 'overhead' was then translated into the English term 'roofing.'"

One day, I visited a Japanese camp on an inspection tour. During the briefing, the battalion commander told me that he had just received his company safes—five of them, one for each company—and he didn't know how he was going to get them into the barracks. He said he was further troubled because he was told American company commanders took their company safes with them into the field. He didn't see how the Japanese could do that. I was surprised since I visualized the typical small metal box that American company commanders are issued to secure their limited papers and items of special value.

"Let me see your safes, Superintendent," I suggested, and he took me to a platform behind headquarters. There they were, five massive upright safes weighing several tons. I later learned that the Japanese logistical section of the General Group Headquarters, in determining allowances for Japanese organizations, used our American table of organization and equipment. This table showed that each unit was issued a "company safe." In the translation and subsequent procurement, General Group Headquarters cornered the market on safes in Japan.

We had a similar experience with absorbent cotton. When the American table of allowances was translated into Japanese tables, NPR Headquarters bought enough absorbent cotton to fill requirements for medical cotton for the force for the next 180 years. I was told that the price of absorbent cotton in Japan went up around 300 percent and the NPR later was able to sell the item at a profit.

While the absorbent cotton transaction was in full swing, Colonel Julian Dayton, a hard-boiled old infantryman, was opening a camp for three thousand Japanese troops. On the day his troops arrived, he called me on the phone. "Frank, damn you," he began. "I have three thousand Japanese sitting in the barracks waiting for chow, but I can't feed them because your damn headquarters hasn't delivered our mess equipment. I've got the rice and fish heads but nothing to put them in."

"Settle down, Julian," I said. "Our G-4 insists you should have the mess kits and other gear there now. He said it was shipped by train and the Japanese should have the train there now on your siding. Look around, will you."

Suddenly Julian broke with, "Wait a minute, Frank. I've just been told that there are four carloads of something on our tracks. Hang on, I'll call you back." Fifteen minutes later when I raised the phone, Julian was coming through the wire. "You dumb son of a bitch. You know what you sent me? Four carloads of absorbent cotton."

Months later, when I saw Julian at an NPR cocktail we downed a goodly number of scotch and sodas laughing about that shipment of cotton.

CHAPTER NINE

LEADERS FASHION ARMIES

Gradually NPR Headquarters (the civilian echelon) and the General Group (the uniformed headquarters) began to fill up with senior government officials. As I reviewed the background and experiences of these new members of the Japanese defense establishment, I noted that all but one of the top appointees were graduates of the Law Department of Tōkyō Imperial University, now the University of Tōkyō. The lone exception was Mitoru Eguchi, who became deputy director general of the NPR and as such was the number two civilian official. Eguchi was a graduate of the Kyōto Imperial University, now Kyōto University. As so many others have observed, the men of Tōkyō University and to a lesser degree those of Kyōto University govern Japan.

    I also noted as I had previously observed in military government, that Japanese executives all enjoyed what appeared to be carefully planned diversified assignments and career experiences. I was told that upon graduation from university, selected young individuals were initially assigned and subsequently moved from one government assignment to another with a view of developing them for high-level positions in the national and local governments. Before the occupation, when all the key officials in the national prefectural and city governments were directly appointed by the Imperial administration in Tōkyō, it was understandable how selected officials could be shifted in the direction of the central government from one prefecture to another, from the prefectures into Tōkyō, or from Imperial Bureaus to prefectural assignments. What amazed me when I served in military government, after we introduced election of governors and other local officials, was to find the chief of the Labor Bureau of Shimane Prefecture, for example, suddenly appear as a chief of the Economic Bureau in Kyōto Prefecture. These shifts I found were being made all over Japan. The governors may have been elected by the people of the prefectures after 1947, but I suspect that their labor commissioners and other officials were being assigned to them by someone somewhere in a central agency controlling such matters in Tōkyō. I do not mean to be critical of the system; it has much to be recommended, and I only mention this situation to illustrate that democracy has many facets. We, of course, view local autonomy as a system in which the people of that area elect and control the officials who govern them. There are other views. Accordingly, if we hope to police the world, as some desire, it is important that we realize that often what seems alien and unworkable to us serves others most adequately in their environment and society.

State Minister Takeo Ōhashi, who came from an illustrious Japanese family and who was serving as the attorney general of Japan, was assigned, in addition to his legal duties, responsibility for the National Police Reserve in the cabinet and became the spokesman for the government on defense matters. Initially, State Minister Ōhashi supervised NPR activities in a detached manner from his office in the cabinet, but gradually his visits to NPR Headquarters became more frequent and his influence increasingly more apparent. By early 1952, he was participating actively with American advisers and former Imperial generals close at hand in arranging for the development and equipment of the future military forces of Japan. In the meantime, Mr. Masuhara, as the director general, had direct responsibility for planning, organizing, and training the NPR.

Both Mr. Masuhara and Mr. Eguchi, as the civilian heads of the force, spent much of their time, as do our own secretaries of defense, appearing before committees of the Diet answering questions. Experienced government officials, their answers addressed to resolving the ambiguities of the NPR, would have qualified either one for the high political tightrope walk in any parliament of the world.

In accordance with our American concept of civilian control over the military, we encouraged the chief of the General Group Headquarters, General Keizō Hayashi, and his deputy, General Yujirō Izeki, a former official of the Foreign Ministry, to stay away from the Diet and Japanese politicians. This created some confusion and at one point caused a severe rift between General Hayashi and Mr.

Masuhara. The director general's office, however, was learning rapidly, and the men in uniform were subordinated to the civilian echelon, particularly on political matters.

General Izeki, who spoke English fluently and handled his scotch adroitly, as a Foreign Ministry official should, was a favorite with Americans. In his relations with the advisers, he assumed a relaxed, indifferent attitude. He remained in uniform for only about a year before he returned to his career as chief of the International Cooperation Bureau (Kokusai Kyōryokukyoku). In the year that he served with the NPR, his major contribution, as far as I was concerned, was to provide a high-level liaison between American and Japanese headquarters. Whenever difficulties or misunderstandings arose, General Izeki would come to me in a frank, forthright talk and present the Japanese position in clear and understandable English terms. I have often speculated what a wonderful world this would be if humanity could communicate in one tongue.

While General Shepard and all of us in the Advisory Group were eager to organize an effective Japanese headquarters and staff for the NPR as rapidly as possible, we nevertheless were more acutely concerned with building a military force in being. With our Army engaged in a death struggle on the Korean Peninsula, the payoff in Japan had to be a viable force that could march and fight. An effective combat battalion of Japanese infantrymen in the field was much more important to the United States and Japan at the moment than a Japanese General Staff in Tōkyō. If the NPR had to fight, our American Advisory Group could in such an eventuality provide command and battle direction. Accordingly, while the new Japanese leaders in NPR Headquarters and the General Group fumbled with strange tables of organization and equipment and tried to grasp the meaning of unfamiliar military terms and training requirements, Colonel Albergotti, our operations officer, whipped out a thirteen-week training program, and the Japanese GIs were marching and shooting as soon as we could cut our Marine shoes down to fit them and get carbines in their hands. The major credit for converting Japanese civilians into paramilitary troopers must be given to the American majors and lieutenant colonels and their sergeant assistants who organized and commanded the Japanese forces in the field. Initiative, ingenuity, and action characterized these wonderful American heroes.

The raw material with which the Americans had to work, that is, the volunteers who joined the NPR in those early days, were well above the average for inductees. To begin with, almost 400,000 young people volunteered for the force, of whom 75,000 were accepted for induction. Over half of those inducted had served in the Imperial Army and Navy. Many of the inductees had been noncommissioned officers, a large percentage combat veterans. Their average age was about twenty-six years. As soon as we dressed them in uniforms, they strongly reminded me of the prewar Japanese army, except we knew their standard of education was much higher. They were generally physically fit, keen of spirit, and eager to make a success in the new organization.

Our immediate problem at the unit level was to select leaders so that we could move and control the unorganized mass. Unable to communicate except through interpreters, our American camp commanders faced a Herculean task. I don't know how they and their Japanese colleagues accomplished the miracle of initial organization. Somehow leaders were found to command squads, platoons, and companies. Four companies were combined into battalions, and overall the American commander ran his troops like a private army. That the companies and the battalions developed in accordance with a common training program and on a prescribed schedule is owing in a great measure to the high level of development and dedication to duty of our officer and noncommissioned officer corps.

While our majors and lieutenant colonels struggled valiantly with their troops at the camps, the Advisory Group in Tōkyō undertook the equally difficult task of selecting and training leaders and instructors for the entire force. Having been stationed as military government chief in the Hiroshima area, I remembered the outstanding school and weapons training facilities our Eighth Army operated on the island of Eta Jima. With General Shepard's approval, I made a hurried visit to my classmate, Colonel Sauer, who commanded the installation. My visit was most timely, as the Eighth Army, under heavy demand for men in Korea, was preparing to close out their operations on the island. It was indeed a master stroke of good luck, and equally important, there was an understanding at Eighth Army Headquarters that the American training facilities and the instructors would be made available for a limited time—enough time to train urgently needed weapons instructors and a few small-unit leaders. Without Eta Jima, it is doubtful that the NPR could have been anything more than an assembly of inadequate police recruits.

A total of 320 potential leaders and instructors, selected from camps all over Japan, attended our first intensive four-week course at the American school. We concentrated on infantry weapons instruction and small-unit leadership. Some technical men were given instruction in demolitions, combat engineering, and communications. Our first class was a vital training cadre that was to have an invigorating impact on the entire force. Distributed like treasured seeds throughout Japan, they became the key instructors and leaders in the NPR camps.

Forty of the first class of Eta Jima, carefully selected by our advisers there and by representatives of the National Rural Police, were ordered into our headquarters in Tōkyō, where they attended a four-week command and staff course conducted by Colonel Albergotti and his officers. Thirty-nine of them completed the course and were commissioned captains. They became our first leaders in the field, thirty-one being immediately assigned to command battalions while the remaining eight were allocated staff duty.

At the same time, Lieutenant Colonel Freyereisen, our comptroller; Colonel Thoulton, our personnel adviser; and Lieutenant Colonel Weetman, our logistics adviser, organized and conducted schools for finance, personnel, and procurement officers. Two months after the first volunteers donned NPR uniforms, several hundred eager young Japanese were enthusiastically assisting American advisers to build a new, enlightened democratic army in Japan. Of course, it was impossible in a few short weeks to develop military commanders and technicians, but we did instill in these high-quality, intelligent Japanese a keen awareness and appreciation of American instructional methods and theory of leadership and a working acquaintance with our infantry weapons and some of our engineering equipment.

Nevertheless, it was obvious to all, American and Japanese alike, that the higher-level leadership needed to command and staff the force could not be found among those who were volunteering as privates for the NPR. Since the decision had been made not to use former officers of the Imperial forces, this leadership had to be recruited from government agencies, from police establishments, and from business executives, professionals, and technicians.

One of the first requests that the director general made upon taking office was to ask for authority to commission by direct appointment initially two hundred, then an additional eight hundred, in the age group of thirty-one to forty, to be offered direct positions in the lower and intermediate ranks. As the GHQ staff, particularly Generals Willoughby and Whitney, was responsible for the clearing of all NPR leaders, the requests bounced around in the Japanese cabinet and American headquarters for more than a month. At one point, when Ministry of Justice General Ōhashi suggested that there were a large number of former Japanese officers who had served in the army of Manchukuo available for these posts (officers in the Manchukuo army had not been purged), the G-2 section of SCAP reopened the whole question of purgees. The matter degenerated into an acrimonious debate between General Willoughby and Mr. Ōhashi regarding the numbers actually available. Eventually, after intervention by the Japanese at the highest political level, the NPR was authorized to induct one thousand civilian executives, professionals, and technicians by offering direct appointments to the force.

The actions necessary to query, interview, and induce one thousand successful individuals who were established in their own businesses, professions, and services to give up their careers and join the NPR consumed many months. In the meantime, the organization, training, and development of a force of 75,000 proceeded under American advisers through the young Japanese officers and noncommissioned officers who were evolving from the ranks in the NPR. As time elapsed, with no severe protests being raised in the United States, among our allies, or even from the communist camp, we cautiously supplied the NPR initially with American carbines, then M-1 rifles and .30-caliber machine guns. As the international and local calm continued, we grew bold, issuing .50-caliber machine guns, 60-mm mortars, and eventually 81-mm mortars, ordnance repair shops, combat engineer equipment, and signal communications. While the creeping rearmament proceeded, the prime minister denied that Japan was doing so, steadfastly maintaining that the NPR was a police force, and we pressed our abundant weapons into the hands of the troopers as rapidly as they learned to use them.

By September 1951, one year after our hectic effort to deploy ten thousand NPR recruits on Hokkaidō to block a rumored communist invasion from Sakhalin, the new organization was beginning to assume some of the qualities of a military force. Based in thirty-seven camps throughout Japan, it was loosely grouped into four infantry-type divisions.

Although the force by this time had undergone nothing more advanced than battalion field exercises, the officers and troops had been given extensive individual and small-unit training. Practically everyone in the battalions had actually fired carbines, M-1 rifles, machine guns, bazookas, and mortars. As individual soldiers and members of small units, the NPR men could have given a credible account of themselves. As battalions of infantry, the NPR could, in the closing months of 1951, have put on a whale of a fight. Beyond that, the capability of the force for war was very limited, although in the opinion of many the organization possessed a great potential for future development.

In November 1951, I was privileged to read a formal report and evaluation of the NPR made by Lieutenant Colonel J. G. Figgess, assistant military adviser of the British Embassy in Tōkyō. In a six-page report, summarizing an extensive visit to the NPR in the fields, he noted, "But perhaps the most outstanding feature of the NPR units is the tremendous enthusiasm of all ranks and their evident keenness to make the most of their training. The junior officers (Lieutenants and Captains) and some of the NCOs were particularly impressive. They had joined the NPR as private soldiers and had risen to their present rank through merit and qualities of leadership." Colonel Figgess concluded his report,

> Judging from the standards of the units visited, the National Police Reserve has made great strides since its formation fourteen months ago and the progress has been particularly rapid during the past six months. Although the value of the force for war is not yet very high, the basic organization and training is sound and in view of the enthusiasm of all the ranks for the task in hand I consider that in another six months the infantry elements of the NPR will have reached a standard which would be acceptable in the modern British or American Army. It will be much later than this of course before the NPR is ready to be committed as a composite, self-supporting force since the technical and specialist training of the artillery, engineer and service elements has hardly begun and no field guns and other specialist equipment has yet been issued or even authorized for issue.

At this stage in the development of the NPR, noisy criticism erupted in the press, especially from former Imperial officers, attacking the quality of the leadership of the force. Most of the former military officers were pressing for immediate liquidation of the NPR as a totally inadequate organization. These individuals deplored the imposition of American concepts upon Japanese troops, urging a fresh start in which obviously they would play creative and controlling roles. Aside from those arguing their special interests, there were many Americans and Japanese who sincerely questioned the wisdom of organizing a military force with former police officers and civilian executives when there were so many highly qualified former Imperial officers available for the task. This argument, of course, could not be lightly dismissed, yet there were sound reasons against wholesale embracing of purgees in the NPR.

In visits to units at the camps, we were tremendously impressed with the effectiveness of the leadership at the company and battalion level. Our advisers with the units had uniformly high regard for their Japanese counterparts and especially the young captains and lieutenants serving in the companies. Moreover, I had learned long ago as a regular army professional to stop sneering at the civilian officers. In World War II, I rapidly discovered that a person who was a successful leader in civilian life usually possessed the intelligence and adaptability to develop into a good military commander or staff officer. Accordingly, many of us in the Advisory Group were convinced that the Japanese civilian leaders, who in most instances had to be urged to join the NPR, possessed fine leadership potential. All they needed to be effective soldiers was experience in commanding troops and carefully planned military schooling.

Most significant, from the American view, the civilian leaders brought to the NPR a freshness, enthusiasm, and flexibility that was indispensable in our effort to fashion a new democratic army in Japan. Recognizing their military limitations, they were eager for knowledge. They had nothing to unlearn and so they jumped to the task of learning with gusto. Highly intelligent and adaptable, they rapidly acquired considerable basic military knowledge and skills from their American advisers. It was amazing how much and how quickly they learned the elements of organization, administration, and logistics. They studied our technical and tactical manuals with a devotion. They loved soldiering, demonstrating a keen interest in weapons and commanding troops.

It was my firm conviction at the time that with intelligent assistance from our American advisers, the Japanese leadership in the NPR, from General Hayashi to the lowest-ranking lieutenant, could build an effective military force. We could probably develop an army more rapidly with former Imperial forces, but in the fall of 1951, I failed to see any violent emergency facing Japan that would necessitate any urgent buildup or expansion of its military forces.

Many argued, with merit, that there was no one in the NPR qualified to command a division or even a regiment in combat. But to be realistic, almost seven years had elapsed since any Japanese officer had commanded a division or regiment in combat. It was doubtful that former Imperial generals, now advancing in age, would be effective in commanding an American-type division organized with strange weapons, vehicles, and equipment. Even the younger Imperial colonels would have to undergo months of reorientation and re-education on new concepts dictated by modern military weapons and equipment. Moreover, it was a fact of life that even with the best military leaders in the world, it would be a year or a year and a half before the NPR would be ready to fight in division strength. Aside from the lack of qualified officers, the force had no artillery, tanks, or other heavy weapons necessary for a combat division. Nor did it possess the signal equipment, transportation, or logistical capability to be employed in divisional units. Even after the heavy weapons and other necessary equipment were issued and the troops trained in their use, months would be required to shake down units and exercise them in division maneuvers. One does not build an army for a nation overnight.

Yet the logic of rearmament could not disregard the former military officers of Japan. As the NPR assumed its potential military character and we celebrated the supply of increasingly heavier weapons and equipment, the Japanese cautiously opened the question of using former military officers in the force. Mr. Masuhara pointed out to General Shepard that some of the younger Imperial officers had recently been depurged and that there were hints that older officers would be removed from the purge lists shortly. Newspapers began to explore the possibilities involved, and American advisers were queried on their views. In February 1951, authority was cleared to induct these individuals, and subsequently we learned that Prime Minister Yoshida and General Ridgway, the new SCAP, were meeting to consider the desirability of depurging former colonels and lieutenant colonels with a view to bringing them into the NPR.

Although there was no serious objection raised to the induction of the younger former officers, the proposal to incorporate senior Imperial officers was greeted less than enthusiastically by some of our advisers and many Japanese. These officers, of course, posed a natural threat to those already in the NPR, but many sincere Japanese resisted their inclusion in the force on principle. Six years of national indoctrination by the occupation did not serve to endear former military leaders in the hearts of the people. I noted that the civilians in NPR Headquarters appeared especially hostile. Several months elapsed while feet dragged. When General Izeki, deputy chief of the General Group, one day requested that I extend the time for submission of certain information on these senior candidates for the NPR, I asked him bluntly what was delaying the decision. He assured me that neither General Hayashi nor himself had any objection, but he said that the young civilian bureaucrats in the director general's office strongly opposed bringing senior Imperial officers into the NPR. Mr. Masuhara, he said, was being pulled in all directions, but he thought a compromise could somehow be arranged. Eventually 243 graduates of the Imperial Army and Navy academies, the younger men initially considered, were enrolled in the first officer training course for depurgees in the latter part of August 1951. In October, 812 former Imperial captains, majors, and lieutenant colonels were brought into the NPR and ordered to attend a two-month reorientation course. The door was now open for the former military personnel to resume their interrupted careers.

The long-debated issue of whether to use former Imperial officers was thus not a matter of principle or even need but a question of timeliness. Nothing that General Willoughby or the G-2 Section could do in 1950 had any impact on the decision to keep these officers out of the NPR at that time. American policy, General MacArthur's directives, Allied attitudes, world opinion, and the Japanese public had grown to accept a military establishment for Japan, and it no longer mattered who served in the force. The Imperial officers who only a short time before had been viewed with suspicion and concern now joined the new army without any fuss or opposition and proceeded with their training as though they had always been a part of the NPR.

Time has the same effect on human attitudes, human behavior, and historical acceptance that it has on any process of erosion. One can chop rocks and stones with an axe until sparks fly and the brain is jarred, but all one can accomplish is to dull the axe. Yet water flowing into the sea in time has gouged out the great canyons of the Colorado. The War of Roses lasted a generation, but how many today know where it was fought? The Christians during the Crusades, bent on seeking the Holy Grail, hated the Saracens so vilely that it is reported they actually ate their enemy in battle, but that long-forgotten hate has turned to compassion and loans to our Arab brothers. And so, as the slaughter in the Holy War against communism escalates, humanity knows that both sides will eventually settle their differences at the conference table, unless time dictates destruction for both.

The circumstance that caused a hiatus in the use of Imperial officers in Japan's military establishment permitted the fashioning of a democratically inclined modern force. The initial leaders of the NPR, inexperienced in military matters, friendly to American leadership, and unhampered by preconceived ideas or ordeals, laid the foundation in the organization for a permissive climate that could not have come about in a force dominated from its inception by former officers of the Imperial military establishment. Brutality as a symbol of toughness, so vital a part of the old army, could not re-establish itself among officers who abhorred its practice; instead there developed in the NPR a new spirit dedicated to the dignity of the individual soldier. When the purgees did join the force, they were inducted in relatively small numbers into an organization that was dominated by American military concepts and that had accepted these concepts as superior to those of the old army. They joined a "going concern" in which they had to move cautiously, picking their uncertain way in an environment not altogether familiar. They were not the "top dogs." They had been in prewar Japan, or they might have been as the creators of the NPR. If they wanted to move up in this new organization, they would have to demonstrate not only military skills and knowledge but tolerance and acceptance. On the other hand, they possessed much they could give the new force: military competence, strength of character, devotion to country, and hopefully a deep understanding of past mistakes.

In December 1951, Lieutenant Colonel Figgess of the British Embassy, after a visit to three NPR installations, had a revealing comment to make in his written report on the newly integrated former Imperial majors and lieutenant colonels he had observed at a field-firing exercise of a company in an attack. He wrote,

> However, the especial factor of interest was the reaction of the former Japanese Army officers to the training exercises and demonstrations. At first they were silent and appeared to be somewhat shy of expressing any opinion and two individuals who I engaged in conversation separately told me that despite their two months staff course at Kurihama, they had been unprepared to find the NPR in such an advanced state of military readiness. Later on, as they shed their reserve, it was clear that they were taking a keen interest in everything that they saw but my impression was that, as a whole, they were surprisingly ignorant of modern infantry tactics and methods of training, and that was as far as these matters were concerned, any of the junior officers of the NPR who had been in the force for just over a year would probably be more competent than these former professional officers. (Most of our advisers subscribed to this observation.) For example, it was clear from the questions asked and the comments offered that the officers, as a body, were unfamiliar with the principle of fire and movement and one of the group told me

that this system was not practiced in the old Japanese Army because the lavish expenditure of ammunition which it involved would never have been permitted.

Interestingly, Lieutenant Colonel Figgess speculated,

> Although their training at the moment is of high order, and the progress made during the past six or eight months is certainly remarkable, the Japanese if left to themselves at this juncture would, I think, tend to slip from the straight and narrow path laid down by the Americans and indulge in training schedules of their own conception. Some of this no doubt would be harmless though time-consuming junketing such as fancy marching, honour guards and ceremonial drill but some might tend to take on the flavor of less agreeable features of the old Japanese Army.

This was a warm compliment to American capabilities and achievements from a sincere soldier. Yet as I read his thought-provoking report, I wondered whether we were repeating in Japan what we had so sadly produced in South Korea—a great paper army with officers highly articulate in military jargon and soldiers suffering from the dry rot of a sterile nothingness in their souls.

I recalled the early days of July 1950 when a small band of bitter American officers watched the South Korean army they had so diligently trained fall apart and flee in terror before the invaders from the North. This was the army that had been lauded in the American press as the best army in Asia. Its officers were schooled in what Brigadier General William L. Roberts, chief of the Advisory Group Korea, had called his "Little West Point." Many of these officers had undergone advanced training in Korean versions of our own infantry school at Leavenworth, Kansas. But there was something very vital missing in the South Korean army. Nor did the communists outnumber our ally, for South Korea, with 25 million people, enjoyed a population two and a half times that of North Korea.

What had occurred was that our South Korean officers and men had learned the synthesis of soldiering. They could recite their classroom lessons well. They talked a good game of war. Everyone worked, practiced, and maneuvered like soldiers, but when the chips were down, they ran like cattle in a stampede.

In the early phase of the Korean invasion, companies, battalions, and regiments retreated in full flight without permission, without orders, and in many instances without making contact with the enemy. They were scattered like chaff before the wind by the same kind of Koreans as they were, except the invaders lived north of the 38th parallel. One must ponder, why did the South Koreans run and why did the "communist gooks" from the north fight?

As I watched our NPR battalions run through their field exercises with their usual excellence, I always reserved a hope that our methods had not spoiled the traditional fighting qualities of the Japanese soldier. At such moments, I always sensed that there was something resilient and tough in the guts of the Japanese. One thing is certain, outer military trappings, those often-lauded characteristics—neat uniforms, shined shoes, sharp commands, articulate officers, and even modern weapons do not make a fighting army.[1]

CHAPTER TEN
SEISHIN KYŌIKU

Napoleon liked to say, "An Army traveled on its stomach," but he also knew that an army fights with its heart. More than any soldier, the Japanese Imperial *heitai* had *seishin kyōiku*, or "military spirit." Spirit, heart, guts, or *seishin kyōiku*, whatever one calls it, is the essence of a fighting force. Without it, no soldier is worth his salt and no army worth its budget.

When Mr. Masuhara became director general of the NPR, he established his family in Tōkyō, a few houses down the street from my quarters. This gave us both an opportunity to become acquainted socially, and although at that time he spoke very little English and my Japanese was limited to enthusiastic "ah-so's," we found that a scotch or two did wonders for communication and understanding.

About nine months after the establishment of the NPR, I found Mr. Masuhara talking more and more about the spirit of the soldiers. He seemed agitated whenever he brought up the subject, and he would go on, beyond my capability to understand, telling me what *seishin kyōiku* meant when he was a lieutenant in the Japanese Imperial Army.

I never got the full significance of the message he was trying to convey to me until one day I read an inspection report sent to me by the chief of the General Group, General Hayashi. Part of the report was in English and apparently prepared personally by the general for my information. In it, he went into some detail describing a parade and review that was held in his honor. Obviously disappointed, General Hayashi concluded, "I was very discouraged. As the men marched in review, I saw no spirit in their eyes."

The strange comment—"no spirit in their eyes"—produced mixed thoughts and emotions within me. "No spirit in their eyes." At first I smiled to myself at the unaccustomed combination of words, but I knew that General Hayashi was a very serious, sincere man, and if he took the trouble to write me that his men did not show spirit in their eyes, something was "bugging" him, and I was determined to find out what.

A few days later, I paid a visit to General Hayashi. As we sat around his low table sipping tea in his office, I asked him what he meant when he reported that the soldiers of the NPR did not have spirit in their eyes. He smiled in his sincere manner, then, talking to his interpreter, he answered with a faraway look in his eyes. "You have often told me, Colonel, that you admired the Japanese soldier in the last war for his will to fight and his readiness to die. In the Imperial Japanese Army, the most important training that a soldier received was spiritual training. We called it '*seishin kyōiku*.' It was a kind of warrior religion of the army. The *yobitai* has no *seishin kyōiku*. I have looked into the eyes of my men but it is not there. All Japan is worried because the *yobitai* has no spirit. Our people ask, 'How can the NPR fight with no *seishin kyōiku*? Who will the *yobitai* fight for? Who is the supreme commander?'"

"To the Japanese," continued General Hayashi, "these are serious questions. I am full of deep concern for our *yobitai*. I have tried to find a satisfactory substitute to take the place of the spirit of the Imperial Army, but there is nothing in Japan that can substitute for *seishin kyōiku*. There is a great void in our hearts. Before the war, the emperor was our supreme commander. Who is our supreme commander now? The soldier of the Japanese Imperial Army was ready and eager to die for his emperor. But now, Colonel, tell me, do I ask my *yobitai* to die for a politician? How can I ask them to die for Yoshida or Ōhashi?"

How does one bridge the centuries of thinking and communicate from one mind to another what one means by fighting and dying for one's country, our way of life, our democracy, and that we fought and many died so these things would endure. I explained that we had no emperor to inspire patriotism, but we were patriotic nonetheless. Our Army was not only a great technological war machine; it was composed of ordinary men and women, who sacrificed, suffered, and died, whose blood flowed just as red and courageously as did the blood of the kamikaze and the dedicated soldiers of the *tennō*, son of heaven.

"Your soldiers fought well and you won the war, but we do not understand democracy like you do. Our soldiers need something more to fight for," answered General Hayashi.

I wondered, could there be something greater than democracy to inspire a people? I was puzzled. Nevertheless, I left General Hayashi with a sense of good feeling. It was apparent that the Japanese leaders of the NPR were as deeply concerned as we were with the development of the moral fiber of their fighting force.

There were others, too, who were thinking about *seishin kyōiku*. Newsman Frank Robertson, writing about the new security force, had also recognized the uncertain spiritual vacuum. "But something is missing," he wrote one time,

> and if it escapes the attention of the American instructors, it is noted with some foreboding by thoughtful Japanese, who ask what is to replace Emperor worship as a source of discipline. Far from being impassive Orientals, the Japanese are highly emotional people, the men particularly. This emotion channeled by Emperor worship made them fight as frantically as they did in World War II. Emperor Hirohito still holds tremendous sway over the Japanese people, but for the time being at least the NPR is not the Emperor's Army.

No, the NPR was not yet the emperor's army. We hoped it would never become his army. But we wanted a viable fighting force, a force that could take its place on the firing line, among American units, if the Korean War ever came to Japan. One thing was certain, if the Japanese needed *seishin kyōiku* to become good soldiers, then we all wanted to know more about it.

My interpreter, Mr. Kitamura, was a veritable encyclopedia on Japanese history, religion, and mores, so I began to question him about *seishin kyōiku*. "*Seishin kyōiku* was very important to Japanese soldier," he began. "Americans say it is 'emperor worship.' True, but it's more. Did you ever hear about *bushidō*, Colonel?" he asked. "*Bushidō*," Kitamura began to explain,

> is what made *seishin kyōiku* work in the Imperial Japanese Army. You have heard about the samurai—the warriors of old Japan? Well you know the samurai were like your knights of King Arthur. *Bushidō* was their way of life. It was a code of ethics, a set of moral principles which guided the

life and behavior of the samurai. It was a mixture of chivalry, Buddhism, ancient Chinese philosophy, and Shintōism. Like your chivalry, it flourished in the soil of feudalism. As a code of behavior for life and battle, it was passed on by word of mouth from father to son. Little boys learned about *bushidō* on their mother's knees listening to stories about the samurai. *Bushidō* was born with the samurai and lived on to inspire the Imperial soldier of Japan. The samurai offered his life to the sun goddess Amaterasu. Our *"heitai,"* the simple soldier of the last war, dedicated his life to the emperor whom he worshipped as "the son of heaven."[1]

"Do you think, Kitamura-san," I interrupted, "that our *yobitai* have *seishin kyōiku?*"

"I don't know," he answered with some confusion. "But all Japanese have *bushidō* in them and the *yobitai* are Japanese."

I had the same feeling about our *yobitai*. Kitamura went on to explain that from Buddhism, *bushidō* passed on to the Japanese serenity, calmness, peaceful contemplation, indifference to pain, a disdain of life, and hopeful anticipation of death. *Bushidō* cooled the hot brow of the warrior and gave him poise and dignity, harmonizing his life with the Universal Being.

From the ancient Chinese philosophies, *bushidō* distilled the politico-ethics of Confucius. It helped to cement the relationship between master and servant and sovereign and subject. It argued the infallibility of conscience and emphasized cleavage between right and wrong.

The native religion of Shintō, or Way of the Gods, gave *bushidō* its special Japanese twist, a filial piety and reverence for ancestors that has no equal in any other creed in the world. It glorified man who indeed was believed to be part god. It taught that the soil of Japan was sacred, the abode of gods where the spirits of the ancestors continued to live and watch over the living. Shintō gave *bushidō* a uniquely Japanese love of race and country. It anchored the warrior to the twin pillars of patriotism and loyalty.

With the flow of generations, these simple precepts became a way of life for the common folk. There was stamped upon the people and the whole nation a deep sense of moral goodness and rigid conformance to strict ethical principles. Japan became a nation of stoics who placed high moral value on endurance, fortitude, and perseverance. It glorified suffering and enshrined those who sacrificed.

There is, for example, a story of a little prince who bravely proclaims, "For a samurai, when his stomach is empty, it is a disgrace to be hungry." And a young mother in a nursery tale reproaches her first born with, "What a coward to cry for a trifling pain! What will you do when an arm is cut off?" This was the *bushidō* of the samurai and of the common man. It helps us understand the banzai charge, the kamikaze, and the Japanese soldier fighting onto death. "All Japanese have *bushidō* in them."

Unfortunately for Japan and also for the rest of the world, *bushidō* was susceptible to easy perversion. In the hands of superpatriots, it became a powerful tool of the militarists. While it could inspire a simple peasant soldier to a hero's death, *bushidō* could also be used indoctrinate a people into believing that they were the chosen of the gods.

Playing on the emotional strings of patriotism, loyalty, and racial superiority, militarists seized the imagination of the Japanese people. After the Russo-Japanese War (1904–5), they kindled in the breasts of the humble farmer and the factory worker a fiery zeal not unlike that which burned in the hearts of the Crusaders. Whereas the Crusaders banded together in the name of Christianity, the people of Japan bowed as one to the *tennō*. A nation of little gods became convinced its number one god, the emperor, would lead the Japanese to world domination.

Probably the question that puzzled Americans during the occupation more than any other was, "How could the nips ever believe that they could whip the United States? Why did they ever get sucked into the war?" I used to ponder this question because during my four and a half years' stay in Japan, I grew to like the people very much. I found them extremely intelligent, practical, and hardworking. I could not understand why these sensible people permitted themselves to get into the war.

The best explanation for their involvement that I heard came from a senior officer of the Japanese Imperial Navy. "It was the stupid army," he said, "that got us into the war. The navy had better sense. We were better informed. Between the First and Second World Wars our navy visited many countries. So did our diplomats and businessmen. We knew the world. We knew the United States. We were very much aware of the economic capabilities of your country and the potential of your people. We in the navy did not believe we had any business fighting you." Continuing, he said, "But the army was stupid. Its senior officers were fooled by their own success in China and Manchuria. They knew only the limited capabilities of the backward Chinese people. They were uneducated men and uninformed about the rest of the world. Because they were able to whip the Chinese, they thought they could whip the Americans. The army generals got us into the war because they were ignorant."

Maybe so, but I often wondered the role of *tennō*, the divine emperor of Japan, and the appointed destiny of a mesmerized people. It is hard to believe today that just prior to World War II, General Senjurō Hayashi (no relative of my friend), then minister of war, could frantically declare to the effect that not only the Imperial Army but the entire nation regarded the emperor as a living god, and that for Japanese it was not a question of historical or scientific accuracy but an article of national faith.

This, mind you, was a public statement made by a minister of a modern nation in the twentieth century. How could anyone believe in a "living god"? I could not understand it, until one day I had an unusual opportunity to get a feeling of how deeply the Japanese felt about their emperor. We were on an inspection tour of camps on the northern island of Hokkaidō, traveling comfortably in a special railroad car. In the group were four Japanese officers of General Group Headquarters, General Hayashi, and myself. Before dinner, we sat down to have some traditional *saké*. I broke out a bottle of scotch and a bottle of bourbon. Before long we all deserted the *saké*, and my friends' faces began to glow with the warm relaxed flush that American whiskey always brought to Japanese faces.

General Hayashi, before his appointment as chief of the General Group, in his capacity as steward to the Imperial household, was very close to the Imperial family and especially Emperor Hirohito. As the evening wore on, I finally found the courage to ask him about his life and experiences at the Imperial Palace. The subject was not taboo, but I noted a reluctance in the Japanese to talk about the emperor. General Hayashi put his glass down and looked at me sternly. Then he began to talk in a low whisper. When he mentioned the emperor, he bowed his head in reverence and the four aides drew in their breaths audibly. They leaned forward as one, listening intently. "Colonel," concluded Hayashi, his face aglow with a beautiful light that only complete faith can bring, "you cannot realize what it is for a Japanese to be in the presence of the emperor. It is like something out of this world. It is beautiful. In his presence, you are overcome with calm and serenity."

The general's face was burning with fever, and his eyes were glazed. His aides sat in a trance, staring into the infinite. Time had stopped for them.

I didn't find out much that evening about life in the Imperial household, but I think I learned something about the Japanese people and their emotional attachment to their emperor. General Hayashi was no ignorant peasant, nor were his officers. They were all intelligent, highly sophisticated men. Nor can I believe that General Hayashi was taken in by any false concepts of race superiority. He was simply a Japanese person reared in the quasi-religious climate of *bushidō* who acquired a heavy dose of *seishin kyōiku* from his military father, and his conditioning was showing that evening. His devotion and that of his officers to the sacred emperor may be fantastic for the Western mind, but it is deeply rooted in the Japanese. It is beyond reason or scientific analysis.

We were indeed well-advised at the time of our victory over Japan in refraining from attacking the institution of the emperor. Our acceptance and retention of the emperor made the task of occupying and governing the country infinitely easier. For belief in the divinity of the emperor was so deeply ingrained in the people of Japan that even in the blackest days of national defeat the son of heaven was able to order his people to surrender to the Western barbarians, and his most fanatical subjects accepted his will without a murmur.

Even Sanzō Nosaka, the oracle of the Japan Communist Party, never once directly attacked the institution of the emperor. It makes one wonder whether Nosaka and the communist leadership could have visualized a communist Japan with an emperor behind the moat in the Imperial Palace at Tōkyō. Some believe that's the kind of communism Japan could accept.

Legend records that the sun goddess, Amaterasu Ōmikami, ordered her grandson, Ninigi no Mikoto, to the Islands of Japan, the Divine Land, to govern the people living there. The warlike tribes that Ninigi found were themselves descendants of lesser gods. According to *Kojiki*, a manuscript written about AD 700–800, Jimmu Tennō, the great great grandson of Ninigi no Mikoto, and, of course, a direct descendant of the sun goddess, finally subdued the warring tribes and established the Imperial throne of Japan. Starting with Jimmu, so the Imperial manuscripts record, his descendants have ruled the Divine Land without interruption for more than 2,600 years.

In time, legend became a national faith, and finally in the nineteenth century, the Meiji constitution transcribed national faith into legal reality. Article 3 of the prewar constitution declared, "The Emperor is sacred and inviolable."

In their dedication to the emperor god, the Japanese people took their cue from the army. The Imperial soldier, or *heitai*, became the natural successor of the samurai. At the completion of his tour of military services, he returned home to breathe fire and inspiration into the hearts of his family and friends. The sacred emperor remained his commander for life, for the Japanese soldier had a very personal relationship with his emperor. That relationship was clearly defined in the Imperial Rescript of Emperor Meiji, and its simple precepts became the soldier's bible. It told the soldier and the nation how to live, how to fight, and how to die. Because the Imperial Rescript had such profound influence on the Japanese fighting force and the nation, I read the document very carefully.

Emperor Meiji begins his rescript with the declarations, "The forces of our Empire are in all ages under the command of the Emperor. . . . The supreme command of our forces is in our hands, and although we may entrust subordinate commands to our subjects, yet the ultimate authority we ourselves shall hold and never delegate to any subjects. . . . Soldiers and Sailors, we are your supreme commander-in-chief."

This left not the slightest question in the mind of the simplest *heitai* as to his relationship with his emperor. The Imperial Rescript as the Holy Writ of the Imperial Forces enunciated five basic virtues. The first was loyalty:

> The soldier and sailor should consider loyalty their essential duty. A soldier or sailor in whom this spirit is not strong however skilled in art or proficient in science, is a mere puppet, and a body of soldiers and sailors wanting in loyalty . . . is in an emergency no better than rabble . . . neither be led astray by current opinions or meddle in politics, but . . . fulfill your essential duty of loyalty, and bear in mind that duty is weightier than a mountain, while death is lighter than a feather.

This virtue, like the other four, was basically a sound military precept, but in practice the officers and the noncommissioned officers who explained the Imperial Rescript to their soldiers perverted its meaning to serve their own purpose. For the militarists, loyalty demanded unbelievable self-sacrifice in the name of the emperor, the ancestors, and the divine land. It often inspired behavior repugnant to the Western minds. In the Pacific War, loyalty became so disoriented it drove Japanese soldiers, writhing in pain, to stab at the helping hand of an American medic who tried to offer assistance. Horrible, inhuman "slaughter battles" were fought in unhappy China in the name of loyalty. And it was loyalty that required officers to fall on their swords and soldiers to blow themselves to bits with hand grenades clutched to their breasts. It was a cruel, savage, senseless, destructive loyalty, but a loyalty nonetheless, that made "good soldiers" of simple, ignorant peasants and workers.

The second virtue prescribed by Emperor Meiji ensured complete and direct control over all members of the armed forces. This virtue enunciated the sanctity of rank and importance of obedience. It enjoined the subordinate to obey the superior: "The soldier and the sailors should be strict in observing propriety . . . juniors should submit to their seniors. . . . Inferiors should regard the orders of their superiors as issuing directly from us."

This last statement enabled Japanese commanders to move squads, companies, and divisions unflinchingly into the face of certain death, for the orders of the superior were in fact as binding on the inferiors as though they were issued by the son of heaven himself. No one could question the orders of a "living god."

There are classic examples in which commanders ordered their men to march without water in maneuvers under such severe conditions that some died from sheer exhaustion. Examination later of their canteens would reveal that they were full but untouched. *Bushidō* and the Imperial Rescript taught the Japanese to prefer death to disobedience.

Yet in other situations, direct disobedience of orders became a virtue. This contradiction resulted from the policy of assigning staff officers to field commanders directly by the Imperial General Staff in Tōkyō with implicit instructions to the staff officers to obey orders from Tōkyō only. Under this policy, an Imperial staff officer on a division commander's staff in the field could and often deliberately defied the orders of his commander on the theory that those in the Imperial General Staff expressed the desires of the emperor. Commanders in the field were frustrated time and again by this senseless interpretation of the emperor's desires, and there are many historical instances of battles being "snafued" by officers of the Imperial General Staff.

This theory was so strongly ingrained in the Imperial Army that when the NPR became the National Safety Force, and later the Self-Defense Forces (Jieitai), and previously purged officers of the Imperial Japanese Army were integrated into the new military establishment, our American advisers had a most difficult time in trying to prevent the re-establishment of this discredited policy in the new force. The Japanese G-3, the officer responsible for operations and training of the defense force, who had been a member of the Imperial Japanese Staff, was especially adamant in his views. He insisted that defense force staff officers be assigned directly to positions in the field with control over them from General Group Headquarters in Tōkyō. When Colonel Albergotti, our G-3 adviser, could not convince him to do otherwise, I finally decided to talk to General Hayashi. After about two hours of discussion, General Hayashi finally accepted our point of view with, "You won the war. We'll try it your way."

I often found that General Hayashi resolved differences in position between his officers and the American advisers with this practical approach. How long they'll try it our way, I'm not sure.

Under the concept of the Imperial Rescript, top military leaders had direct access to the emperor as their supreme commander in chief. This permitted the top generals and admirals to circumvent political leadership and undermine uncooperative ministers and governments. This close association of the emperor and the military ensured that no one would rise in opposition to the army or navy budgets or military policies the militarists supported. They could always lean on a directive "issuing directly from us." But, after all, power is relative, and the power of those who govern is directly proportional to the indifference of the people. Some believe that in the United States, a catastrophic war can be launched by the president without the aid of an Imperial Rescript. As Congress has permitted its constitutional powers to erode, the president has acquired frightening authority. Today, many believe that the president has greater and more immediate power than the Japanese emperor-god to plunge the nation into a nuclear holocaust.

Returning to the Imperial Rescript, courage was the third virtue. In enunciating this concept, Emperor Meiji was uniquely prophetic: "The soldier and sailor should esteem valor. But there is true valor and false. To incite to mere impetuosity, to violent action cannot be called true valor. If you affect valor and act with violence, the world will in the end detest you and look upon you as wild beasts. Of this you must take heed." As victors in a savage, fanatical war, we could strike a righteous attitude and accuse, "You should have heeded your emperor."

It was in the name of valor, nonetheless, that the Japanese men reached their apex of self-sacrifice. The story of the "Three Human Bombs" is a classic of human valor.

During the fighting in China in the early 1930s, a Japanese attack was brought to a halt before strongly fortified Chinese emplacements. Three soldiers were selected from a large number of volunteers to breach the position. To ensure that the breach was properly placed, three men carried a "bangalore torpedo" (a long tube loaded with explosives), carefully placed it in the assigned location, and exploded the device, blowing themselves to bits. Their act immortalized them. They went to their ancestors in the spirit of the samurai who while dying raises himself and with his last breath shouts, "Tennō Heika, Banzai!"

In the last two virtues, the Imperial Rescript enjoined the soldiers and sailors to value faithfulness and righteousness and to live a simple life: "Faithfulness implies keeping one's work and righteousness the fulfillment of one's duty. . . . The soldier and sailor should make simplicity their aim. If you do not make simplicity your aim, you will become effeminate and frivolous and acquire fondness for luxurious and extravagant ways. . . . We hereby reiterate our warning. Never do you soldiers and sailors make light of this injunction."

In Japan, bursting with people, limited in material resources, lacking food for its masses, and possessing only the bare necessities of life, this last virtue was the easiest for the military and the populace to achieve. It was also a very practical injunction, warning the subjects to be content with their lot.

This then was the Imperial Rescript of Emperor Meiji. Its spiritual force had its roots in *bushidō*. Each day this force was rekindled in the young *heitai* by the officers and noncommissioned officers of the Imperial Japanese Army and Navy. It put "spirit in their eyes" and valor in their hearts. It gave the Japanese *heitai* a spiritual reason for being. It inspired them to emulate the samurai and the nation to endure heroic sacrifices.

The delicate problem that the new leaders of Japan faced in building their defense force was to balance and integrate their ancient *bushidō* ethics with the new, still unfamiliar precepts of democracy. It is interesting to note that seven months after the establishment of the NPR, General Hayashi was trying to accomplish this intricate balance. In addressing one of his regiments in the field, he said, "The fundamental spirit of the NPR I firmly hold to be patriotism and love of our race. We love our parents, our brothers with whom we are one blood, and our wives and children. By extending this love, we love the Japanese people; we love the land of Japan. We love our fatherland which we were entrusted by our forefathers to turn over to our posterity. This is a traditional sincere feeling deep-rooted in the life of the Japanese people."

He was stressing patriotism, love of race, love of country, and obligation to ancestors and posterity. He had not as yet mentioned the emperor, but this omission was to be short-lived. A few months later, on the auspicious occasion of the emperor's fiftieth birthday on April 29, 1951, in a speech to his forces, General Hayashi found it appropriate to deplore the lack of respect for the Imperial family. On this occasion he said, "This source of our (national) distress, however, is found less in the material damage to our country than in the lack of goodwill towards one another, in the lack of patriotism, and in the lack of respect and affection for our Imperial family—a central symbol of our national unity."

Finally in a stirring speech to his soldiers, he made a gallant effort to link the new military organization with the Japanese people. In this speech titled "Let us be the peoples' defense force," he bridges an ancient gap: "Needless to say, if this organization [Japanese defense force] is to play its rightful role in the new Japan, it must be 'an organization of the people.' This must be the fundamental principle upon which this defense force should be established."

On that note, I take hope that the American occupation brought a new dimension and that the new democratic military forces of Japan may yet demonstrate that "storms make oaks take deeper root."

CHAPTER ELEVEN
YOBITAI

The National Police Reserve, having been organized in pseudo-secrecy, suffered some real and imaginary crises, but one of the most vexing minor problems was to find a suitable name for the recruits, the privates of the organization. Always conscious of the troublesome fact that the NPR officially was a police force, we scrupulously avoided using any words or showing any signs that might suggest that it was an army. General Shepard, I recall on one occasion, seriously considered relieving an American lieutenant colonel because on welcoming new recruits to his camp the officer had referred to them as soldiers.

Heitai, the Imperial equivalent for "American GI," was taboo for the Japanese. Various American and Japanese word combinations were tried. *Keisa*, the Japanese word for "patrolman," was used occasionally. However, *keisatsu* neither appealed to the Americans nor was it popular with the Japanese. At times, when we called them "patrolmen," all of us experienced a mental revolution that only a soldier can feel in thinking of another soldier as a police officer. In some units, the Japanese used the words *ippan taiin* for GI. This translated into "common member of a unit," leaving much to be desired in a name for a nation's warrior. *Shihotō*, a kind of abbreviation for "sergeant-patrolman," gained some popularity among the Japanese people. The name that finally won out because it appeared most logical and least objectionable to both Americans and Japanese was *yobitai*, meaning "reservist." Taken from the name of the force, it referred to the police nature of the organization. At the same time implying a supporting element of an army, it became an acceptable substitute for *heitai*. The children and the farm folk, however, not comprehending the delicate difference between the NPR and an army, innocently continued to call the members of the NPR *heitai-san*.

Yet in the eyes of the nation, there was a great difference between *heitai* and *yobitai*. At best in the early days of the NPR and the National Safety Force into which it developed, the *yobitai* was regarded as a hired employee of the government, whereas the *heitai* had for generations been an honored son of the people. The *yobitai* had the earmarks of a mercenary, the *heitai*, even in the defeat, was the hero-warrior. This difference was deeply rooted in the traditional glorification of the Japanese Imperial soldier.

The Imperial Army had been bound by strong ties of heritage to the Japanese people. Gathering sons and husbands from the remotest villages of the country, there was hardly a thatched roof or crowded city shack that did not house a family who had a close personal association with the Imperial Army or Navy. The Japanese people had great confidence in their army because it was a fluid organization, a representative cross section of the nation. The bulk of the officers came from the lower classes, mainly from the families of small landowners, store owners, and small-shop operators. The military leaders, recognizing the political importance of identifying the army with the people, played on every human heartstring to mirror the *heitai* as the soul of the nation.

On the day of his induction into the service, the *heitai* became a local hero. Dressed in the best kimono the family could afford, the *heitai* was accompanied to camp by relatives, friends, and special delegations from the community. On these occasions, the army opened its camps to the public. It was a day of rejoicing and festivities. The new recruits and those who came to camp with them were assembled by the military to hear the most stirring patriotic speeches. The new *heitai* were portrayed as young heroes, who in serving the emperor brought honor to their families and communities. Everything was done to tie the people to the soldiers and the Imperial Army.

In contrast, the NPR, having gone through an unfortunate secret formative period, was unable to identify with the people. Everyone was aware that the basic plan for the force had been developed by the occupation forces, that General MacArthur's directive to the Japanese government initiated the organization, and that it had been trained and deployed under active American leadership. At the time the force was recruited, only a minimum of information was disclosed to the public, and the average Japanese knew little about the nature and the purpose of the NPR. Even some of the senior officers who joined the organization initially volunteered under the misapprehension that they were being recruited into a national police establishment.

In the early formative days, the public was prohibited from visiting NPR camps, and strict orders were given to keep civilians, except those on business, out of the camps. The Communists, Socialists, and other opposition groups made the most of this difficult situation, fanning the fears and natural distrust of the people. Later when political objections to the new force were aired in the Diet and in the press, many of the students and working men and women were turned against the organization. Under these circumstances it is little wonder that the *yobitai* had difficulty in capturing the hearts of the people.

About a year and a half after the NPR had been organized, I visited several camps in the northern areas of Japan. On this visit, I took every opportunity to talk to the soldiers, trying to get some feeling of what they thought of their organization and how they viewed themselves. I talked to them in small groups, four or five *yobitai* in a group. Usually after we broke the traditional icy reserve and tendency to behave "in a military manner," we had some very interesting conversations. I am sure the answers were staged somewhat, but I found that these answers were generally corroborated by other observers, including news reporters.

The *yobitai* told me that in the early months of the NPR, they were reluctant to visit home because the older men laughed at them, calling them "toy soldiers." Even now, after a year and a half, the *yobitai* didn't like to wear their uniforms in town. The people stared at them, they said, and not in a friendly manner. They thought the children and the old ladies liked them, but the young girls were not impressed with the *yobitai*. Most of them agreed that the farmers were much friendlier than the people in the large cities. The farmers called them *heitai-san* and that made the people appreciate the *yobitai*.

> Well in my case my home is in Tōkyō. They sent me up here to Hokkaidō. I'm like a fish out of water. At first, no one came to visit me here in camp. When I went to town, people would turn cold eyes at me. My friends in the NPR and I had nothing to do so we would go to town to have a drink of *saké*. The people called us drunks. We didn't like being talked down like that. One Sunday, there was a fire in town. We rushed to the scene,

helped put out a fire, and saved some furniture and other property. After that the people looked at us with changed eyes.

Two newspaper articles that were translated for me show the interest of the Japanese press in the *yobitai*. The first was titled "Earth and Soldiers." I have reproduced both of them here as they were translated for me. Both articles, one favorable and one critical, appeared the same week.

The story begins with a young farmer who had some four acres of farmland to be tilled by him and his ailing mother-in-law, who needed his care. The cultivation of four acres, plus the care of his ailing mother, had been too heavy a burden to be borne by him. As providence would have it, however, one day last May, a ministering angel appeared before him in the uniform of the NPR. Patrolman 2nd class Kamata Take, 23, assigned to Camp Utsunomiya in Tochigi Prefecture, while walking along a field lane around the barrack, happened to meet this young farmer who was working in the field. A casual exchange of greetings made them friends. Told of the young farmer's hard luck, he was moved to sympathy. So he made up his mind to help the poor farmer and took the trouble to have his farm clothes sent from his home. Then, he made a point of visiting the young farmer whenever he had leave, to help him in his farming; at the outset, however, the young farmer hesitated to accept his kind offer, but eventually he did. In this way, two young men were seen working together in the field. This cooperation continued even during the scorching days of summer until their concerted efforts were rewarded with rich crops in autumn. Now Takashima Yoshio, 22, the young farmer, is happy because his mother, Nayo-san, 68, has recovered and got well again. Nayo-san, too, is happy because she not only recovered her health but also discovered what the NPR really is through Patrolman 2nd class Kamata. This story was shared throughout the village and its vicinity, which deeply moved the villagers.

The second article was critical. It was titled "Bad Manners of NPR Personnel." According to it,

A camp for the personnel of the NPR has recently been built at Kita-machi, Nerime Ward, Tōkyō, and the members have moved into the building. However, there are no accommodations for baths and they use the local bathhouse. We are very much surprised at their bad manners in the bathhouse. They fling their shoes everywhere and while bathing they sing songs which are obscene and can be heard by the children. Such disturbances take place for about one hour every day. Of course we do not agree with the unreasonable regulations that restrained of the army of bygone days, however, we hope that they become members of the community with better social manners and common sense.

I found that the *yobitai* blamed their uniforms for the lack of acceptance of the NPR by the people. Most of them liked the uniform personally, but they thought that the people didn't like it. One of the *yobitai*, however, was very specific in his criticism: "I don't like to wear my uniform. The people stare at us whenever we travel in uniform. It lacks Japanese style. It is foreign design."

I had to smile when I thought of the long, drawn-out discussions we had with Mr. Masuhara about the uniforms. When General Shepard asked him one day about a design and color for the uniform, the director general didn't hesitate a moment, declaring himself immediately for an American-type uniform, except that he wanted an Eisenhower jacket that by 1950 the United States Army had discarded. General Shepard, on the other hand, was eager to have the Japanese adopt a green uniform somewhat like the one the Germans wore during World War II. He also wanted a loose, field-type jacket, which he considered much more serviceable than the Eisenhower jacket. However, Masuhara was a determined man, and he refused to give in. No color would do except olive drab, and he insisted on an Eisenhower jacket. General Shepard finally suggested that he would provide a sample jacket slightly different from the Eisenhower type. Masuhara agreed to consider it.

When the director general left, Shepard turned to me and said, "We can't have that stupid Eisenhower jacket. It will make them look like little bellhops. You get me an Australian jacket; it's loose, serviceable, and practical. But for God sakes, don't tell the Australians that we're going to use it as a model for the Japanese army. The Aussies would go nuts."

It required considerable maneuvering among my Australian friends to secure one of their jackets. Before we showed it to Mr. Masuhara, we removed all insignia and markings. When he saw it, his eyed brightened. Two weeks later, he returned the Australian jacket and brought in the first NPR uniform. Its color approximated our American olive drab, but the design was a compromise between the Eisenhower and Australian jackets. If the *yobitai* considered his uniform modeled on a foreign design, they were correct, but I assure them and the Japanese people reading this that the Americans had little influence in its selection.

The decision on the field cap was an ordeal. We had no difficulty with the so-called dress cap. Mr. Masuhara and his advisers adopted a dress cap similar to the one we wore. A dress cap, however, has a stiff visor, is expensive, and is limited in its utility. Accordingly, in the past two wars, Americans have worn what has come to be known as an overseas cap. It is cheap, flexible, and easily stuffed into a back pocket or shoulder strap when not on the head. We thought the NPR should have them. But there was nothing we could do or say to convince the director general to accept our overseas cap. He was determined to dress the *yobitai* in the Imperial Japanese field cap.

This was a cloth cap somewhat peaked and with a soft brim over the eyes. It had been worn by the Japanese *heitai* and officers for several generations. It was also cheap, flexible, and very serviceable. But it had become identified in the Western world with the Japanese invasion and conquest of Manchuria and China. It represented colonialism and imperialist Japan in the eyes of the Allies. We were, therefore, very much concerned that the NPR, decked out in the hated Japanese Imperial field cap, would bring the wrath of the British, French, Australian, and even American people down upon us. We hesitated, dragging our feet, holding off a decision on this part of the uniform.

Finally General Shepard, in exasperation, turned the field cap project over to me. I was to continue to try to sell Mr. Masuhara. One evening I dropped in on the director general at his home. I had my overseas cap with me. "Masuhara-san," I began, "try my cap on. You see how light and soft it is. It's inexpensive and very practical. Put it on, you'll like it."

Reluctantly he took the cap from me and placed it squarely on his head. He turned to his wife for approval, but when she bowed her head to snicker into her hands, the director general turned around sternly. "No," he boomed. "Your cap has no sex appeal." This ended all discussion on the uniform, and that is why the *yobitai* wore a uniform of American olive drab, with an Australian-type jacket and a Japanese Imperial Army sex appeal cap.

Probably the greatest contribution the American advisers made to the new Japanese army was to bring dignity to the individual *yobitai*. As the Japanese NPR members told me themselves, military customs in the Imperial Army were purposely designed to demean the *heitai* and all juniors. The Imperial officers were deliberately arrogant and often sadistically mean. The difference was eloquently described by an NPR sergeant who told me, "I served in the old army. The *yobitai*, today, as an individual is treated like a human being. In the old army, I would describe the training as fierce in a barbarous sense. Officers and noncommissioned officers kicked and slapped the *heitai* around. The horse was often treated better than a soldier. My sergeant in the old army was a brute. He taught with his fist and boot. Today, I am a sergeant. I teach our *yobitai* from a manual and they discuss their instructions and ask questions."

It is interesting how the past lives on, even reflecting upon a nation. During the Korean War, I visited a training center behind the front lines to observe new recruits being trained for the South Korean army. To my amazement, I saw a South Korean major brutally slap a young recruit several times in the face because the youngster wasn't learning to shoot as rapidly as the officer thought he should. When the major stopped slapping, a sergeant punctuated the instruction with several well-aimed kicks to the young man's behind. Puzzled at this brutality, I turned to an American adviser and asked, "What the hell is going on here?"

"Oh that's nothing, Colonel," answered my American escort. "I've seen a general slap the hell out of a colonel. They tell me they picked that up from the Japanese army when it occupied Korea."

"And you're not trying to stop it?" I ventured.

"Hell no, we're fighting a war here you know."

After this experience, I was determined that there would be no slapping in the NPR. To my surprise, on return to Japan I read in a Tōkyō paper (by translation) that an NPR captain had slapped and kicked a Japanese civilian on a streetcar because the citizen had not risen to offer his seat to the captain. Shocked at this apparent resurgence of military arrogance and brutality, I asked General Hayashi to come over to my office. When I related the incident, he was disturbed but informed me that he had been previously apprised of the slapping. "What are you doing about it?" I asked General Hayashi.

"We are investigating the incident," he replied.

"That's good," I agreed. "You know, General Hayashi, we cannot tolerate this undemocratic and brutal behavior. Please tell me what action you propose to take after you investigate the matter."

A week later, General Hayashi came in to report on the incident. He advised me that the investigation substantially confirmed the newspaper account. After considering all facets of the situation, General Hayashi said he was going to fine the captain two weeks' pay.

I couldn't hold back my indignation. "I don't understand you, General," I began. "This is a very serious incident. It is serious because what you do in this case will determine policy and behavior for the future. Is the Japanese Army going to become a viable military force of a democratic people, or are you going to permit the officers of the new force to slap, kick, and push your citizens and soldiers around?"

"But," protested General Hayashi, "The captain comes from a very influential family."

"So what, General?" I retorted. "Is his family, and is he, more important than the NPR? Is he more important than the dignity of an individual citizen? This captain doesn't look to me like an officer and a gentleman." When I finished, General Hayashi appeared shaken. Three days later, he came into my office with a smile on his face. "We are going to try it your way, Colonel," he said. "The captain has been dismissed from the NPR."

I was pleased, and so was General Hayashi, to note that several Japanese newspapers carried complimentary editorials congratulating NPR Headquarters for its dedication to democracy and concern for human dignity. They cited the dismissal of the captain as a fundamental difference in the attitudes of the old and new armies.

Like all people the world over, the *yobitai* appreciated being treated as human beings. We may have been slow in bringing a martial spirit back to Japan, but we did inspire a sense of individual dignity and respect for the person of the *yobitai*. As one of them said, we set an example that was taking root in the nation:

> When I became a *yobitai* I was especially pleased by the concern our American advisers showed for us. About a week after I joined, I cut my leg severely. Having served in the old Japanese army, I bandaged it as

best I could, and went about my duties. Our American adviser stopped me and when he saw my wound, he immediately took me in his jeep to an American doctor. Why, you would think I was a governor of a prefecture the way they treated me. I now find that our own officers and doctors follow the American example.

I found that the *yobitai* liked their training and appreciated the fundamental differences between the old and new methods and tactics. Some seemed to regret that the new army was not as tough and severe as the old, but they thought their time was used much more effectively. Transportation to and from rifle ranges and maneuver areas saved hours of laborious marching. And there were no silly drills as in the old army, fighting airplanes with bamboo sticks. As one of the sergeants commented, "We don't charge around madly in the old days. Today we practice firepower and movement. Our officers are now concerned about keeping casualties down. In the old army, no one cared about the life of a soldier."

Some, nevertheless, were critical that the *yobitai* had no one to hate. At best the enemy was identified as insurgents or rioters. And they missed the old bonds of comradeship of the old army. One *yobitai* remarked, "No matter how hard you quarreled and exchanged blows in the old army, we all felt a close affinity for each other. Friendships in the NPR are very thin."

Periodically, the newspapers would criticize the leadership of the NPR. The criticism was in a great measure justified in the case of officers at the higher echelons. Most of these were either police officers or inexperienced civilians. But at the company and battalion levels, I found the young officers eager, alert, hardworking, and as professional as any young officers I have ever known.

I was in the field one day watching an NPR company in an infantry attack exercise. The young Japanese company commander was especially aggressive in pushing his troops. Just before they made their final assault on the objective, an American umpire came up to the company commander and said, "Captain, you are receiving withering machine gun fire from the enemy; you have lost about 30 percent of your men. What do you do?"

"I continue the attack, sir," answered the young officer.

A little later, the American umpire approached the captain again and he said, "Your attack is stopped. Enemy artillery is falling on you. What do you do?"

"I fight here," answered the company commander.

Once again the American umpire came up to the company commander. "Captain, you are under heavy artillery fire. Enemy attack planes are diving on you. What do you do now?"

Without a moment's hesitation, the captain answered, "I die here." As a Japanese man, he was responding to a national conditioning that is deeply rooted in the people. There was no question in my mind that he would have died there whether he had on the Imperial uniform of the emperor's army or the battle green of the NPR. As my trusted interpreter, Kitamura-san, once said, "Every Japanese has *bushidō* in him."

There has remained also a unique spirit in the new Japanese army that has its roots deeply in the soul of a self-sacrificing people. This spirit tends to surface in many diverse ways. It is Asian in source and cannot be understood by the Westerner. It assumed varied forms in the soldiers of new Japan.

A few weeks after the establishment of the NPR, a young *yobitai* met a tragic death emulating his samurai forebears. Before dying, he had carefully written a note to his village. In his letter, he related that disturbed by the hard life he and his family were forced to live after the defeat of his country, he had joined the Japan Communist Party. He worked diligently for communism, spreading propaganda against the Americans. But soon he became disillusioned with the communists. To pay for his infidelity, he volunteered for service in the NPR. He was amazed at the efforts of the Americans to make the new Japanese army an effective military force. He tried to emulate them and worked with all his heart and soul to be a useful soldier of Japan. But he was unhappy and unworthy. There was only one thing he could do to expiate his terrible crime against his family, his village, his nation, and the Americans. He decided to commit "hara-kiri," otherwise known as *seppuku*.

When the company one morning went out to drill, he stayed behind in his barracks. He took a clean sheet from his bed and spread it on the barracks floor. Then, kneeling on the sheet before his ancestors and gods, he disemboweled himself. With his life oozing out, he scribbled his last words, "Makaasaa [MacArthur] Banzai!"

By October 1951, the purge was partially lifted and selected former army and navy officers began to be inducted into the NPR. At first, only captains were permitted to join. Later, commissions were offered to a limited number of majors and lieutenant colonels. Finally, the NPR opened to a few former colonels of the Imperial Army. At this point, some of the newspapers in Japan became deeply concerned. On October 15, 1951, an evening edition of one newspaper carried a piece under the heading "Revival of the Old Army."

> It is reported that now some of the purgees may participate in public life, former army and navy officers have been commissioned in the NPR. Since there are many outstanding men among the old officers, we raise no objection to their employment, recognizing their capacity to serve Japan well. Our only concern is that they shall not revive the old ideology and methods of commanding troops. In fact it would be terrible, if there remained such ideas in the minds of these officers. Indeed, if there are such men among those who have now joined the NPR, the future of the new army will certainly be contrary to the expectations of the nation. The new generation which fought colonial battles is gone. We cannot again tolerate an army of ignorant unscientific leaders who brought upon us the miserable defeat of World War II. The present generation would be mad to contemplate revival of a past age.

A year later, by the middle of October 1952, the new embryo army of Japan had completed its first phase. The National Police Reserve had been expanded and the name changed to the National Safety Force. The *Asahi* reported the event:

> This was the day on which the National Safety Force was born. The men had gone to bed as *yobitai*. They assembled now for a review to commemorate the inauguration of the immediate phase of rearmament of Japan. The National Safety Force has at last assumed the role of a national defense force in name as well as substance. The original NPR which was organized to maintain peace and protect the nation against subversion from within has finally dropped its outer "police" garment and stands now in full armor. The men of the new force are beginning to assume the rugged features of the samurai—the defenders of Japan today.

CHAPTER TWELVE

CONFUSION AND CONFLICT

"Ambiguous" is perhaps the best word that can be used to describe the NPR in its formative days. I have already indicated that initially only a few Americans and the topmost leaders of the Japanese government really knew the true purpose of the organization. General MacArthur and the American Advisory Group conceived a broad general blueprint for the development of the force into an army, but this vague plan depended upon many uncertain factors: world opinion, Japanese reaction, availability of American weapons, and Prime Minister Yoshida's mood. On the Japanese side, violent political forces pulled the cabinet and the government first in one direction then another. The Socialist Party and the splinter groups on the left held the government's feet close to the fire, demolishing all the proposals for rearmament of the nation by raising the prohibition against war and war potential. Accordingly, officially and legally, Yoshida had no choice but to maintain that the NPR was a police force. Even as the organization was being equipped with artillery and tanks, government spokesmen steadfastly denied that Japan was rearming.

In every country of the world, governments officially deny what may be an obvious fact in order to avoid diplomatic embarrassments. But in Japan, the leaders of Yoshida's administration, on the matter of the NPR, had to lie through their teeth to their own people and to their friends and opposition in the Diet. This created many critical and embarrassing situations in the country.

In the public double-talk that was so much a part of the history of Japanese rearmament, I was especially sympathetic with the role that Mitoru Eguchi, deputy director general of the NPR, played. An experienced governmental official, Eguchi participated in these political encounters as becomes a professional, never losing his equilibrium or fine sense of humor. After each interrogation, on returning to headquarters, he would come down to my office to advise me of the questions he had been asked and how he had answered them.

I gathered from these meetings that although the Communist Party members of the Diet were often obnoxious in their queries, neither Eguchi nor the government was disturbed by what the Communist Party said or did. The left Socialist Party, however, enjoying a strong following among the people and forming the core of the opposition, forced the government to run for cover every time its members began to ask questions about the NPR. With Socialists maintaining that the NPR was an army, established in violation of the constitution, their questions invariably generated unfavorable publicity in the press for the government. Typical of these encounters was an interrogation of Eguchi in a Diet hearing about a year after the organization of the NPR.

On that occasion, a Socialist Party member of the Diet was obviously looking for headlines. With Eguchi in the witness chair, he began, "According to the newspapers, the NPR is now armed with bazookas. If that is so, the NPR is an army. Why is it then camouflaging as a police organization and using the name of a police reserve? You are only trying to fool the people of Japan."

Eguchi responded with the official Japanese government position: "The NPR is a police reserve. It was established to assist and support the nation's police reserve. It is organized into units and equipped with weapons to provide necessary support for the police."

But the Socialist interrogating was not to be shaken off the trail so easily. "If that is so, why don't you teach the members of the NPR so-called police spirit which the others policemen are receiving? Why doesn't the NPR send men to the Police College [Keisatsu Gakkō]?"

Eguchi continued his well-drilled answers, prepared with the care and logic of a politician in the United States. "The NPR, as a police reserve, is not responsible for supervising traffic or census taking. It is trained to operate in units. Therefore, it is not necessary to send individual NPR men to the police college for individual training as policemen."

As the questioning proceeded, it developed that the Socialist Party member of the Diet was a citizen of the town of Takada in Niigata Prefecture. The NPR at that time was negotiating with local authorities there for the release of a tract of land that had been a former artillery range. Referring to these negotiations, the Socialist addressed himself to Eguchi: "I have been advised that your camp commander of Camp Takada has approached our local administration office and requested release of the former imperial army artillery training areas there. The camp commander said he needed the land in the very near future for artillery practice. Is the NPR going to have artillery?"

At the time he recounted the incident to me, Eguchi admitted with a smile that the question floored him, and for a while, he didn't know how to answer. Finally, he told the Diet committee that the camp commander was obviously not well informed or he was exaggerating the situation in order to make a good case for his request. The fact was, Eguchi informed his interrogator, no one in NPR Headquarters knew for sure whether the police reserve was to be armed with artillery. The key words in his answer were, of course, the words "for sure."

At this point, the Socialist broke in: "Well, if the NPR is not getting artillery, it has no need for an artillery range and I'm going to tell the local administrator in Takada not to release the training area to the NPR."

"No, don't do that," cried out Eguchi. "The NPR truly needs additional training areas." Everyone in the hearing room laughed. No one was fooling all the people.

While these maneuvers were going on in the Diet, GHQ and the American Advisory Group were urgently pressing the Japanese government to expand its embryo army and to rewrite the defense ordinance to provide for a more effective military organization. By the end of 1951, the NPR had developed to the stage where we thought that it was ready to be equipped with artillery and tanks. The official statements of the prime minister, however, created some doubts about the government's willingness to expose itself to further criticism from the opposition by accepting such obvious military weapons. Indeed, a police force armed with artillery and tanks would be an odd police organization even in Japan. Accordingly, it was suggested that I feel out Mr. Masuhara and General Hayashi on the question of equipping the force with these heavy weapons.

A favorable opportunity presented itself during a social call I made on the director general one evening in his private railroad car while he was on an inspection visit in Hokkaidō. As we were all concerned about the constitutional question, I asked Mr. Masuhara and General Hayashi whether they thought that the constitution would have to be amended before the NPR could be converted and expanded into a modern military force.

Mr. Masuhara had not the slightest doubt. "Japan," he said, "can build an army, navy, and an air force without any need to change the constitution." Then more cautiously he added, "But, politically it would be more desirable to revise the constitution so that we could have the Japanese people behind our program."

General Hayashi smiled his approval, adding optimistically, "We will change the constitution in the summer." He didn't say what summer.

I then posed the question that motivated my visit. "Mr. Masuhara," I asked, "if we were to give artillery, right now, to the NPR, would you anticipate any unfavorable reaction?"

The director general made no attempt to conceal his pleasure, and General Hayashi beamed. Both answered together that there would be no unfavorable reaction. Mr. Masuhara waxed enthusiastically, "We are waiting anxiously for your 105 and 155 artillery." Then he asked excitedly, "Do you think the NPR can have tanks soon?"

I said yes, and the staff applauded. But I wanted to make sure the government had no objections. "What about your government?" I asked. "What will Mr. Yoshida say about artillery and tanks?"

Mr. Masuhara's response was immediate: "I talked with the prime minister only a few days ago and advised him that the Americans might equip the NPR with artillery and tanks in the near future. He answered, 'Then that's good.'"

Then, with everyone laughing, the director general asked, "When are we going to get some jets?" It was quite obvious that the NPR was ready for rearmament.

By the spring of 1952, everyone in Japan was talking about rearmament. All over the country, roundtable discussions and open panel forums were being held on the radio and in public assemblies. The opinions of former army and navy officers were given wide coverage. The views expressed ranged from hope and peace and order through an international police force to traditional dependence upon national arms and salvation through the emperor. The discussions and debates were cleverly reinforced by rumors circulated to support the views of the contending groups.

The specter of international communism played its customary frightening role. In the days of monolithic communism, Russia was the enemy of Japan, as it had been in the eyes of the Japanese people for several generations. Now reports were heard on the debating platforms that Russia was bolstering its forces in Far East Asia. There were rumors that Russian air force and airborne units were being deployed on Kamchatka, Sakhalin, and the Kurile Islands. According to those who said they knew, the Russians were preparing for the invasion of Japan. With the United States committed in Korea, immediate, massive rearmament was the only hope for Japan.

Those who opposed rearmament argued, on the other hand, that Japanese military forces would become the mercenaries and tools of the United States. The Socialists and other leftists contended that after the peace treaty, the NPR would be rapidly equipped with heavy weapons of war and would be dispatched to help the American forces in Korea. An unfortunate comment by Mr. Ōhashi, state minister in charge of the NPR, suggesting the possibility of extending the term of service of soldiers completing their tours of duty unleashed furious attacks in the press. Despite repeated denials by the government, the opposition charged that the Liberal Party planned to re-establish the reserve system so that NPR members could be bound for life service and for eventual duty overseas.

While the public listened to the arguments and debated the rearmament issue, Prime Minister Yoshida steadfastly refused to acknowledge in his statements to the press and in the Diet that the NPR was an army. "Our present policy," he insisted, "remains unchanged—not to rearm ourselves."

As the weeks went by and the newspapers continued to feature stories of the proposed expansion of the NPR and speculated on the plan of the government to convert the present organization into a National Safety Force with a Defense Agency, or Bōeichō, in July 1954, the prime minister's insistence that Japan was not rearming seemed meaningless. When leaks began to appear in the press that the NPR was being equipped with artillery, tanks, and aircraft, the opposition in the Diet could no longer be contained. The constitutional question plagued the prime minister wherever he appeared. Finally, finding his position politically intolerable, Yoshida apparently decided to make a clean breast of the whole matter. On March 6, 1952, while testifying for the proposed expansion of the NPR before the Upper House Budget Committee, the prime minister declared that the constitution did not outlaw "war potential for self-defense." He insisted that "Article

9 of the constitution bans war potential for settling international disputes but not war potential for self-defense. We must do our utmost towards preparing to defend our country against those threatening our independence."

His statement was greeted with a howl of protests in the Diet and in the press. The loudest and sharpest criticism, as could be expected, came from the left-wing Socialists, who charged, "Up to now the government has hoodwinked the people on rearmament by using the expression, 'gradual increase of self-defense power.' It has now quit falsifying the issue with words and disclosed its true intention to rearm. This certainly violates the war-renouncing provision of the Constitution."

The new justice minister, Tokutarō Kimura, in an effort to soften the criticism, complicated the problem by insisting that when Yoshida talked about "war potential (*senryoku*)," he did not mean "war potential" as used in Article 9 of the constitution. This explanation convinced no one, and the prime minister did not help his case any by declaring, "Since the government holds that rearmament will not be undertaken, I do not think it necessary to amend the constitution."

As a result of this exchange of sophisticated views in the Diet, the newspapers enjoyed a field day interpreting and explaining what Yoshida said and what he meant. The opposition was merciless. Having painted himself into an impossible political corner, Yoshida asked for permission to amend his statement before the committee. This only infuriated the opposition, which insisted on restudying the stenographic notes of the committee hearing before listening to an explanation from the prime minister.

Four days after his initial testimony on "war potential," Yoshida appeared again before the Upper House Budget Committee. In correcting his previous statement, the prime minister now admitted that even "war potential for self-defense" amounted to rearmament and so requires a constitutional amendment. Clarifying his views, he reasoned cautiously: "When Japan gains strength, acquires enough economic assets and foreign powers acknowledge Japan's right to self-defense we may then resort to a referendum for constitutional revision in order to possess fighting potentiality."

The explanation left the nation precisely where it had been before the hassle in the Diet began. Japan remained in a kind of twilight zone of rearmament. The prime minister had acknowledged that the constitution would have to be revised before the nation could acquire "fighting potentiality," but the NPR, in the meantime, continued to be equipped with artillery, tanks, and aircraft.

Justice Minister Kimura, in the course of his reply to the Diet, gave a new twist to the constitutional argument by defining "war potential" as something much more powerful than rifles, machine guns, mortars, and artillery. He contended that in a modern world, a nation could not be considered to possess "war potential" if it did not have the A-bomb and jet airplanes. Kimura proposed that since the NPR did not possess these weapons of mass destruction, it could not be construed to be in violation of the constitution, which, according to the justice minister, denounces war as a means of settling international disputes.

Hitoshi Ashida, former prime minister of Japan, leader of the Progressive Party (Kaishintō), and a strong proponent of rearmament, supported the attorney general's view, arguing, "Although Article 9 of the Constitution renounces war, recourse to armed threats and maintenances of an army, this refers strictly to means of settling international differences. When this is interpreted in everyday language, it means war of aggression. Therefore, war and recourse to arms for the sake of self-defense is not denied by this article in the constitution. Likewise war as a punishment against aggression is exempted from application of this article."

Ashida and the Progressive Party thus faced the rearmament issue squarely, and the Progressive Party was the first political party to make a forthright declaration for rearmament of the nation. Though Ashida's interpretation of the constitution seemed to permit Japan to establish military forces, the Progressive Party urged that the constitution be revised.

The right Socialists found themselves on the horns of a dilemma. The party platform was pledged to support the constitution, upholding Article 9, but many of the party members believed that in order to have a meaningful defense establishment, the constitution had to be amended.

The hard core of the opposition to rearmament was concentrated in the left-wing Socialists, the Labor-Farmer Party (Rōnōtō), and the Communist Party. This bloc argued that the NPR was an army and as such was in violation of the constitution. The Socialist Party raised the legality of the NPR in the Supreme Court in 1951, but the court avoided the constitutional question. Under these political circumstances, the government proceeded with its gradual rearmament of the country while the parties of the Left, possessing more than the required one-third of the members in the Diet, managed to block all efforts to revise the constitution.

One of the major fears of the people, especially students, teachers, and trade unionists, was that the NPR and whatever military organization eventually evolved in the country would become a political tool of those in power. These groups had suffered too recently at the hands of the militarists to forget what the military was capable of doing to a nation. In their view, rearmament was being supported by the same fascists and rightists who had stifled democracy in the past.

But all government institutions tend to try to stifle democracy, and the struggle for freedom is endless. I thought the responsibility for maintaining democracy and freedom was placed in proper perspective by a prophetic answer given in reply to a question from a newspaper reporter by Colonel Kiyohara Chihara, commander of Camp Himeji in Hyōgo Prefecture. Colonel Chihara was asked, "Don't you fear that the NPR will be utilized as a tool for political strife in the future?" Chihara pondered the question for a long time, and then he quietly responded, "It is the responsibility of the people to guard against such an eventuality."

The answer demonstrated that at least one formal Imperial officer had acquired a deep understanding of democracy. As the time for the 1952 election campaign approached, the people were to discover that Japan was to experience still another new exercise in democracy. This came in the form of instructions from General Group Headquarters to camp commanders advising them that all qualified NPR personnel would be authorized under the new law to cast absentee ballots. The personnel in the Imperial forces did not vote in prewar Japan. On learning of these instructions, newspaper reporters flooded the camps to record the views of the soldiers on rearmament. One view became immediately clear: they knew they were in the army. A Sergeant Senda gave a typical answer: "We know where we stand. Two years ago when we joined the NPR, we didn't know whether we were going to be policemen or soldiers. Now we know we are in the NPR to defend our country."

Many concurred with the views of a young captain who declared emotionally, "I don't care what the government calls us. As long as we have arms we are troops. Even a three-year-old kid has the instinct to defend himself. If there is a chance that Japan may be attacked by a foreign power, we better have troops."

While the newspapers featured the comments of various soldiers and officers serving in the NPR, there were many, especially among the Imperial officers who had recently joined the NPR, who were reluctant to become involved in political controversies. These people were uncomfortable with the press. They generally agreed with the view of a former lieutenant colonel who declared forcefully, "It may be all right for some to be interested in politics, but it would be better for the NPR and the country if we did not have the right to vote as was the case in the old army."

A vocal minority, on the other hand, opposed rearmament in strong and sometimes embarrassing outbursts. Many of the NPR personnel came from the industrial centers where the trade unions and leftist political parties exerted strong influences. These people followed the Socialist line and their replies to queries left no doubt of their feelings. A comment of a senior sergeant of the force summarized their views: "If there is money for rearmament, let us make it available for social welfare programs. We are rearming," he argued, "because the Americans demand that our government rearm."

Both the Left and extreme Right found common ground in Japan in criticizing American motives on rearmament and the way it was being carried out. The Left objected to the pressure the U.S. government was reported to be exerting on the Japanese to escalate the military forces, while the extreme Right, mostly former militarists, was critical of American dominance in organizing, training, and equipping these forces. The mass of the Japanese people, whether they supported or opposed rearmament, were deeply concerned and often embarrassed by the obvious presence of American officers in the NPR Headquarters in Tōkyō and more particularly in the camps throughout Japan. In the light of these political evasions, contradictions, and endless bickering, it is understandable that the Japanese people were hopelessly confused regarding the nature of the NPR and the government's intentions on rearmament. Almost two years after the establishment of the NPR, it is astonishing how many of the Japanese believed that the organization was actually a police force.

During this formative period, I made it my responsibility to watch carefully Japanese opinion polls reflecting national attitudes toward the NPR, the constitutional prohibition on military forces, the rearmament program, and the presence of Americans in Japan. I was advised that some of the early polls left much to be desired scientifically, but most were acceptable as indicators of public opinion and national trends. In reading and analyzing these polls, I found that reality in public matters was not always easily discernible. For example, I knew that we were rearming Japan, the Japanese officials knew we were building a Japanese army, and the NPR and its armament were obvious to anyone except a blind person.

But the national opinion polls showed that the people were senselessly befuddled. Though a sizable segment of the population was able to cut through the fog of political nonsense, a large percentage of the people believed their national leaders. Japanese, however, are not unique in this regard. Millions of Americans have shown similar disposition, especially during the Vietnam War, to accept their leaders' announcements as gospel truths. This tendency to believe without questioning must be a kind of dependence on authority, probably an extension of our childhood faith in parental omnipotence.

There was nevertheless considerable independent thinking. A surprisingly heavy percentage of the people seemed committed to the Japanese constitution. These people were indicating their support of the provision against war and military potential. Many professed a strong commitment to peace through international law and order. The polls significantly demonstrated a deep suspicion of any movement back to prewar aspirations. Logic in the difficult international environment called for defensive measures and some kind of military machinery, but the majority of the Japanese people were not going to follow any harebrained militarists down a road anything like the one that took them into the Pacific War.

In the latter part of August 1950, as our four-division force was being assembled in NPR camps throughout the country, the *Mainichi Shimbun* asked a sampling of 3,552 people (of which 3,220 responded) the question: "Do you think the police reserve force (Keisatsu Yobitai) can protect Japanese security?" The respondents split almost evenly; 36.4 percent answered yes and 35.2 percent no. Disturbed by the communist invasion of Korea, Japanese had little enthusiasm for the new force being organized in Japan.

A year and a half later, in February 1952, when the *Asahi Shimbun* asked a sampling of 3,000 people (of whom 2,614 responded) the question, "For what purpose do you think Japan has its police reserve?" one-third of those answering believed the organization was established as a police force to maintain law and order. Only 3 percent thought the NPR was an army, and another 16 percent suggested that it was a substitute for an army or a preparation for rearmament. When this question was asked, the *yobitai* were armed with M-1 rifles, machine guns, rocket launchers, and mortars, and there was talk in the newspaper that the troopers were receiving training in artillery and tanks.

It was not surprising then when the *Asahi* asked the same people, "Premier Yoshida said, 'I will never rearm Japan.' Do you believe this?" 48 percent, or about half, said they did not believe the prime minister. Most of the respondents did not feel they could answer the question or said they believed him. Men were more skeptical than women. Only about a third of the women said they did not believe Yoshida, whereas about two-thirds of the men who answered doubted the prime minister's veracity.

During the latter part of 1950, 1951, and early 1952, there were numerous public opinion polls conducted by the *Mainichi*, *Asahi*, *Yomiuri*, *Yoron Kagaku*, *Yoron Chōsa Renmei*, and other agencies on the question of rearmament of Japan. There were variations in the questions asked, so a simple summary of the answers cannot be presented here. In most of the polls, about half of those answering favored some kind of rearmament for Japan after the peace treaty. A strong third opposed any rearmament. A *Mainichi* public opinion poll published April 14, 1952, or two weeks before Japan regained its sovereignty, showed that only 38.3 percent wanted Japan to have a military force, while 41.4 percent of the women opposed the formation of such a force.

In a February 1952 poll, the *Asahi* posed the proposition, "The government has a plan of strengthening the NPR. Do you think this is necessary?" Only 45 percent answered that it should be strengthened. The women again were more afraid of rearmament; only 32 percent supported a strengthening of the force. When the *Asahi* in a later poll asked whether the NPR should become a foundation for a new Japanese army, the respondents were not enthusiastic, with 38 percent supporting the view.

On the question of whether Japanese forces should have compulsory or voluntary service, the Japanese people were overwhelmingly against the draft. In a poll on this question conducted by the *Mainichi* in September 1951, only 18.5 percent approved a draft whereas 69.2 percent favored voluntary recruitment, if there were to be military forces. A similar poll by the *Asahi* taken five months later found only 17 percent supporting compulsory service, with 64 percent for a voluntary program.

While the Diet debated Article 9 of the constitution and acrimonious arguments raged throughout the nation, several opinion polls surveyed attitudes of the people. Practically everyone in Japan accepted General MacArthur as the author of the "no war, no war potential" provision of the constitution. Moreover, most of the people recognized that this provision was forced upon the nation. Nevertheless, a large segment of the people hung tenaciously to this idealistic concept. In April

1952, the *Shimbun Yoron Chōsa Renmei*, querying a sampling of 3,000 people (of whom 2,907 responded), asked the question, "If a plebiscite is held on the revision of the constitution to pave the way for rearmament, will you support revision of the constitution?" Only 42.5 percent said they would support such a revision. It is interesting to note that when the *Asahi* in early 1953 asked a similar question, "The Japanese Constitution has a clause according to which Japan renounces war forever and promises never to have an army. Do you favor this clause?" a bare 15 percent answered that they favored this clause.

Opinion polls taken in the spring of 1952 demonstrated that the Japanese people, after seven years of occupation, were becoming tired of American controls. Though a heavy percentage of the people queried recognized that they were dependent upon our military protection, they nevertheless wanted our military forces withdrawn from Japan as soon as possible. In many people, this uneasiness stemmed in part from a fear that the Soviet-American struggle in Asia would overflow from Korea into Japan, and they wanted none of that.

In discussing the attitudes of the Japanese people concerning armament with Mr. Masuhara, the director general, he minced no words:

> You know, Colonel, for five years prior to the Korean War, you Americans preached disarmament, painting the glories and the wonders of a peaceful world. You gave us an impossible constitution. For a while you even took the pistols away from our policemen. You gave the women the right to vote. You encouraged them to march through our stores, destroying our so-called war toys. Well, the women have the power now. It's going to be a long time before there can be a referendum on the revision of the constitution. In the meanwhile we'll have to build some kind of defensive force as best we can.

Throughout these crucial months, Prime Minister Yoshida alone maintained an irrepressible determination that moved Japan slowly but continuously forward. He could neither be hurried by American pressure nor stopped by the vociferous opposition on the left. "One Man" Yoshida had set a calculated course for his country, and he never wavered from his purpose. Navigating through tricky waters, he accepted American artillery, tanks, and aircraft; denied that he was rearming the nation; and refused to budge at American pleas and coercions to increase inordinately the size of the Japanese forces.

It is reported that when Mr. Dulles urged Mr. Yoshida at the San Francisco Peace Treaty Conference and later in Japan to speed up rearmament, the prime minister at first pleaded economic difficulties, and then cleverly confused the issue with innocuous promises. At the time, the United States was urging Japan to expand its force to 300,000 troops. The prime minister refused to budge beyond a force of 110,000 men. Even when Mr. Dulles, in a counteroffer, suggested economic assistance to Japan, he could obtain nothing more from Yoshida than an uncertain promise to increase the country's "war potential." He left the meaning of this promise to others to define.

There were many important political and economic considerations, of course, operating on the prime minister, but for those who looked behind the scenes, something much more profound than politics or economics seemed to motivate Yoshida. Before returning to the United States in May 1952, I had a revealing talk with one of the top politicians of Japan. "I can't understand," I began, "why the prime minister refuses to increase the defense forces of your country when we are willing to assume the costly burden of supplying weapons and equipment. Surely, this is all to the advantage of Japan. All you're asked to furnish is manpower and you have a lot of that."

Responded my friend, "We will strengthen our forces, but not until 1955."

"Why 1955?" I asked.

"By then the Korean War will be over."

"But why must you wait until the war is ended?" I persisted.

This politician explained,

Mr. Yoshida does not want Japan to become involved in the Korean War. If we organize 300,000 troops as your Mr. Dulles wanted us to do, your government will insist that we send some of these troops to Korea. That is why the prime minister agreed to expand our forces only to 110,000. Mr. Yoshida shudders every time he recalls how the Japanese army was bogged down in China. In that the people share his fears. Should Japan have 300,000 ground troops, a strong argument would be made that we don't need that many to defend Japan from attack and the United Nations, under your influence, would ask us to cooperate by sending at least a hundred thousand to Korea. Once these troops are dispatched, there is no telling when they will be withdrawn.

Even more important is Mr. Yoshida's view—and many Japanese agree with him—that China should be left alone. China may turn red or black, all the same. Be it the people's revolution of Dr. Sun Yat-sen or Mao Tse-tung's communist revolution, leave this to China. What is an affair of China should be left to the Chinese. It will all settle down in the long run. That is the history of China, and it is not a business in which other people should interfere, Mr. Yoshida thinks.

Whatever the reason, "One Man" Yoshida held the Japanese rearmament machine in low gear.

CHAPTER THIRTEEN
THE IMPERIAL MILITARY

The preceding chapter abundantly demonstrated that on the whole, the Japanese people viewed rearmament and military forces as a necessary evil rather than as a national aspiration. Many equated rearmament to war and they were touchy about war; 106,000 had died in two atomic blasts alone. Rearmament, many thought, could prove to be an invitation to disaster.

Soviet pressures in the world, however, culminating in the communist invasion of Korea, forced radical changes in American objectives and policies in Japan. Occupation reform programs were hastily abandoned. The scorn and exposure that had been so studiously focused on the Japanese militarists and ultranationalists was now turned furiously upon communism and the Japanese left. As we shifted into a "reverse course," previously purged and discredited enemies of democracy suddenly became friends, and former war allies became our enemies.

Though the Potsdam Declaration called for removal of purgees from public life "for all times," the new conditions in the world and specifically in Japan necessitated greater acceleration on the "reverse course." A mass depurge in October 1951 removed thousands of former Imperial Army and Navy officers from purge restrictions. By the time Japan had regained its sovereignty in April 1952, only about five thousand former military officers remained on the purge lists. With their full citizenship restored, thousands of these former officers, who for the past six or seven years had been seeking out their stifled existences as fishermen, farmers, and toilers, now raised their eyes and voices to Tōkyō for recognition.

Conscious of their military education, training, and experience, they were convinced that the United States needed them and that their own government would have to use their services in the new military establishment that was forming.

I think a look at these men, who they were, what political and military views they espoused, and what some of them tried to do will add to our understanding of the environment in which the rearmament of Japan was initiated.

As a group, the former Imperial officers were honorable, dedicated, forthright men. Most of them had difficulty, however, in shedding the mental shackles of their early indoctrination, and too many seemed unable to catch up with the modern world. A few were more concerned about their personal ambitions than the welfare of the country.

To me, their most disturbing weakness was their inability to grow above their narrow concentration on the importance of a national military posture. Their vision of the political aspirations and hopes of the people, Japan's economic limitations, and its commitments to other nations were as misplaced after the surrender as they had been in their delusionary prewar days. Although many of their spokesmen embraced the principle of civilian control of the military, they never quite grasped the true meaning of a concept that permitted a former operator of haberdashery (Truman) to sack a five-star general (MacArthur). They argued correctly that the civilian leaders of the NPR did not have the needed military "know-how," and so it was necessary to use former military officers in the new forces. But they also rigidly contended that since they possessed military "know-how," they were the best qualified to organize and formulate the rearmament policy of the country. In this regard, they had learned nothing from the tragedy of the Pacific War.

The military of Japan has enjoyed long centuries of hegemony over the affairs of the nation. Rising to power in the twelfth century, the shoguns (generals) subjugated the emperor and ruled Japan for seven hundred years. They were finally overthrown in the Meiji Restoration. Under the influence of Western political concepts, the privileged position of the military was torn down and civilian authority grew dominant. During the past hundred years, their fortunes and powers waxed and waned with changes in the world situation and the ability of the civilian political forces to suppress them. Governed by strong civilian leaders and moving carefully under a cautious foreign policy, Japan emerged from World War

I with its territories enhanced and recognized as a world power. For a decade its military receded. Then in the 1930s military leaders assassinated the civilian leadership and banded together into *gunbatsu*, or "military cliques," and seized control of the government and direction of the nation's foreign policy. Qualified to command, ready to die, but unfit to rule, they reaped a horrendous devastation.

In the purge that followed the Pacific War, the militarists and ultra-nationalists, directly responsible for having misled the people of Japan, were shorn overnight of their power and prestige. The bureaucrats, who were generally untouched by the purge, stood to gain by the liquidation of their erstwhile bosses and eagerly joined the occupation forces in the indictment. The people too no longer found the military to be heroes, and they accepted the foreigner's explanation of Japan's degradation. Hundreds of top military officers were tried as war criminals, and all 122,235 career military officers were purged. Not only was the leadership of the nation completely changed, but the former military elite became national outcasts, unpitied, unwanted, and distrusted by the people.

Understandably, when the purge restrictions were lifted and the former Imperial officers were inducted into the NPR in 1951 and 1952, they were not greeted with popular enthusiasm. Although the recruitment was limited essentially to young captains, some majors and lieutenant colonels, and a few carefully screened colonels, the people nevertheless were suspicious and watchful. The civilian leaders of the NPR received the new officers into the organization with reserved caution. The young *yobitai*, having found American tutelage pleasantly acceptable, viewed the former Imperials with mixed emotions. Officially, however, everyone hoped they would bring leadership and the badly needed military "know-how" to the new military establishment.

In the meantime, outside the NPR, the former military community was fermenting with disappointment and distrust. Senior officers of the Imperial forces became disgruntled when they were not called by the government to serve. Many organized and joined rightist groups, which have plagued Japan into the present. When they found themselves unable to influence the rearmament program, they turned on the government, became critical of the United States, flooded the news media with militaristic statements, and did their utmost to undermine the morale and integrity of the young *yobitai*. It is difficult to predict what role the younger militarists of the rightist organizations may play in their country's future. But the senior Imperial leaders, now elderly men, are fading away. In the early 1950s, however, they pressed their views furiously.

The nationalist movement has its roots planted deeply in tradition. Japanese literature is replete with accounts of gruesome assassinations every time the "patriots" and *rōnin* "masterless samurai" got together. Genyōsha, or Dark Ocean Society, the first modern nationalist organization in Japan, was organized in 1881 by a band of self-righteous men incensed at what they considered to be a sellout by the Japanese government, which was revising its treaties with foreign powers. The band carried on a violent campaign that instigated a terrorist, Tsuneki Kurushima, to throw a bomb at Shigenobu Ōkuma, the foreign minister. Though the "incident" shocked the nation at the time, Kurushima set a pattern for a steadily increasing series of bloody assassinations and attempted killings. As the nationalists became more sophisticated, their murderous outrages were cleverly justified as having been carried out "for the sake of the country," "for the emperor," or "for the prestige of the army."

The purge disbanded these organizations, but many thoughtful Japanese wonder whether the roots have been torn out. The threat of external communist attack and internal subversion, political strikes of the labor unions, riots, and excesses of leftist students have all stirred violent emotions in the breasts of former senior officers, many of whom belonged to the Cherry Blossom Society (Sakurakai) or the East Asia League (Tōa Renmei), or were the proud and unresurrected veterans of the Kwantung Army (Kantōgun). Some of these nationalist organizations have surfaces with new foliage, but like the bamboo, they get their sap from a common root.

In 1950, as the Korean War grew in ferocity and the United States and the Japanese government shifted their programs and policies into a "reverse course," the former military officers banded together throughout the country, generating a plethora of organizations. Initially, army and navy academy graduates formed classmates associations for social and informative purposes. These were followed by various service groups to promote mutual benefit interests, such as pension rights. Gradually, groups were organized that were concerned with fighting communism, providing security for the country, advocating rearmament, establishing foreign policy, and promoting nationalism. Like soap bubbles, some burst and others expanded or grew by combining and absorbing smaller groups. In time all these associations became involved in the rearmament program of Japan and the new forces that were being organized.

Pulled by a common emotional magnet, these organizations of former Imperial officers all pointed to the right. Despite this general orientation, there were important differences between them, which inhibited effective cooperation.

Many of the splits and rivalries that existed in the prewar Imperial forces persisted into the 1950s. The hardened military views on the conflicting missions, capabilities, and comparative importance of the army and navy continued to divide the former officers of those services. Programs initially developed by Kanji Ishiwara projected one group of his followers into commitments to international peace while a second group of followers supported a program of "armed neutrality" for Japan.

Interestingly, a significant split developed between senior Imperial officers and the younger officers. After an interlude of six or seven years as citizens of a democratic Japan, the young group entertained a decidedly different view of their country and the future than did their former superiors. Whereas in the prewar Imperial forces the young officers of the army and navy general staff were the extremists, pushing their seniors, evolving bold national strategy, and projecting their generals and admirals upon the national stage, it was the senior officers now who pushed for political action, attacked the government, and were the extremists. The younger former Imperial officers did not find democracy odious; they became acclimated to American innovations and found no difficulty in integrating into civilian society. While the former generals, admirals, and colonels pressed furiously to the right, the younger officers looked cautiously about their surroundings.

Attitudes on rearmament, and specifically concerning the new forces, differed drastically. Men like former general Sadamu Shimomura and former lieutenant generals Eiichi Tatsumi, Shuichi Miyazaki, and Yoshio Kotsuki joined Prime Minister Yoshida to advise him regarding the release of former officers from the purge and to assist in screening officers for acceptance into the NPR. Former navy admirals Yoshio Yamamoto and Sadatoshi Tomioka cooperated with the government in organizing the coast guard. These men, however, had little influence with the mass of the Imperial officers who for a long time regarded the NPR with hostility. After 1951, when former officers were inducted into the NPR and professional military leaders were assigned important posts, most Imperial military officers began to accept the new defense forces as something better than nothing. They continued, however, to differ on the broader aspects of rearmament.

Attitudes on the United States, our military capabilities in the Far East, the impact of the occupation of Japan, and the effect of American training methods on the discipline and the spirit of the new establishment divided the former military officers into a variety of camps. Except for their common slogans against communists, they were pro-American as well as anti-American, favored the new democracy, argued for the liquidation of the NPR, and urged the return of the emperor system. Their views of democracy and Americans influenced their thinking on basic military concepts, polarizing their attitudes on the question of supreme command (*saikō shireikan*). While the arguments against democratic control of the future military forces by the prime minister were subdued, many nevertheless advocated return of the supreme command to the emperor. These groups contended that neither the power of the law nor institutions alone were sufficient to build a dedicated military force or to inspire the troops. Some were willing to compromise, urging the establishment of a National Defense Council (Kokubō Kaigi) headed by an appropriate member of the Imperial family.

While these differences in views and attitudes generated rivalries and divisions among the various military groups that surfaced during the "reverse course" environment, their fundamental rightist orientation encouraged wide agreement on many issues. Uniformly, as in the prewar days, they argued that the crisis in Japan was spiritual and the people had to be aroused to the dangers confronting the nation. American tutelage had lulled the Japanese into a false sense of security, and the new liberal concepts of democracy were destroying the traditions of the country. An apathetic Japan was exposing its borders and the soul of its people to alien ideological subversion, from the West to American democracy and from the Soviets to communism. Of the two evils, the more immediate danger to the nation and the people was communism. Duty therefore demanded that the former Imperial officers in this crisis act to save Japan.

This patriotic anticommunism fit nicely with our own views of the world situation. Though the former Imperialists grossly exaggerated the strength of the Communist Party, they gained a warm reception in many American quarters. Arguing that rearmament was the only hope for resisting communist aggression, the new militarists were applauded by Americans. As so often happens in human endeavors, views that coincided were motivated by completely different objectives.

On the one hand, the Americans were urging swift and extensive rearmament primarily to build up a strong military force in Japan in the hope that in an emergency we would have massive Japanese ground forces to throw in against the communists in Korea. Most of the nationalists, however, considered such an adventure totally inimical to Japan's interests.

As the nationalists grew stronger, they began to favor with increasing conviction a military force for Japan independent of all foreign powers. They wanted neither domination by the United States nor commitments to the West. They admitted that Japan would need American weapons and equipment for the initial rearmament, but they argued for early restoration of Japanese armament factories and facilities. Firm in their determination that professionals should make decisions on the buildup of Japanese forces in Japan's interest, they resented bitterly American supervision of the rearmament program. Most of the nationalists demanded that the NPR be disbanded and that a fresh start be made under professional supervision. Critical of the civilian leadership in the NPR, they urged wholesale firings of the amateurs.

Refraining from a direct attack against the parliamentary system, the nationalists did not spare the whip against the new democratic ideas. Deploring the emphasis on the rights of the individual, they contended that the family structure was being undermined and the hearts of fighting soldiers weakened. They urged a massive Japanese revival of traditional virtues. Soft civilian concern for the rights of the people had no place in the military forces of Japan. They advocated revision of the constitution, restriction of the civilian bureaucracy, and rededication to ancient Japanese virtues of discipline, obedience, and self-sacrifice.

Within CASA, the ideas of the nationalists were supported mainly for the reasons previously mentioned, to accelerate rearmament for immediate American military purposes. Personally, I considered these objectives too shallow and lacking an appreciation of long-term human and American interests. Because I was concerned with the impact the nationalist groups might exert, I kept myself carefully informed of their activities.

Colonel Takushirō Hattori and his associates, who in time became known as the "Hattori Agency" (Hattori Kikan), were a unique group that played an important role in those crucial days. As I have mentioned in a previous chapter, Colonel Hattori and his colleagues, with access to the records of the Demobilization Bureau, controlled the main depository of Japanese resources and knowledge. For years after the surrender, Hattori and his fellow officers from the Imperial Army and Navy served as the main point of contact between the occupation forces and the Japanese professional military leaders. Major General Willoughby, General MacArthur's intelligence officer, who had been the supervisor and sponsor of this clique of former Imperial elite, had promised and did his utmost to deliver to Colonel Hattori the command of the NPR. When this did not materialize and the American Advisory Group refused to incorporate the Hattori element into the CASA organization, Colonel Hattori switched his approach, moving the Hattori Agency into the political environment of Japan.

The core of the group at the time consisted of ten or so former Imperial colonels and lieutenant colonels, most of whom had served in the Demobilization Bureau. They were supported by some three hundred members in the prefectures. The announced purpose of the agency was to collect and disseminate information on the rearmament of Japan. The group's slogan was freedom, independence, and self-defense. In their hidden agenda, the members continue to visualize themselves eventually filling the command structure of the new army. Joining other groups of former military officers, they found the NPR wanting in many categories.

Steeped in the emotional traditions of the Imperial past, these groups viewed the NPR and American supervision and training methods with skepticism and aversion. They were critical of American discipline and fighting spirit. Ignorant of modern military concepts, they deplored the use of massive equipment and heavy consumption of ammunition. They accused the NPR of being paid mercenaries who, like the American soldiers they tried to imitate, would not fight unless they were served ice cream daily. They argued that Japan could not afford to pay for the great volume of ammunition that the Americans were requiring the Japanese to expend in training. Suspicious of heavy equipment, they pointed out that bridges in Japan would collapse under the weight of our tanks, artillery, and engineering equipment. They urged the government to disband the NPR and start anew, building ground, sea, and air forces designed for the special defense of Japan. Though they grudgingly acknowledged that under the circumstances then prevailing in the world, American weapons, aircraft, and naval vessels would initially be required, they wanted to be free of any American controls.

Some Americans were surprised to find that Colonel Hattori and his group not only criticized the adequacy of the NPR but questioned overall American military capability in the Far East. Hattori contended that in Asia, which was important to Japan, the Russians were militarily far superior to the United States. The war in Korea, he pointed out, was demonstrating that although the Americans were equipped with superior weapons, they were hardly holding their own against the Chinese, who were fighting with second-grade equipment. His point was that he feared that Japan would find itself as unprotected and unprepared as the Philippine Islands had been against Japanese assaults in the Pacific War.

I was told that in 1951 Colonel Hattori had submitted a fantastic recommendation to GHQ SCAP suggesting that Japan immediately organize twenty infantry divisions, with former company grade officers as the nucleus. He is said to have estimated that such a force could be formed in one month and that given two or three months' training, these units would become as effective as any American troops. If he really made such a recommendation, he certainly knew nothing about the logistics of equipping, housing, deploying, and training a force of this magnitude. Yet he went on to suggest that in the event of an emergency Japan could field fifty divisions.

These ideas were so far out of line with the modest four-division force that Prime Minister Yoshida was trying to nurse along that they were rejected firmly and inalterably. When in the autumn of 1951, after many of the former military officers were depurged, the government refused to call Colonel Hattori and his associates to the command of the NPR, the agency turned bitterly against the new organization. Attacking the civilian bureaucrats in the NPR, the Hattori group sent a circular to prospective candidates among the former officers advising them not to join the NPR. I am informed that later, when the depurged cadres became integrated into the military forces, Colonel Hattori became reconciled to the new organization.

In 1956, following the formation of the National Defense Council, Colonel Hattori was suggested for the important post of councillor, in which he would have been responsible for coordinating defense planning. By this time, however, he had made many powerful enemies. His opposition to civilian control of the military had been so uncompromising that it became a major issue in considering him for the council. The civilian officials in the Defense Agency were irrevocably against his candidacy. Moreover, he had also become unpopular in navy circles for advocating a unified command structure for the ground, sea, and air forces. Ironically, his close association with the occupation forces in the end militated against his appointment. Colonel Hattori came very close to the top in his many efforts to project himself into the rearmament of Japan, but somehow fate, each time, acted to shut him out of the establishment.

A man who sometimes collaborated with Colonel Hattori—but who had his own wide following among Japanese nationalists—was former army colonel Masanobu Tsuji. Colonel Tsuji belonged to many organizations and formed several of his own, but he was never a member of the Hattori clique. An aggressive propagandist, he inspired a movement not unlike those of the prewar extremists. After the purge restrictions were lifted, Colonel Tsuji became a successful politician and was repeatedly re-elected to the Diet.

A dynamic young officer, Colonel Tsuji, beginning as an instructor at the military academy, served in many important assignments in the Imperial Army. At the outbreak of the Pacific War, he was chief of the Operations Section of the First Division of the General Staff (Rikugun Sanbō Honbu Daiichibu Sakusenka). He has been credited with being one of the most ardent protagonists of war with the United States. He gained fame as a shrewd strategist, planning the Japanese campaign that resulted in the conquest of Singapore. On the cessation of hostilities, the British listed Colonel Tsuji as a war criminal, but Tsuji would not permit himself to be shot or to rot in an Allied prison. Disguising himself as a Buddhist monk, Colonel Tsuji remained hidden in Southeast Asia and China for three years—until the war crimes trials were over in Japan.

On his return home, Colonel Tsuji avoided the occupation forces. He became active in numerous military nationalist organizations. One of the early organizations he joined was a group headed by the notorious former major general Takeo Imai. This group advocated disbanding the NPR and urged former military officers not to cooperate with the civilian-dominated organization. Colonel Tsuji and General Imai evolved a fantastic program designed to give Japan an independent military force. They pressed the government to demand weapons from the United States, and if the United States would not cooperate, then the group urged the government to appeal for military aid to the Russians. They considered the situation in Japan so critical that martial law should be declared and a crash rearmament program launched. As a clincher, they wanted the commander of the new military forces to assume control of the economy, administration, and judiciary of the nation. In 1951, despite his efforts to stay away from the occupation forces, Colonel Tsuji was indicted for violating the purge directive.

Basically, Colonel Tsuji was a follower of Kanji Ishiwara and his East Asia League philosophy. With Ishiwara, Tsuji believed that Japan's future was in East

Asia, in a federation or at least a coprosperity sphere with mainland Asians. After the war, he contended that it would be impossible for Japan to enjoy prosperity as a satellite of the United States. Abhorring the Russians, he advocated armed neutrality, proposing a Japan strong enough to stand independently between the Soviet Union and the United States. He stressed the need for cooperation among Asian people and contended that Japan's destiny lay with neither the Russians nor the Americans. This view, especially during the Korean War, had a strong appeal to both extreme Right and extreme Left.

Unlike Hattori, Colonel Tsuji consolidated his support throughout the country. He waged an aggressive political campaign. Pleading for an independent, neutral, armed Japan, he built strong support among neutralists and nationalists as well as among the extremists on both the left and the right. It is difficult to estimate the extent of his following. As the elections developed, his main support centered in Tōhoku and Kyūshū. He was elected to the Diet time and again by a large vote. Although he was initially very hostile to the NPR, he mellowed as more and more of his followers joined the organization and were given important posts. He nevertheless persisted in demanding an independent, self-sufficient, neutral military force free of "interference" from the United States.

By the time I departed Japan in May 1952, I was informed that in addition to approximately sixty fairly well-known nationalist groups centering on former generals, admirals, and colonels, there were upward of four hundred others in various stages of formation and existence. "They are growing like mushrooms after a rain," said my informant.

The far-reaching inspirational teachings of Ishiwara created a movement that deserves our attention because it motivated not only former military officers, but farmers, religious leaders, educators, and the general public. Disillusioned with Japan's aggressive program in Manchukuo (Japan's name for Manchuria), which at the time was alienating Asians from Japan, Lieutenant General Ishiwara proposed a cooperative approach for building an Asian federation that would include Japan, China, and Manchukuo. Organizing his East Asia League in 1939, General Ishiwara developed his theories for a coprosperity sphere in Asia. General Tōjō, having little sympathy for cooperative forces, bypassed Ishiwara during the war, but the "Ishiwara thesis" had many supporters in the nation. After his death in 1949, his broad concepts became increasingly popular with various groups of former military officers. In addition to his views on a coprosperity sphere, Ishiwara predicted what he called a "Final War" between Asian forces and the

Western world. Motivated by strong religious convictions, Ishiwara also preached a form of Buddhist pacifism. As Korea polarized the world into two power camps, Ishiwara's predictions seemed to be fulfilled and followers seemed to move in two directions. One group urged Japan to prepare for the Final War, while another organized the Harmony (Peace) Party (Chōwa [Heiwa] Tō). Though the Harmony Party opposed rearmament, it was also antigovernment, distrustful of Americans, and advocated Ishiwara's program of Asia for Asians. As the party became increasingly pacifist, an aggressive minority that included Colonel Tsuji broke away to form the East Asia League Comrades Association (Tōa Renmei Dōshikai). Subsequently, Colonel Tsuji and some followers split away from that association to form their own self-defense league. The Harmony Party and the splinter groups evolving from it included many influential officers who worked with the public, and some pushed impatiently at the highest level of government for a massive ground force, while others opposed rearmament completely, putting their hope of security in international authority—both views inspired by Ishiwara.

By the spring of 1952, as it became evident that the Yoshida government planned to expand the initial NPR force, the views of the former military officers received wide coverage in the press, especially the ideas of Colonels Tsuji and Hattori. Wondering what the senior Imperial leaders who were now helping the government with plans for the expansion thought of some of the loudly acclaimed programs, I asked a former Imperial general about Colonels Tsuji and Hattori.

"Ah so," he responded. "Some say that it was the Hattori-Tsuji team that persuaded General Tōjō to start the Pacific War. All I can say is that those two flunked the test once. They should never again be allowed to jeopardize the nation."

I think it is fair to say that the organizations created by the former Imperial officers had little influence on American thinking and moved "One Man" Yoshida not a mite. Their arguments were noisy, attracted attention in the press, and caused some trouble for those of us working with the NPR, but they had little impact on the speed or the nature of the rearmament program. Many of the proposals they advocated were acceptable to both the United States and Japan, but at the time they were made, neither the world situation nor the political environment in the country were favorable for their implementation. The Japanese people wanted security, but they were more concerned with their human wants. What may be important for the future, however, is that the Imperial officers in their public and private debates hammered out some very significant national positions.

CHAPTER FOURTEEN

DAWN OF A NEW ERA

The cycle of events was closing upon itself. Six years and eight months had passed since Emperor Hirohito, on September 2, 1945, sadly declared, "We command all our people forthwith to cease hostilities, to lay down their arms and faithfully to carry out the provisions of the instrument of surrender and the general orders issued by the Japanese government and the Japanese Imperial General Headquarters hereunder."

Some, apologizing to their emperor for their real or imagined failure in the war, committed *seppuku* in the tradition of the samurai. The mass of the people, obeying their emperor's instructions, continued to work, suffer, and endure.

On April 28, 1952, Japan regained its sovereignty. Robert D. Murphy, the first American ambassador to Japan since December 8, 1941, correctly timed his arrival in Tōkyō with the official closing of the doors at the headquarters of the supreme commander of Allied powers. At 10:30 p.m., the occupation government was abolished. In a prepared statement made on debarking from the Pan-American clipper *Good Hope*, Ambassador Murphy said, "This is a day for rejoicing and I rejoice with the people of Japan on this happy occasion. Our two nations have joined hands in a new partnership dedicated to the preservation of peace."

But there was no peace and there was no rejoicing. There were few signs of spontaneous jubilation. There was a strange uneasiness in the land.

As I drove through Tōkyō on my way to NPR Headquarters, I observed no outward display of any emotions. I expected and wanted to see joy on the faces of the Japanese people, happiness on their first day of independence from foreign rule. But there was none. The little people who before and during the war dragged their overloaded, unbalanced carts through the streets of metropolitan Tōkyō continued on the day of liberation as they had during the occupation to strain their plodding way, harnessed to the same carts and the same loads. Though the automobile population, acquired with American dollars, had more than doubled since the war, workers in Tōkyō were undernourished and ill-clad. Rice was still rationed. On the historic day of independence, the Ministry of Agriculture and Forestry (Nōrinshō) announced a rice production goal of 13.5 million bushels, an increase of half a million bushels above normal yield. The squeeze was on Japan. The announced quota would be met only through the sweat and toil of the farmers.

Prime Minister Yoshida called upon the people to "march joyfully, courageously, and resolutely on the broad highway of peace and democracy." But there was no marching. Few bothered to hang out flags. The flag-waving spirit, so much in evidence in Japanese newsreels before the war, was nowhere to be seen. Yoshida himself, driving through Tōkyō, is quoted to have remarked, "Hinomaru flags are too few." His cabinet hastened to reassure him that the situation would be remedied, not by compulsion as in the past but through "recommendation" to the people.

Only the little ones seemed moved by the occasion. The most enthusiastic was a group of primary school children, a beautiful post-hostilities crop. As I drove past them, they shouted greetings happily, skipping, jumping, playfully waving their little paper flags of Nippon. These were the fortunate ones who had been spared the horrors of the bombings.

I had removed my GHQ shoulder patch, which to the Japanese was a symbol of the occupation of Japan, but as I drove through the gate the Japanese guards saluted me as smartly as they had for the past two years. The old men and women who cleaned our offices and so conscientiously polished our desks seemed not at all moved by their new day of freedom.

I was later to learn dramatically one day that people who worked hard at routine tasks, day in and day out, find little to be joyous about in their drudgery. I was campaigning for Congress in 1958 in Connecticut one early morning at a factory gate, shaking hands and asking the workers to vote for me. Suddenly an old man stopped in front of me, looked me squarely in the eyes, and asked, "Why should I vote for you? What difference will it make to me whether you or your opponent is elected? I have been walking through this gate every morning for forty years. Tomorrow it won't make a damn bit of difference to me whether you're elected or not." I wanted it to make a difference, but I suppose the old fellow was right. One man has little impact on matters in Washington.

So nothing seemed changed in Japan on its day of liberation. I reached for my *Nippon Times* and was immediately reassured. Japan had indeed been drastically changed and more dynamic changes were on the way. Its lead editorial was reflective:

> It is well that the people should recall those dreary, hopeless and fearful days immediately following the Japanese surrender. The future at that time offered no pleasant prospects. It was not even a thing to be talked about, except in hurried whispered snatches; the world had seemingly come to end. The people lacked even those basic requirements of food, clothing and shelter. . . . Only later history can give a true and final evaluation of the Japanese occupation. But it would be safe at this time to point out that while mistakes were inevitable, the results on the whole were beneficial not only for Japanese people but also for the world at large. Certainly, no greater tribute can be paid the occupation and its policies than the fact that an entire nation and people were awakened to the political and ideological concept of democracy. It is true, to be sure, that democracy has still a long course to run in Japan, but a start has been made which only a major revolution could halt. The ideas of human rights, popular government, women's suffrage, land reform, local autonomy, decentralized educational system, and free labor movement among others are here to stay.

Sovereign Japan began its new era with 81,540,000 people, 20 percent more than the prewar population of the islands. These people were living on an area slightly more than half the territory controlled by Japan before its defeat.

One indicator of the future of Japan was the combination of statistics relating to the birth and death rates and the life span of the people. The death rate dropped from 15.7 per 1,000 to 10 and the birthrate surprisingly dropped from 31.3 to 25.6. The life expectancy for men had risen from a 1936 level of 46.9 years to 60.8 years and for women from 49.6 to 64.8.

Japanese were eating more protein than before the war, and the average daily intake of 2,125 calories was approximately that of 1941. Consumption of sugar was down, however, from 18 pounds annually to 9.81 pounds. Average clothing consumption also decreased from 7.59 to 6.97 pounds annually.

Industrial statistics were encouraging and were a harbinger of things to come. The number of factories had increased 10 percent. Electric power output was up 26 percent. Textile production had almost doubled, but coal and steel production were both down.

The number of compulsory schools had jumped to keep pace with the population increase. Radio sets had almost doubled to ten million and newspaper circulation soared from 11 million to 29 million. Crime was increasing. The number of female criminals had doubled and the number of juvenile delinquents was increasing alarmingly.

My attention was drawn to a sad commentary. A newspaper looking for comments on this day of liberation from people on the street approached a former lieutenant of the Japanese Imperial Army. The lieutenant had been wounded in the head and stomach in North China. Now, out of the hospital, he was reduced to begging on the Ginza. His response to the reporter's question was bitter: "I don't anticipate a sudden change in the attitude of these passersby toward me."

It was a great day nevertheless for those who received pardons under the general amnesty declared by the prime minister. More than 2 million Japanese benefited from this order. Criminal charges against approximately half a million were dropped, 270,000 received reductions in their prison terms, and 470,000 regained their civil rights. The remainder were persons on parole, serving suspended sentences, freed on payment of fines, and evaders on taxes. In the last category were many big businessmen. Most of these were aware that the grand pardon would come in the spring with the signing of the peace treaty. The legal trick was to negotiate and wait out the government. This had been the traditional procedure for big business, and now it was paying off with millions of yen. I was not surprised that under the general amnesty, the government forgave the *zaibatsu* (cartel) firm of Mitsubishi Chemical Company for nonpayment of 290 million yen, Kokobō Industry Company 27 million yen, and Yokohama Rubber Company 30 million yen. When I recalled how the Japanese tax collector in Ōsaka confiscated pieces of furniture and even *hibachi* (grills or stoves) from the small businessmen who failed to pay their taxes in 1949, I shuddered at the gross injustice.

The abolition of the occupation government helped those on the left as well as those on the right. *Akahata*, the Japan Communist Party publication "Red Flag," appeared on the streets of Tōkyō for the first time since its suppression by General MacArthur on July 18, 1950. The justice minister acknowledged his office anticipated the publication of *Akahata*, but in sovereign Japan, there was no prohibition against the Communist Party or its official publication.

The right-wing Socialists joined the two conservative parties in welcoming independence and sovereignty for the nation. Declaring their rededication to democracy, they announced their determination to increase their efforts to re-establish international confidence in Japan. Kaneshichi Masuda, secretary general of the Liberal Party, said his party proposed to rebuild Japan as an independent, self-sufficient nation determined to defend itself. Takeo Miki, secretary general of the Progressive Party, rejoiced at liberation from a foreign occupation. Mr. Miki declared that Japan had to re-establish international confidence and internal harmony by adhering to democratic principles and social justice within the nation. The right-wing Socialists were jubilant over the return of sovereignty but announced dissatisfaction with the treaty terms regarding security, territorial possessions, and reparations.

Left-wing Socialists found no occasion for rejoicing. They anticipated no change in the condition of Japan under the terms of the peace treaty from what had been the situation under the occupation. They contended that the failure of the government to conclude peace treaties with the Soviet Union, Red China, and other Asian countries left Japan in an unstable international position. The peace treaty with the United States, they said, was bought for the price of the security pact, which made Japan an advance military base for American strategy in the Far East.

Yet the return of sovereignty to Japan, at a time when the United States was involved in a worldwide Cold War struggle with the communists and engaged in a bloody war in Korea, represented a deliberate gamble for our foreign policy. Those who were willing to gamble rested their stakes on the contention that freedom and independence would make a better and more dependable ally of Japan than would continued occupation. As might be anticipated, the Pentagon and the State Department argued opposing points of view. The State Department, supported by General MacArthur, who had repeatedly declared that no occupation could profitably last more than five years, wanted an early peace treaty. The military, on the other hand, cautioned that an independent Japan could not be explicitly counted upon to support the Korean War. The Pentagon feared that after Japan regained its sovereignty, the United States could no longer tell it what to do. The gamble was minimized when Japan agreed to have the security pact with the United States come into force simultaneously with the peace treaty. As has been pointed out, the Left deplored the price Japan had to pay for the peace treaty, but in its state of economic and military impotence, Japan had no alternative. Its survival as a nation depended on trade with the United States and the protective military umbrella America was willing to extend.

Prime Minister Yoshida thanked the Allied powers for "a magnanimous peace unparalleled in history" and set the mood for his administration:

> Unfortunately our horizon is darkened by the menace of communism which seeks to conquer the world through insidious propaganda and infiltration by force—by open armed aggression. That is why for the protection of unarmed Japan as well as for the common defense of the Pacific we have concluded a security pact with the United States, under which American land, sea and air forces, at our request, will be stationed within and about our territory. Obviously such an arrangement cannot be continued indefinitely. That is why we must undertake to build up a self-defense power of our own, gradually, according as circumstances and resources permit.

Conscious of international concern and not wishing to alarm other countries, the prime minister cautiously elaborated, "We will not rearm in such a way as to arouse suspicion and apprehension on the part of foreign countries." Those who may now be critical of Yoshida's reluctance to build a larger military force should not overlook the world situation that faced the sagacious prime minister in the early 1950s.

Eighteen nations of the noncommunist world recognized Japan as a sovereign state. Great Britain, Australia, New Zealand, the Philippines, Singapore, and India, among others, greeted Japan's re-emergence into the world as an independent nation with varying degrees of acceptance. There was deep concern about future trade relations and unabashed fear of Japanese competition.

The communist world reacted predictably. Mr. Alexander Panyushkin, the Soviet ambassador in Washington, denounced the San Francisco peace treaty as "illegal." He demanded that American troops be withdrawn from Japan and notified the world that the Soviet Union "cannot bear any responsibility whatsoever for the situation created in Japan." Red China echoed the Soviet Union's renunciation of the peace treaty, declaring that China "cannot recognize it any way." Though most Americans were unconcerned about the communist response, the Japanese people, conscious of their Asian environment, were deeply apprehensive about both their security and economic welfare. To the merchants, manufacturers, and financial circles of trade-hungry Japan, "ideology was politics, but trade was business." Ishiwara's philosophy of a coprosperity sphere embracing Japan, China, and Manchuria was so potentially appealing to the Japanese that no ideological obstacles could be permitted to stand in the way of the good life the theory promises.

There were some thoughtful men among the Japanese who compared the emergence of Japan as an independent nation with the Meiji Restoration. These men highlighted the similarity in the world situations that faced a small, isolated island country in 1868 with the plight of a weak, defenseless, debilitated Japan in 1952. It was useless, they said, to think about the fact that Japan had been a "first-class power." The disastrous Pacific War had destroyed that power. Japan in the twentieth century faced the same problems that the pioneers of the Meiji era solved under severe limitations of national power. The difference between the Meiji Restoration and new Japan was that in the former period only the country's leaders and statesmen deliberated and planned the policies for the nation, and the people followed, while in democratic Japan the people had the power and the responsibility to determine the future course of the nation.

About noon on the first day of sovereignty, Director General Masuhara invited the senior American officers of the Advisory Group to join his staff at NPR Headquarters in a small gathering to commemorate the San Francisco peace treaty. The tables were set in the customary Japanese fashion in the form of a "U." There were no chairs; guests were invited to eat and drink standing at the tables, which were decorated with ceremonial packages of seaweed tied in interesting little bows of "friendship." Plates of sliced meats were scattered among brown bottles of excellent Japanese beer.

Mr. Masuhara presently raised a toast to the United States and its great military forces, thanking Americans for considerations extended during the occupation and the helpful assistance and guidance in organizing the NPR. We responded by wishing Japan prosperity and the NPR success in achieving its mission.

The little party became lively, and shortly American officers and NPR civilian officials and senior men in uniform were enjoying the comradeship of people who work together. I joined a small group including Mr. Masuhara; Mr. Eguchi, the deputy director general; and General Hayashi. I had been reading about the Japanese constitution and the circumstances of its formulation and acceptance by the Japanese government. I wondered how much of this idealistic document would remain now that Japan had acquired its independence. Mr. Masuhara assured me that the fundamental concepts of the constitution would remain. Some changes were necessary. Article 9, of course, would have to be eliminated. In addition, he thought, the article concerning the dissolution of the House of Representatives would have to be revised. When I pointed out that these amendments, together with changes proposed in Article 18 and 22, would require major surgery, he smiled in agreement. He acknowledged, with Mr. Eguchi's concurrence, that the women of Japan, so thoroughly indoctrinated against war, would oppose revision most strenuously. Mr. Eguchi volunteered that the political parties would have to launch a broad educational program, not only among women but among the entire electorate, to get the people to support rearmament.

As we discussed the constitution, I asked whether it was a fact that the "no-war, no-army" provision had actually been included in the constitution at the direction of General MacArthur. The "no" that boomed out of the director general disturbed some of the Americans with us. Mr. Masuhara went on to explain that Baron Shidehara had told the director general personally that although the Japanese people think that General MacArthur directed the provisions of Article 9 be included in the Japanese constitution, actually he, Baron Shidehara, suggested that the provision be placed in the constitution.

Having read several pieces in the press speculating on the future of Emperor Hirohito, I asked whether the emperor planned to abdicate. General Hayashi blanched, assuring me there was no truth in the rumor. "The emperor," he said, "will lay to rest all these speculations when he speaks to the people on May 3."

"The emperor will stay," volunteered the director general. "But the prime minister will remain as the head of our defense forces. Japan must have an army responsible to all the people."

The opposition parties had entirely different views about revision of the constitution and rearmament. The left Socialist Party, holding a meeting in Itami, Hyōgo Prefecture, on April 3 and 4, 1952, had announced a "struggle policy" of steadfast adherence to Article 9 and irrevocable opposition to rearmament. The party pledged its opposition to rearmament. The party pledged its opposition to "militarization" of the NPR and promised to wage a struggle against American military bases in Japan. Opposing any consideration of the conscription system, the Socialists announced their determination to uphold Article 18, against involuntary servitude, and Article 22, the freedom to select one's own occupation and change of residence. More significant, the Socialists were girding for an all-out struggle against Prime Minister Yoshida's legislative program designed to accelerate the "reverse course." The program of the conservatives to force through the Diet the controversial Subversive Acts Prevention Bill to revise the trade union law, the labor standards law, and the labor relations adjustment law was headed for a rough fight.

While the press debated the propriety in a democracy of politically motivated strikes, and some of the labor leaders urged legislative action in the Diet rather than demonstrations in the streets, most of the labor movement fermented violently. Yoshida's "reverse course" threatened their newly born political power. The extremists hardened their position against the government, and the ranks of the unions closed. Focusing their opposition on the Subversive Acts Prevention Bill, they called for massive demonstrations on April 12. The effort, however, fizzled when at the eleventh hour, Tanrō, the nickname for the Nihon Tankō Rōdō Kumiai, or the National Federation of Coal Miners Unions, gave lukewarm support. When the conservative leadership of Tanrō was replaced by leftist leaders, it became evident that sparks would fly on May Day, the fourth day of Japan's new independence.

With the ratification of the peace treaty, the Japan Communist Party, which at the time had twenty-two elected representatives in the Diet, made a determined effort to seize the nation in the streets. I lived only a few blocks from the national headquarters of the party. Every day on my way to work, I could see their tattered flag flying over their headquarters building. On April 29, the first day of independence, I was amused to see not one but a flock of red flags, all flying at half-staff, symbolizing a day of humiliation. On May Day, however, the flags had all been pushed to the tops of their poles. I drove to my office apprehensive of coming events.

Early in the afternoon on May Day, NPR Headquarters advised me that more than 400,000 working men and women and students had gathered in a massive rally in the Meiji Outer Gardens. There had been violent scuffles throughout the rally, and now there were reports of serious trouble expected at the Imperial Palace Plaza. Requests had been made to use the NPR to keep the peace. Headquarters had dispatched a reconnaissance unit to keep the director general informed. I was disturbed, not so much by the May Day gathering, which was expected to be troublesome, or even the clash that might result in Tōkyō, but by the eagerness with which the employment of the NPR against the workers was sought. Counseling caution, I urged the NPR to leave the situation to the Tōkyō Metropolitan Police and the National Rural Police. I reminded the officials that the NPR was an army, not a police force, and that its premature commitment against the Japanese people would give the organization a black eye and would aggravate the opposition. Determining to take a personal look at the situation, I jumped into a jeep and took off for the Imperial Palace Plaza.

Pushing through a mass of humanity, I worked my way into the Dai Ichi Building and climbed to its roof. From there, I could see thousands milling around, some trying to force their way onto the Imperial Palace Plaza and other groups pushing their way along Hibiya Park. The people were swarming. There was a profusion of signs and banners, with many in the crowd carrying bamboo sticks. Small, detached groups were throwing rocks and smashing windows in American cars parked near the Dai Ichi Building. In a sudden rush, the rioters seized American cars parked near the curb and turned them over. An enterprising rioter struck a match, and the cars burst into flames. The pattern was repeated over and over until the police, arriving in force, finally stopped the destruction. The situation was terrible, and one could be critical of the police for permitting the action to get out of hand, but the police were reinforced rapidly and the rioters were brought under control. I ran down from the roof to make my report to headquarters; again, I urged caution. I saw no reason to commit the NPR.

Later, I learned that ten thousand May Day demonstrators led by Japanese and Korean communists broke from the main rally and, defying the police, engaged in citywide rioting. The major attack was launched on and near the Imperial Palace Plaza. Early estimates reported more than four hundred persons injured, including several Americans. About twenty American automobiles had been overturned and set afire. Many more American and Western automobiles had been stoned. Several American soldiers had been mauled.

The Japanese press uniformly deplored the violence and apologized for what appeared to be an anti-American complexion in the riots. I personally considered the attack on the American automobiles to be a matter of chance. The mob, milling near the Dai Ichi Building and Hibiya Park, attacked the cars as targets of opportunity. It is true that some Americans were mauled, but hundreds of Americans who found themselves in the melee were unmolested. I was especially unhappy about a Scripps-Howard report that was critical of the government for not using the NPR. The reporter urged that the next time the force should "move more effectively to smash future attempts to undermine Japan's internal security."

After the confusion of the riots cleared, I had a long talk with General Hayashi. On a visit to my office, he informed me that he was deeply worried about the attitude of the government. Prime Minister Yoshida was very short-tempered, he said, and it required all the force of argument that Mr. Masuhara and he could muster to prevent the commitment of the NPR during the riot.

I showed General Hayashi a newspaper article in which State Minister Ōhashi, who at the time had cabinet responsibility of the NPR, was quoted as saying, "But in the future, NPR will go into action in case of such riots or in case of danger of outbreak of such riots, after receiving the Prime Minister's permission, even if no demand for NPR action is made by those in charge of the Metropolitan or the Rural Police."

"That's what I mean," answered General Hayashi. "That's our problem."

He went on to say that the prime minister wanted to alert the NPR for the emperor's appearance in public on May 3. I could see that the chief of the General Group was deeply disturbed.

General Hayashi said he thoroughly agreed with me and asked me to explain in detail under what circumstances federal troops were employed to quell civil disturbances in the United States. I outlined for him our statutes, procedures, and restrictions on the use of the National Guard and the regular army. We spent several hours discussing American relations with local police, state responsibility, and federal authority and obligations. Then we explored how these concepts could be applied in the Japanese environment.

I was delighted with General Hayashi's attitude and thinking. He was sincerely concerned about the rights of the people and was determined to seek procedures and statutes that would ensure those rights without jeopardizing law and order. He assured me that the view we discussed would become Japanese law.

In the ordinance that changed the NPR into the National Safety Agency (in October 1952) and the statute that later converted the NSA into the Japan Defense Agency, the views of General Hayashi prevailed, for the rules, which were adopted for the employment of the Self-Defense Forces of Japan, incorporated the essential elements we discussed during the days that followed the May Day riots. I often wondered what those rules might have become had the chief of the Central Group been someone other than the intelligent, thoughtful, and sensitive General Hayashi.

The immediate impact of the May Day riots was political. The Japanese, traditionally a disciplined, law-abiding people, were shocked at the senseless violence and bloodshed. The newspapers, crying for law and order, fanned the fires, attacking not only the radicals and communists, but the labor unions and students for permitting themselves to be used by the lawless. The primary beneficiaries of the riots were the conservative groups, which accused the Socialists and trade union leadership of irresponsibility and cited the riots as precisely the kind of disorders and lawlessness their legislation was designed to prevent. As a result, the Subversive Acts Prevention Bill and other "reverse course" legislation became law. In the fall elections that year, the Communist Party, which went into the elections with twenty-two members in the lower house of the Diet, was unable to elect a single member. The left Socialists and the right Socialists, running on anti-American platforms, opposing rearmament, and urging independence and neutrality, gained a total of sixty-five members in the Diet and became a solid core of opposition to the conservative bloc, which was formed essentially of liberals and progressives.

The historic first week of Japan's independence, packed so full of tragic and dramatic events, closed on Saturday, May 3, in quiet ceremonies commemorating throughout the land the fifth Constitution Day. The emperor and empress led the national celebration in a ceremony attended by 30,000 people assembled on the Imperial Palace Plaza, where the police two days previously had met communist-led rioters in a bloody clash. I was in the crowd because the NPR was there in formation to add color to the ceremony and to prevent any disorders that might break out.

When the emperor and empress stepped upon the temporary platform, the people in the assembly grew deadly quiet. This was the emperor's first appearance at a public gathering since the war. More significant, the day marked a unique and historic change in Japan. The people standing in the warm sun, for the first time in the nation's history, could actually see and look upon His Majesty. Up until this day, the Japanese had not dared to look directly at the descendant of the longest unbroken line of rulers in the world. Even when the emperor passed in a train, the Japanese people bowed and averted their eyes from his august presence. Now, some in the silent assemblage cautiously looked up, then directly, at the emperor and empress. I sensed the people liked the unassuming couple that stood so quietly and solemnly on the platform.

Prime Minister Yoshida spoke, as did the chief justice of the Supreme Court, the speaker of the House of Representatives, the president of the House of Councillors, and the governor of Tōkyō, but the eyes of the people were on the emperor.

Finally, His Majesty stepped forward and began to read in a quiet, subdued voice, unrolling the scroll to pace his address. I wanted to know what he was saying, but I never would have dared to talk or listen to my interpreter on that occasion. When the emperor finished his address, there was some muffled applause. Then the emperor and empress raised their arms, leading the people in the traditional banzai cheers. Still the audience seemed politely unresponsive.

As the emperor stepped back to leave the platform, the crowd stood quiet, unmoving. Then as he took another step backward, the emperor in a very human gesture twirled his hat lightly over his head. The crowd burst into a cheer. The emperor, seeing that he had struck a chord of empathy with his people, gave his hat a second and a third twirl. The gathering went wild. Surging forward, an excited mass of humanity crowded round the emperor's automobile. I was afraid for a moment he would be mobbed from sheer enthusiasm, but the automobile moved on, with the people not only looking at His and Her Majesty but enjoying them.

The NPR, having turned out with carbines by order of the prime minister to protect the emperor and empress on this day, looked sheepish in their ranks, watching the people joyfully running after the emperor's automobile. A new day and a new era had dawned in democratic Japan.

CHAPTER FIFTEEN
CONCLUSION: A CRITIQUE

Having brought the Japanese rearmament program up to the uncertain present, I think it is desirable for us to review the achievements and mistakes that were made in the evolution of Japan's military establishment.

In making our judgments, one must never forget that during the critical period of the establishment and development of the NPR, Japan was an occupied country. Though the United States was tolerant and perhaps even benevolent, we nevertheless were in every sense the conquering power. Into 1952, not only did American troops occupy Japan, but the supreme commander's staff in Tōkyō continued to control the Japanese government. Civil affairs (CA) teams and counterintelligence corps (CIC) operators continued to observe and report on local Japanese institutions and governmental entities. In every aspect, Japanese sovereignty was delimited by American military power and surveillance.

Today, we can argue the legality of Japanese rearmament, but in July 1950 the need for a Japanese defense force was so urgent that neither the Japanese government nor the United States could allow any obstacles to stand in the way of organizing such a force. On the Japanese side, the government was not so much concerned with launching a rearmament program as in organizing a force that was immediately needed to defend the government and its institutions. For the United States, the NPR, though limited in its initial capabilities, provided sufficient protection for our dependents, and air, naval, and logistical bases in Japan permitted us to deploy all our ground forces to Korea. In brief, Japan needed the

NPR to defend the nation against insurrection and foreign attack, while the United States needed the NPR to protect our bases. Whether the NPR was adequate for the task is immaterial now, since it was never put to the test. The first achievement, then, was that the NPR filled a very vital need for Japan and the United States.

Whether it was so intended or not, the NPR became the first step in the rearmament of Japan. In this light, it is highly important that we examine any mistakes that may have been made in establishing the organization and evaluate contributions the NPR may have made to the future military forces of Japan.

In my opinion, which I held at the time the NPR was established and which today is reinforced by history, the constitutional question of rearmament was badly handled by the United States, the Japanese government, and the opposition parties in Japan. All three violated important moral principles for exigencies of the moment. All three are plagued today by the consequences of their shortsightedness. The successive conservative governments of Japan, by trampling upon their constitution, created for themselves difficult constitutional obstacles that have forced the development of a military establishment that exists in the twilight zone of legality, hobbled and weakened by that constitution and by the hostility of the people. The United States has become a foreign culprit, allying itself with the conservatives to circumvent the law. The opposition parties, especially the Socialists, in their pseudo-purity, have failed to face up to reality and, by leaning as partisans upon the constitution, have confused and soured the electorate.

To begin with, the United States was wrong to order the Japanese government to organize an army in violation of a constitution that our own commander dictated and that we all interpreted at the time as prohibiting the maintenance of an army, navy, or air force. Recent interpretations may or may not justify the view that the constitution permits self-defense forces or that neither General MacArthur nor the United States forced the no-war, no-arms provision in the constitution on the Japanese. The fact is that in 1950 in Japan, neither General MacArthur nor any official of the United States even hinted that Article 9 of the constitution meant anything other than a prohibition against war, war potential, and military forces. Moreover, no one at that time in Japan suggested that Article 9 had not been proposed to the Japanese by the supreme commander. It was not until three years later, when in November 1953, Vice President Richard M. Nixon, visiting Tōkyō, raised the question of American involvement in the disarmament of Japan. At that time, he said that "the United States did make a mistake [in disarming Japan] in 1946."

There was no question in the minds of the American echelon that was organizing the NPR that we were building an army, yet we were required to camouflage the new force as a police organization. Officers in the NPR were denied military recognition and were designated inspectors, superintendents, and other silly ranks, while the soldiers were called patrolmen. It was a serious offense for an American officer to refer to the NPR as an army or to address Japanese officers as captain, major, or general. When we distributed American tanks to the NPR, the Japanese were admonished never to refer to these weapons as tanks but to call them special vehicles. This, as previously pointed out, caused ridiculous difficulties for those who had to prepare Japanese training manuals. The American advisers and the Japanese leaders were thus required to talk out both sides of their mouths.

Similarly, the prime minister and all the officers and officials of the NPR were seized with a sudden stupidity that was shameful for otherwise honorable, intelligent Japanese leaders. Time and again, top Japanese officials were compelled to deny in public, to their own people, that they were building an army, when the prime minister and the senior officials in the NPR knew without qualification that the force being developed was an army. At one point, the Japanese government contended that the constitution was not violated because the NPR was a self-defense force and not an army. This argument, too, was difficult for some people to swallow when the facts were that in 1946, while the constitution was being debated in the Diet, Prime Minister Yoshida himself, in response to questions in the Diet, clearly stated that the official position of the Japanese government at that time was that rearmament—even for self-defense—was prohibited by Article 9. Anyway, though the Japanese Defense Agency may be defended today as not violating the constitution because it is held to be a self-defense establishment, in 1950 the Yoshida government argued that the NPR was legal because it was not an army.[1] Neither machine guns, mortars, rockets, tanks, artillery, nor aircraft made any difference in the arguments of the government when they were issued to the NPR. Amazingly, as I pointed out in a previous chapter, opinion polls showed that a large percentage of the Japanese people, especially women, believed—or at least said they believed—the prime minister when he declared that the NPR was not an army.

At the same time, the opposition parties in the Diet played a deplorable game of politics by refusing to acknowledge reality. The reality, apparent to the Socialists, as well as to the conservative parties, was that after American ground forces were deployed to Korea, Japan was a gaping power vacuum. The government, whether it was to be Conservative or Socialist, could not exist without some kind of a force to protect it against insurrection, if not attack from abroad. Moreover, since it became evident early that despite the constitution and despite the most determined opposition, nothing would stop the Yoshida government from organizing a military force, the Socialists were in an untenable political position. After recognizing that they could not prevent the formation of the NPR, they should have accepted the situation and devoted their energies to controlling the way the NPR was organized. Had the Socialists, for example, agreed to a minor revision in the constitution in 1950 or 1951, they would have received the support of SCAP in any efforts that they might have made to limit the revisions. At the time the NPR was being established, the occupation forces were still in control of Japan, and it is inconceivable that at that time the United States would have permitted the conservative parties to amend drastically the American-inspired constitution. From a practical political point of view, the Socialists had little to lose and much to gain by supporting a reasonable revision of the constitution. By opposing revision of Article 9, they assumed a rigid political stance, confused the people, and sacrificed for years any chance to head a government in Japan.

The political struggle in 1950 between the Socialists and the conservative parties generated such violent distrust that meaningful dialogue between "One Man" Yoshida and the Socialists was impossible. Yoshida publicly lumped the Socialist opposition with the Communists while the Socialists regarded Yoshida as an enemy of the people. Unlike the Republicans and the Democrats in the United States, who on many domestic issues fight to the bitter end but who resolve differences on national defense and foreign policy, Japanese political leaders seemed devoid of any disposition to reach a compromise. The issue of rearmament, so vital to the nation, deserved the most thoughtful consideration of all the politicians. Watching the political action in 1950, however, I gathered that the conservative leaders wanted the Socialists to have nothing to do with building the defense forces and the Socialists, locked in their ideological dilemma, refused to consider the critical international situation that faced the country.

The basic moral responsibility, nevertheless, seemed to rest with the United States. Legally, and in accordance with international agreements, General MacArthur, as the supreme commander of the Allied powers, was placed in Japan to carry out the will of these powers. After the occupation forces decided that Japan was to be permitted to establish a military defense force, the United States, as the principal occupying power, had a joint obligation with Japan to ensure that the Japanese government executed our directive in compliance with the constitution. No sophistry can now be invented to justify the United States' joining the conservatives in disregarding the Japanese constitution. As an occupying power, we had an obligation to uphold and support that constitution. To argue, as some did at the time, that Great Britain, France, Australia, Nationalist China, and other Allied powers would not agree to rearmament of Japan was to raise the following conundrum: If the United States could induce most of its former allies to fight in Korea, it is inconceivable that we could not convince these same nations that it was necessary to organize a Japanese force to protect United Nations bases in Japan.

Though it would have been difficult, the supreme commander had the authority and the prestige to call in Prime Minister Yoshida and appropriate Socialist leaders to acquaint them with the military situation facing Japan and to urge them, for the good of the nation, to build a limited military force. Since Article 9 and certain other provisions in the constitution operated against a viable military establishment, the supreme commander should have insisted on a limited revision of the constitution. Unfortunately, the supreme commander allowed Yoshida to convince him that the prime minister did not need the support of the minority parties in the Diet for implementing legislation. Moreover, the Americans and the government wanted to avoid telling the opposition anything about the rearmament program. This unprincipled approach to a problem that was most vital to both the United States and Japan was unworthy of American democracy.

America, in the interest of Japanese and our own requirements, had a unique opportunity to open channels to the parties on the left in Japan. This, of course, does not mean collaboration with the Japan Communist Party, but it was important for the United States not to isolate itself from the Socialists and other opposition parties, which we Americans should have realized would be around today and may tomorrow be heading the Japanese government. This shortsighted political rigidity on the American side in 1950 created difficult obstacles for our national interests in the Far East. I was repeatedly shocked at the political ignorance displayed by our military commanders in Japan. Time and again, when the Japanese trade union members and Socialists marched in Ōsaka under their red flags, the American division commander and his provost marshal went out of their minds screaming about those "damn communists."

Whatever reasons may be ascribed to our conditioning and that of the Japanese government to violate the constitution, the results of that action are disturbing. The NPR in the 1950s, and the Self-Defense Forces today, did not and do not now have the enthusiastic support of the Japanese; the people remain suspicious. In addition, the legal obstacles of the constitution have blocked healthy development of the military establishment, undermining its legal base and weakening its professional structure. Most significant, our close association with the conservative elements has alienated intellectuals, progressives, students, and trade union members who initially turned to us for guidance and understanding.

No one, neither the Americans nor the successive conservative governments and the Socialists and other opposition parties, can point with any pride to the way they jointly and individually handled the constitutional question regarding the rearmament of Japan.

Without question an equally important problem, which deserved the searching attention of all the politicians and the Japanese people, was the matter of selection and training of the leadership for the future military forces. Japan had suffered a devastating war precisely because the leadership of the Imperial forces had gone astray. Yet the tremendously important questions regarding qualification, selection criteria, promotion requirements, and training policies for the officers of the new force were never considered by the Diet and never debated in public. All criteria for officer qualification and development was left to the determination of the cabinet, that is, in the control of the party in power. Whereas the U.S. Senate confirms original appointments and all promotion of officers, giving both the Democrats and the Republicans an opportunity to consider the qualifications of each new candidate for military commission and the records of the officers being promoted, the Diet has no such authority. The decision to induct former Imperial officers, the timing of their recruitment, and their rank and qualification criteria were all matters determined by the prime minister with the help of his advisers. Unquestionably, the former military officers brought valuable skills and knowledge to the NPR. Nevertheless, their selection, future training, and schooling deserved the closest supervision by an appropriate committee of the Diet.

Unfortunately, the ideological nature of Japanese political disharmony made it impossible for the politicians to reason together even on this vital issue, pointing up again the basic failure of national politics in Japan. The majority and opposition parties were unable to find a mutually satisfactory arrangement for studying and determining the best way to organize the new military establishment, because the opposition was ideologically against such a force. Nevertheless, failure to revise the constitution and the one-sided decision regarding leadership in the NPR determined the kind of military establishment the nation has today and what it will be in the future. Although the Socialists and opposition parties refused to consider the revision of the constitution or to participate in solving the leadership problems, their resistance was too weak to prevent the establishment of the NPR or the development of the present military forces. It should have become apparent that political decisions affecting national institutions cannot be endlessly put off by any political party nor can they be arbitrarily made by any one element in the country. The politicians in any country must find a way to hammer out the difficult issues, recognizing that in a democracy, "politics is the art of the possible."

A critique enables one to isolate and analyze mistakes and open avenues for corrective action. An examination of achievements, on the other hand, affords opportunities for building on past successes for more effective performances in the future. There were obviously many mistakes made on the American side and by the Japanese in establishing, training, and deploying the NPR. We have examined two, which I considered major deficiencies in our decision making. I think we can also learn much from a consideration of what was accomplished by the NPR and the way the buildup of Japanese forces was achieved.

For the Japanese government, the NPR was the difference between helplessness and a means for maintaining authority. As the new force moved into vacated American camps and grew and developed, confidence, dignity, and independence returned to Japanese officials. Though it never became necessary for the Japanese government during those uncertain days to call upon the NPR, the force was there, available to maintain law and order and to defend the nation, if that had become necessary. To those Japanese critics who today point an accusing finger at the inadequacies of the civilian leadership of the NPR, I can only say that the fledgling organization did its job well enough to maintain national tranquility without the fuss of the prewar military.

Though a military force organized by former Imperial officers would have served equally well the purpose of the Japanese government and the needs of the United States, there was born in the NPR something new and different, something former Imperial officers on their own initiative could likely not have given the new Japanese army. The unique difference was that the individual member became the most important concern of the NPR. Unlike the *heitai* of the Imperial Japanese Army, the *yobitai* became an individual, dignified and respected as a person. Officers and noncommissioned officers treated the *yobitai* as intelligent and capable of learning and doing anything their superiors could accomplish. I was most favorably impressed in those days on visiting the NPR units to find young soldiers taking notes during instructions and referring to notes previously taken in discussing weapons, tactics, and equipment. No longer did a sergeant or officer dare to strike or kick a soldier in ranks. Nor did the *yobitai* or the officers behave superior to the civilian citizenry of Japan. What was especially gratifying to me was the deep concern the public demonstrated when on occasion some officers resorted to abuse practiced in the Imperial Army. This respect for the dignity of the individual fighter is undoubtedly the most important contribution the NPR made to the future of the nation.

Yet the *heitai* of the Imperial Japanese Army was a great soldier, a courageous fighter, ready to die for the emperor and the country. Many believe that the new soldier of Japan is better educated and more reliant than was the simple *heitai*, but there was something very tough in the fiber of the fighting soldiers of the Pacific War. They acquired this quality through centuries of human refinement. No country can afford to squander these assets by soft, fuzzy thinking. Discipline is as important in an army of a democracy as it is in the army of a dictator or an autocrat. Spirit is as vital a force in the new Self-Defense Forces as it was in the Imperial Japanese Army. Courage and valor are as indispensable today as they were in yesterday's heroes.

The time may now have come to take another look at the Imperial Rescript. In my opinion, there is nothing in the rescript that would negate the dignity of the individual soldier. To me, there is nothing inconsistent with respecting a soldier and at the same time demanding obedience from that soldier. Superiors can command subordinates without abusing them, and soldiers can be disciplined without the need to have them grovel.

The Imperial Rescript was promulgated thirteen years after the Imperial Army was formed. Eighteen years have now elapsed since the formation of the NPR. Perhaps the time has come for a new rescript to be delivered to the new military forces of the nation, one that will incorporate the inspirations of the past with the democratic concepts of the new era.

Civilian control of the military establishment is an equally important new concept the NPR contributed to democratic Japan. In the broadest sense, civilian control means civilian supremacy in politics. Democratic theory proposes that control of the military of a nation by appointed or elected civilian officials makes it impossible for military leaders to seize the reins of government. Steadfast commitment to the principles of civilian control will, in time, lead to intelligent institutional arrangements and procedures that will permit the maximum utilization of the professional skills and knowledge of the military without jeopardizing the independence of the government from the will of the military. In this arrangement, the military must always be placed in a subordinate position to the elected representatives of the people. They will accept this subordinate position, as they have in the United States, only through indoctrination at all levels in the military and in the nation's total society. Our American generals today and throughout our history have accepted civilian control because they were conditioned to this concept as cadets in the United States Military Academy and throughout their services in the Army. If the Japanese cadets in the National Defense Academy (Bōei Daigakkō) are encouraged to doubt the desirability of civilian control, and if the officers of the Self-Defense Forces dispute the validity of this principle, the generals and admirals will soon find a way to again seize the government of Japan. In a democracy there of course can be no objection to a retired military officer or one who has left active duty running for elective office. In the final analysis, if representative government continues in Japan, then the principle of civilian control will rest with the people.

In practice, civilian control tends to place civilian officials and the military in adversary positions. The system should not degenerate into control by bureaucracy nor should all planning and administration be the sole province of the civilians. Civilian control could mean leaving the battles to be fought by the generals and reserving to the elected representatives of the people the discretion and the direction of wars. The most effective way to control the military is to control the funds they can expend and the appointment and promotion of all military officers.

Another important achievement of the NPR was the great leap forward Japanese rearmament made by accepting new military concepts of training, tactics, logistical procedures, and budgetary controls. All these concepts have played a role in developing the new defense forces. Had the views of Colonels Tsuji and Hattori and some of the other former Imperial officers prevailed, Japanese rearmament would have followed the road of building a massive army of twenty or more Imperial-type divisions organized and trained in accordance with traditional Japanese concepts. Under those concepts, Japanese rearmament would have started where the surrender armies were disbanded. By initially accepting American equipment, training methods, tactics, and logistical systems, the NPR provided a proving ground where the best from both American and Japanese military thought could be viewed, studied, analyzed, and integrated to suit the new requirements. During the past eighteen years, this sifting process has proceeded cautiously and intelligently and has served the best interests of the United States and Japan.

The slow, gradual, carefully timed rearmament initially conceived by Prime Minister Yoshida and faithfully carried out by successive Japanese governments has allowed Japan to advance its economic and strategic interests without arousing suspicion among its former enemies and without ever provoking the Far East communists. Though the pace of rearmament has not been rapid enough to please some Americans, the program has not neglected vital defensive measures of mutual concern to Japan and the United States. The Japanese Imperial generals and admirals, likewise, have not been satisfied with the speed or magnitude of the rearmament. The mass of the people, however, seem to be quite happy with what has been done. Jobs, family security, education, welfare, and national prosperity are more on the minds of the people than heavy appropriations for armaments. Many are convinced that their phenomenal industrial expansion was owing in a great measure to their small national investment in weapons and troops.

The limited nature of rearmament, moreover, has served to keep Japan out of overseas involvements. Throughout 1951, pressures mounted from the American side to accelerate the armament pace. While Prime Minister Yoshida grudgingly agreed to expand the NPR to 110,000, American planners were urging a force of 300,000. Had Japan in those days expanded her forces to 300,000, instructions surely would have come from the United Nations to send an expeditionary force to Korea. How long and how deep such an involvement might have become is, of course, impossible to determine. Similarly today, Japan with its limited forces cannot be expected to support the United States in Vietnam.

It is important to recognize that the rearmament of Japan is closely integrated with the mutual security treaty the nation has with the United States. The pact signed in 1960, currently in effect, provides American military protection for the home islands of Japan and permits the United States to maintain military bases on Japanese soil for the purpose of mutual security. The pact requires the United States to consult with the Japanese government before committing any of our forces stationed in Japan to hostile action against an enemy. This requirement, together with the provisions of Japanese law that prohibit the presence of nuclear weapons in Japan, create political difficulties time to time when American carriers and submarines visit Japanese ports. In general, however, the mutual security treaty, by providing a military umbrella over Japan, has permitted Japan to proceed with its rearmament program at a leisurely pace.

In summary, the NPR adequately and effectively provided the urgent defense needs of the United States and Japan in 1950. It was conceived and established in the exigencies of war rather than as a deliberate first step in the rearmament of Japan. In the formation of the NPR, the United States and the Japanese government trampled upon the Japanese constitution, deliberately confusing the truth and sadly violating moral commitments. The Socialists and opposition political parties of Japan refused to recognize the dangers facing the nation, assumed a rigid political stance, confused the electorate, and in the end achieved little of positive value. Nevertheless, the new Self-Defense Forces of Japan have imbibed deeply of democracy and are committed to an abiding concern for the individual soldier and a firm resolve to make civilian control effective. Within the limitations imposed by the structural deficiencies of the constitution, Japan is developing a small, modern, highly effective military establishment and a significant armament industry. This quiet and reasonable approach to the rearmament program has been achieved without ruffling the national feathers of Japan's former enemies, the neutral bloc of nations, or even the communist Far East. Thus, while remaining under the protection of the American military umbrella, Japan's inoffensive rearmament permits it maximum latitude to seek again a place, if it so decides, in a new East Asian coprosperity sphere.

NOTES

Editor's Preface

1. "Letter from Douglas MacArthur to Prime Minister Yoshida Shigeru, July 8, 1950," in *Correspondence between General MacArthur, Prime Minister Yoshida and Other High Japanese Officials, 1945–1951*, ed. Rinjiro Sodei (Tōkyō: Hosei University Press, 2000), 203–4.
2. The at-large seat for Connecticut traditionally went to a candidate of Polish descent. The at-large system was abolished by Congress in 1967.
3. E-mail correspondence from Carol Reidy to Robert D. Eldridge, April 22, 2012. Unless otherwise cited, personal and family information about Kowalski has been provided by Carol and her brother, Barry, in a series of e-mails and other interactions between April and December 2012.
4. Furanku Kowarusukii, *Nihon Saigunbi: Beigunji Komondan Bakuryocho no Kiroku* (The Rearmament of Japan: The Records of the Chief of Staff of the U.S. Military Advisory Group) (Tōkyō: Chūō Kōron Shinsha, 1999), 4–5.
5. Katsuyama Kinjiro, "Yakusha Maegaki (Translator's Preface)," in Kowarusukii, *Nihon Saigunbi*, 9.
6. Carol thinks it might have been someone from the Japanese Embassy in Washington, D.C., who assisted with locating a publisher, but Katsuyama may have made the connection for him.
7. Furanku Kowarusukii, *Nihon Saigunbi: Beigunji Komondan Bakuryocho no Kiroku* (The Rearmament of Japan: The Records of the Chief of Staff of the U.S. Military Advisory Group) (Tōkyō: Simul, 1969).

8. Katsuyama, "Yakusha Maegaki," 8–9.
9. An incomplete first chapter of the manuscript was donated with the rest of the papers to the Library of Congress, but for some reason, the whole manuscript was not. The original was likely provided to the translator to work from, and a copy resided with his daughter, who generously shared the manuscript with me through her brother, a well-known prosecutor in the Department of Justice specializing in civil rights cases. Carol believes there had to be more copies than just the one she has. She thinks her mother had one but supposes it must have been inadvertently discarded during house cleanings or moves. Barry added that since the manuscript was addressed to Carol, their father did not keep it in his own papers and thus it was not a part of the collection given to the Library of Congress. A former State Department official who wrote a book about the occupation period stated that the English version of the memoir is available in the National Diet Library (Kokkai Toshokan) in Tōkyō, but that appears to be incorrect. See Richard B. Finn, *Winners in Peace: MacArthur, Yoshida, and Postwar Japan* (Berkeley: University of California Press, 1992), 367 n28.
10. The translator also published the first one in the series as Robert D. Eldridge, ed., *Secret Talks between Tokyo and Washington: The Memoirs of Miyazawa Kiichi, 1949–1954* (Lanham, Md.: Lexington Books, 2007).
11. See Robert D. Eldridge and Charles Tatum, eds., *Fighting Spirit: The Memoirs of Yoshitaka Horie and the Battle of Iwo Jima* (Annapolis, Md.: Naval Institute Press, 2011).
12. Undated essay by Barry Kowalski shared with editor.
13. Undated essay by Barry Kowalski shared with editor.
14. "Ex-Congressman Kowalski Dies," *Washington Post*, October 15, 1974. The "peacemonger" label was possibly related to his efforts to seek controls on nuclear weapons and reduce waste in military manpower. In one unpublished collection of random thoughts, he wrote, "No man or group of the ancients or in Roman times possessed the power of the President of the United States or of the controlling group in the Soviet Union to give the command to destroy not only his enemies but his own country, his own countrymen, and the world. The power to unleash a nuclear holocaust which would eradicate millions of human beings, destroy life itself, and, that which may not be destroyed would be changed into horrible proportions. The men of dignitas

today truly possess the power of anti-Christ." Untitled, unpublished, undated ten-page document shared with the author by Barry Kowalski, written by his father on the latter's thoughts about ethics, politics, international affairs, and man's relationship with God.

15. "Ex-Congressman Kowalski Dies."
16. For more on the riots and the cancellation of the Eisenhower visit, see George R. Packard, *Protest in Tokyo: The Security Treaty Crisis of 1960* (Westport, Conn.: Greenwood Press, 1966).
17. "Letter from Frank Kowalski to President Eisenhower, June 29, 1960," Central Files, 611.94/62860, Record Group 59, National Archives II, College Park, Md. Kowalski received an immediate, if pro forma, reply from Jack Z. Anderson, the administrative assistant to the president, noting that "the thought which prompted you to make this suggestion is appreciated. You may be sure it will have appropriate consideration." It is unclear what the final disposition of the letter and suggestion was, but Eisenhower was not particularly close with MacArthur, for whom he had once worked, for many years. For a recent book on the latter years of Eisenhower's life, see David Eisenhower, *Going Home to Glory: A Memoir of Life with Dwight D. Eisenhower* (New York: Simon and Schuster, 2010). In it, the reader learns that the radical Japanese student organization, Zengakuren, had announced in March 1961 it would not demonstrate again if Eisenhower chose to visit Japan in his capacity as former president of Columbia University. He never made it to Japan.

Chapter 1. Grace of Heaven

1. *Koku* was a historic measurement for rice used in Japan. A *koku* was the equivalent of 150 kilograms, or 330 pounds, of rice, or about the amount an average person ate in one year then.
2. "Old" in the sense that Kowalski had previously served in the Ōsaka area.
3. An *ukase* was a decree or edict issued in Imperial Russia by the czar.
4. For more, see William F. Dean, *General Dean's Story of His Three Years Captivity in North Korea* (New York: Viking Press, 1954).
5. One might include the phrase "even against his own earlier wishes" here because MacArthur had directed in early 1946 that Japan adopt a clause in

its constitution that said, "War as a sovereign right of the nation is abolished. Japan renounces it as an instrument for settling its disputes and even for preserving its own security." See chapter 4.

Chapter 2. Japan before Korea

1. George F. Kennan, who was the first director of the Policy Planning Staff at the Department of State, had similar ideas, including the neutralization of Japan upon stabilizing it internally. See George F. Kennan, *Memoirs: 1925–1950* (Boston: Little, Brown, and Company, 1967), chapter 8, and his subsequent *Memoirs: 1950–1963* (Boston: Little, Brown, and Company, 1972), chapter 3.
2. For more on letters, petitions, and gifts to MacArthur, see Sodei Rinjirō, *Dear General MacArthur: Letters from the Japanese during the American Occupation* (Lanham, Md.: Rowman and Littlefield, 2001).

Chapter 3. Basic Plan

1. This school was known as Tōkyō Kōtō Shōsen Gakkō in Japanese and was located in Ecchūjima, Tōkyō.

Chapter 4. Constitution Bans War

1. Atcheson died in August 1947 in a plane crash off the coast of Oahu on a trip to the United States and was succeeded by his deputy, William J. Sebald.
2. The SWNCC was created in December 1944 and is considered the forerunner to the National Security Council, established in 1947.
3. The Japanese name of Matsumoto's committee was Kenpō Mondai Chōsai Iinkai. The committee was formed on October 25, 1945. There was no official disbanding of it per se, but by February 1946, Matsumoto's work was essentially superseded by the draft prepared by MacArthur's staff.
4. Takayanagi's committee was established on June 11, 1956, within the cabinet. It was made up of up to fifty members, thirty of which were members of the Diet and twenty were outside scholars and intellectuals. It submitted its report on the constitution on July 3, 1964, and disbanded a year later. For more on the committee, see Harold S. Quigley, "Revising the Japanese Constitution," *Foreign Affairs* 38, no. 10 (October 1959): 112–20. Shidehara died in March 1951, so he was unavailable to answer any questions the committee may have had for him.

Chapter 5. Yoshida's Views

1. *Tabi* is a sturdy Japanese sock. When elegant, it is used in the home. It is also used at the construction sites in place of Western-style boots, allowing workers to be much more agile.
2. Prime Minister Tsuyoshi Inukai was assassinated by eleven junior naval officers on May 15, 1932, in an attempted coup known as the "May 15 Incident." They also attacked, among other places, the residence of the Lord Keeper of the Privy Seal Nobuaki Makino, who was Prime Minister Yoshida's father-in-law. The plotters were only mildly punished. This incident followed the March assassination of a former finance minister and head of the Constitutional Democratic Party (Rikken Minseitō), Inoue Junnosuke.
3. There are many books in Japanese about Yoshida. The only biography of him in English is John Dower's *Empire and Aftermath: Yoshida Shigeru and the Japanese Experience, 1878–1954* (Cambridge, Mass.: Harvard University Press, 1988). It stops short, however, of covering his entire life, including his post-prime-minister years (he lived until 1967) and in this sense is incomplete. Fortunately, Yoshida left several writings. An abbreviated version of his 1957 memoir (*Kaisō Jūnen*, or Reflections on Ten Years) was translated into English by his son and published as *The Yoshida Memoirs: The Story of Japan in Crisis* (New York: Houghton-Mifflin, 1962). An expanded version was edited thirty years later by Hiroshi Nara titled *Yoshida Shigeru: The Last Meiji Man* (Boulder, Colo.: Rowman & Littlefield, 2007).

Chapter 9. Leaders Fashion Armies

1. In his original manuscript, Kowalski references the Vietnam War and the challenges the Lyndon B. Johnson administration was having: "Other wise, why do the Viet Cong in ragged pajamas, without tanks, without artillery, and without air support fight unto the death the best American troops we can muster, while our South Vietnamese allies, equipped with most modern weapons we can produce, prefer, like Ferdinand the Bull, to sniff flowers?" Because they were not directly related to Japan and the NPR, the editor decided to remove those last few lines from the actual text and include them here as a footnote.

Chapter 10. *Seishin Kyōiku*

1. One of the most famous books on the way of the Japanese warrior is Inazō Nitobe, *Bushidō: The Soul of Japan*, first published in 1900 for the benefit of non-Japanese readers.

Chapter 15. Conclusion

1. The JDA became the Ministry of Defense in January 2007.

INDEX

Acheson Line, 8–9
Advisory Group. *See* Military Advisory Assistance Group
agriculture, 2, 3, 18–19, 159
aircraft, 136, 138, 143
Akama, Bunzō, 7–8
Albergotti, William M.: as G-3, MAAG, 30, 73, 80, 81, 98, 100; NPR organization, 61, 80; NPR staff and, 88–89, 118; at Yoshida dinner, 47
Allied Council for Japan, 16–17
Allies. *See* occupation; peace treaty; supreme commander for Allied powers
Almond, Edward M., 74–75
Amaterasu, 1, 46, 112, 115
amnesty, 161
anti-Americanism, 167–68, 169
anticommunism, 14–16, 20, 151–52, 175–76. *See also* communism
Article 9: as constraint, 33, 43; debates on, 39–40; effects of violation, 43–44, 172, 173, 175, 177; idealism, 46; interpretations, 33, 136–37, 138, 172; justification of NPR and, 41, 137–38, 181; MacArthur's authorship, 38, 41, 142, 165; need to abolish, 135, 137–38, 165; origins, 34–35, 36–39, 52; prohibition of military forces, 24, 38–39, 135, 136–37, 172; public support, 29, 142–43; purpose, 33; right of self-defense and, 33, 39–40, 41, 42, 136–37, 138; Socialist support, 43, 166; "war potential," 46, 136–38; Yoshida on, 52–53. *See also* disarmament
Asahi Shimbun, 131, 141–42, 143
Ashida, Hitoshi, 40, 138
Atcheson, George C., Jr., 34, 35

Basic Plan, 23–24, 27
Biedelinder, W. A., 22, 23
black market, 3
Bradley, Omar N., 13, 19, 20
Bratton, Rufus S., 67
Buddhism, 112, 157
Bunker, Laurence E., 64
bureaucrats, Japanese, 48–49, 90, 96–97, 148
bushidō, 111–13, 115, 117, 119, 130
Byrnes, James F., 34–35, 37

Cabinet Order No. 260, 31, 87–88
CASA. *See* Civil Affairs Section Annex
Chiang Kai-shek, 12

189

chief medical officer, 91–92
chiefs of staff, 74–75. *See also* Kowalski, Frank, Jr.
Chihara, Kiyohara, 139
China: civil war, 12, 145; forces in Korean War, 154; Japanese independence and, 164; Japanese rearmament and, 53, 113–14; Japanese war in, 52, 119, 155
Civil Affairs Section, GHQ, xviii, 21, 23–24, 28–30, 77, 171
Civil Affairs Section Annex (CASA): establishment, 31; headquarters, 30–31, 75–77, 78; Kowalski as chief of staff, 23, 73–74, 75–77; nationalist groups and, 152–54, 157; reports, 63–64; staff, 30, 73–74. *See also* Military Advisory Assistance Group
civilian control of military: acceptance by former Imperial officers, 147, 151; advantages, 179; constitutional provisions, 34, 37; explaining to Japanese, 87, 88–89; in Japan, 34, 37, 72, 147–48, 179; in NPR organization, 72, 87–90, 97–98; officer appointments and promotions, 89–90; opponents, 154; in United States, 89, 179
civilians: American, 6; NPR headquarters staff, 87–89, 90, 94, 95, 96, 98, 104–5; NPR officers from civilian backgrounds, 101, 102, 103. *See also* Masuhara, Keikichi; public opinion
coffee *sukoshi*, 76–77
Cold War, 11–12, 146, 162
communism: in Asia, 8–9, 12; in Japan, 13–16, 59; as threat, 8–9, 136, 151–52, 163, 175–76. *See also* China; Cold War; Japan Communist Party; North Korea; Soviet Union
Confucianism, 112
conscription, 42, 142, 166
constitution, Japanese: amendments, 43, 165, 174; American draft, 38–39; American instructions, 34–35; Article 18, 42, 43–44, 165, 166; Article 22, 165, 166; Article 76, 42–44; civilian control of military, 34, 37; debates in Diet, 39–40; idealism, 44, 46; Matsumoto draft, 37–38, 39, 41; Meiji, 37, 39, 115; provisions, 5; public support, 141; ratification, 40; reform process, 35–41; resistance, 40–41; U.S. objectives, 34–35, 37. *See also* Article 9
Constitution Day, 169–70
Constitutional Problem Investigation Committee, 36
courage, 118–19, 178
court-martial systems, 42–43

Dai Ichi Building, 15, 18, 22, 24, 167–68. *See also* General Headquarters
Dayton, Julian, 95
Dean, William F., 8
Defense Agency, Japanese, 154, 173
Defense Department, U.S., 162–63
defense ministry, Japanese: NPR Headquarters as, 86–87; prewar, 87
demilitarization, 5, 35, 93. *See also* disarmament
Demobilization Bureau. *See* Japanese Demobilization Bureau
democracy: criticism of, 152; elections, 51, 139–40, 169; in Japan, 15, 97, 119, 139–40, 150, 181; objective, 5; voting rights, 52–53, 139–40, 143. *See also* civilian control of military
Derevyanko, Kuzma, 16
Diet: committee hearings, 72, 97, 132–34, 136–37; communists in, 13, 133, 166, 169; constitutional amendment procedure, 43; debates on constitution, 39–40; former officers in, 155–56; House of Councillors, 40, 43, 52, 89–90; House of Representatives, 40, 43, 165; rearmament debates, 136–38; socialists in, 31, 43, 133–34, 169
disarmament: effects, 9; as mistake, 172; objective, 5; order, 35, 56;

women's support, 52–53, 142, 143, 165. *See also* Article 9; rearmament
draft (conscription), 42, 142, 166
Drinkent, John, 83
Dulles, John Foster, 13, 20, 144

East Asia League, 155–56
East Asia League Comrades Association, 157
Eells, Walter C., 14–15
Eguchi, Mitoru, 84, 96, 97, 133–34, 165
Eisenhower, Dwight D., xvii, xx
elections: of 1949, 51; of 1952, 139–40, 169. *See also* democracy
emperor: constitutional provisions, 34; as living god, 111, 113, 114–16; public appearances, 169–70; as supreme military commander, 37, 116–17, 118, 151; symbolism, 120. *See also* Hirohito, Emperor; Meiji, Emperor
Endō, Nicky, 60–61, 85, 86
Eta Jima, 99–100

field caps, 126–27
Figgess, J. G., 102, 106–7
food supply system, 2, 3–4, 17–18, 159, 161
Fox, Alonzo P., 64, 65
Franco, Francisco, 58
Freyereisen, Paul A., 30, 88–89, 100

General Group, NPR: chief, 66–69, 71–72, 90; establishment, 90; officers, 91–92, 96, 98. *See also* Hayashi, Keizō
General Headquarters (GHQ), SCAP: building, 15, 18, 22; Civil Information and Education Section, 14–15; closing, 158; G-2 (Intelligence) Section, 28, 29, 58, 59, 60, 63, 64; G-3 (Operations) Section, 28, 29; Government Section, 28, 38–39, 60, 66, 67; Korean War and, 21; political parties and, 13; reporting lines, 74. *See also* Civil Affairs Section; supreme commander for Allied powers
Genyōsha (Dark Ocean Society), 149

Glover, Wellington, 24, 79
Grew, Joseph C., 50

Harmony (Peace) Party (Chōwa [Heiwa] Tō), 157
Hatoyama, Ichirō, 50–51
Hattori, Takushirō, 60–61, 62–65, 69, 152–55, 157
"Hattori Agency" (Hattori Kikan), 152–54
Hayashi, Keizō: accomplishments, 71–72; American advisers and, 93–94, 118; appointment to head General Group, NPR, 66–68, 69; career, 66, 68, 91; criticism of, 71; discipline, 127–28; on emperor, 114–15, 120; inspection tours, 114; Masuhara and, 67, 72, 97–98; May Day demonstrations and, 168; peace treaty commemoration, 165; Pulliam and, 68–69; on spirit of soldiers, 109–11; weapons plans, 134–35
Hayashi, Senjurō, 114
heitai (Imperial soldiers): later service in NPR, 99; new recruits, 122; self-sacrifice, 116–17, 118–19; spirit, 92, 109, 111–12, 116–17, 119; toughness, 178; treatment by officers, 127; use of term, 121, 122. *See also* Imperial Army
Higashikuni, Naruhiko, Prince, 35
Hirohito, Emperor: abdication rumors, 165; Constitution Day ceremony, 169–70; constitutional reform and, 39; Hayashi and, 66, 114–15, 120; MacArthur and, 74; surrender, 158. *See also* emperor
Hirota, Kōki, 50
Hokkaidō, 83, 114, 123–24, 134–35
Honna, Fuminori, 91–92
Hoover, Herbert C., 12

Imai, Takeo, 155
Imoto, Kumao, 63, 64–65
Imperial Army: demobilization, 56, 59; discipline, 178; "Manchuria Clique,"

62; misconceptions of strength, 113–14; as model for NPR, 92–93; national importance, 122; noncommissioned officers, 99, 127; officers, 127; spirit, 92, 109, 110, 111–12, 113–14, 116, 119; strength, 92; uniforms, 126; war in China, 52, 119, 155; weapons, 92–93; Yoshida and, 50. See also *heitai*
imperial family. *See* emperor
Imperial forces, former officers: acceptance into NPR, 105–7, 117–18, 130–31, 148, 150–51, 154, 176; beggars, 161; criticism of NPR, 70–71, 72, 102, 152, 153, 154; Diet members, 155–56; divisions among, 70, 150–51; efforts to bring into NPR, 57–58, 60–65, 104–6; excluded from NPR, 29, 50, 56–57, 69, 100–101, 102, 103–4, 105–6; influence on occupation, 59; intelligence activities, 59; military know-how, 147; in rightist groups, 148–50, 151–54; senior, 148–49, 150; views of NPR, 150–51; war crimes trials, 35, 148, 155; worldview, 147, 150, 151–52. *See also* Japanese Demobilization Bureau; purged officers
Imperial General Staff, 57, 61, 62, 117–18, 155
Imperial Household Agency, 66, 91, 114
Imperial Navy, 56, 59, 99, 113, 122. *See also* Imperial forces, former officers
Imperial Palace Plaza, 15, 167, 169–70
Imperial Rescript of Emperor Meiji, 116–17, 118–19, 178
Initial Postsurrender Policy for Japan, 35, 56–57
Intelligence Section (G-2), GHQ, 28, 58, 59, 63, 64, 65, 69. *See also* Public Safety Division; Willoughby, Charles A.
interpreters, 48, 60–61, 85–86, 93, 94, 111–12
Ishiwara, Kanji, 150, 155–57, 164
Izeki, Yujirō, 97, 98, 104–5

Japan: agriculture, 2, 3, 18–19, 159; conditions at end of war, 1–4; food supply system, 2, 3–4, 17–18, 159, 161; industries, 2, 3, 93, 161; life expectancies, 160; military influence, 147–48; mutual security pact with United States, 163, 180–81; national security threats, 82–83, 136, 163; political failures, 176–77; population growth, 2, 160; rebuilding, 1, 3, 5–6; sovereignty regained, 146, 158–65; surrender, 4, 158, 160; trust in authority, 141; U.S. bases, 41–42, 166, 181. *See also* Diet; emperor; Imperial forces; occupation
Japan Communist Party (Nihon Kyōsantō): acceptance of emperor, 115; Diet members, 13, 133, 166, 169; MacArthur's purge of Central Committee, 16, 17; May Day demonstrations, 166–69; members, 130; opposition to rearmament, 138; popular support, 4, 13–14, 51; potential infiltration of NPR, 69–70; publications, 162; surveillance by Demobilization Bureau, 59
Japan Self-Defense Forces (JSDF; Jieitai), 42–43, 169, 176, 178, 181
Japan Socialist Party. *See* Socialist Party
Japanese Commission on the Constitution, 37
Japanese Demobilization Bureau (Nihon Fukuinkyoku), 28, 59–61, 62–64, 65, 69, 153
Japanese Supreme Court, 41–42
Jimmu Tennō, 115
Johnson, Louis A., 13, 19, 20
Johnson, Lyndon B., xx
Joint Chiefs of Staff, U.S., 8, 13
JSDF. *See* Japan Self-Defense Forces

Kennedy, John F., xix
Kimura, Tokutarō, 137, 138
Kitamura (interpreter), 111–12, 130
Knowlton, Charles E., 30
Kojiki, 115

Konoe, Fumimaro, Prince, 35
Korean War: Chinese strength, 154; effects in Japan, 7, 46, 146; Japanese support of U.S. military, 7–8; North Korean victories, 8, 51–52, 107–8; potential use of NPR, 52–54, 152; Republic of Korea Headquarters, 21–22; surprise attack, 20; U.S. deployments from Japan, 9, 21, 23, 30–31, 82, 83; U.S. units, 8, 9; Yoshida on, 1, 4, 51–52, 55, 144
Kowalski, Frank, Jr.: assignments in Japan, xviii, 21, 22–23, 29–30; as CASA chief of staff, 23, 73–74, 75–77; childhood and family, xiv–xv; children, xvii, xviii, xxii; death, xxii; education, xiv–xvi; health, xvii–xviii, xxi–xxii; inspection tours, 94–95, 114, 134–35; interest in Japan, xx–xxi; inventions, xxi; marriage, xvi; military career, xv–xix; political career, xix, xx–xxi, 159–60; political views, xx
Kowalski, Helene Amelia Bober, xvi, xxi, xxii
Kurushima, Tsuneki, 149

labor unions, 166, 169, 175–76
land reform, 6
language issues, 93–95, 98, 99. *See also* interpreters
Liberal Party (Jiyūtō), 13, 136, 162
loyalty, 116–17

MAAG. *See* Military Advisory Assistance Group
MacArthur, Douglas: accomplishments, 5; Asian defense plan, 20; chief of staff, 74–75; inaccessibility, 74–75; on Japan Communist Party, 13–14; Japanese constitution and, 34, 35–39, 40–41, 142, 165, 172; Japanese view of, xx–xxi, 18–19; Korean War, 8–9, 22, 51; letters, 25; life in Japan, 18; National Police Reserve and, 25–27, 31, 41, 174–75; on occupation, 6–7; on peace treaty, 12, 162; police force expansion, 25–27; rearmament order, 10; relations with troops, 18; relieved of command by Truman, 78, 147; Whitney and, 28, 74; Willoughby and, 28, 58, 74. *See also* supreme commander for Allied powers
Mainichi Shimbun, 37, 38, 141, 142
Makino, Nobuaki, Count, 49
Manchukuo, army of, 100–101
"Manchuria Clique," 62
Mao Tse-tung, 12, 145
Maritime Safety Board, police forces, 26
Marquat, William F., 74
Masuda, Kaneshichi, 162
Masuhara, Keikichi: appointment, 84; criticism of, 71; Hayashi and, 67, 72, 97–98; headquarters staff, 87–88, 90; inspection tours, 134–35; NPR organization and, 86–87; officer appointments, 100–101, 104; peace treaty commemoration, 164–65; personality, 84–85; on rearmament, 143; relations with Americans, 86, 109; on spirit of soldiers, 109; uniform designs, 125–27; weapons plans, 134–35
Matsumoto, Jōji, 36–38, 39, 41
May Day demonstrations, 166–69
Meiji, Emperor: birthday, 40; Imperial Rescript, 116–17, 118–19, 178
Meiji constitution, 37, 39, 115
Meiji Restoration, 49, 164
Miki, Takeo, 162
militarists: *bushidō* and, 113; excluded from NPR, 50; ideology, 116–17; in postwar period, 148–57; preventing resurgence, 87; support of rearmament, 54; during war, 54–55. *See also* Imperial forces, former officers; nationalist organizations; purge
Military Advisory Assistance Group (MAAG): Kowalski as acting chief,

87; officers, 29–30; potential leadership of NPR, 98; relations with civilian leaders of NPR, 84–85, 86, 88, 103, 125, 126, 164; training role, 99. *See also* Civil Affairs Section Annex; Shepard, Whitfield P.
military spirit. See *seishin kyōiku*
Murphy, Robert D., 158
mutual security pact, 163, 180–81

Nambara, Shigeru, 13, 15
Napoleon Bonaparte, 109
National Defense Council, 151, 154
National Police Reserve, director general. *See* Masuhara, Keikichi
National Police Reserve (NPR; Kokka Keisatsu Yobitai): accomplishments, 177–81; American advisers, 78–81, 98, 101, 103, 118; American officers on staff, 29–31, 45–47, 73–74, 82, 98, 100, 140; Americans in charge, 73, 78, 81–82; assistant director general, 84, 96, 97, 133–34; Basic Plan, 23–24, 27; cabinet supervision, 97; cadre list, 61; camps, 77–81, 83, 94–95, 123, 134; conference on operational policies, 31; corruption allegations, 70; criticism of, 27, 70–71, 72, 123, 129, 131, 152, 153, 154; differences from Imperial forces, 177–80; discipline, 42–43, 178; equipment and supplies, 27, 81, 82, 83, 95; establishment, 25–26, 31–32, 41, 87–88; evaluation, 102, 106–7; expansion, 72, 131, 180; General Group, 66–69, 71–72, 91–92, 96, 98; goals, 51, 53; headquarters, 30–31, 73–74, 86–89; headquarters staff, 87–89, 90, 94, 95, 96, 98, 104–5; induction centers, 61–62, 77–79; infantry divisions, 27–28; legality, 27, 41, 173, 174–75; manuals, 93–94, 103, 173; military nature concealed, 27, 93–94, 121, 122–23, 132–33, 173; need for, 171–72, 173–74; number of personnel, 87–88, 180; organizing, 27–28, 77–83, 85, 86–89, 92–93, 98–101; as police force, 86–87, 88, 93–94, 101, 132; potential communist infiltration, 69–70; potential use in Korea, 52–54, 152; prime ministerial control, 28; public perceptions, 176; readiness, 102, 104, 106; relations with people, 122–25, 127–28, 139, 140–42; as self-defense force, 53, 139, 173; Shepard's role, 23, 28–31; significance for rearmament, 137–38, 172; use in domestic disturbances, 167, 168–69; Yoshida's policies, 52, 55, 136–37, 143. *See also* Civil Affairs Section Annex; weapons; *yobitai*
National Rural Police (Kokka Chihō Keisatsu): American supervision, 60; director general, 68–69, 86; officers transferred to NPR, 82, 90; recruiting for NPR, 60, 78, 79, 80; size, 25
National Safety Agency (Kokka Hoanchō), 87
National Safety Force (NSF; Kokka Hoantai), 72, 131, 169
nationalist organizations, 148–50, 151–54, 155–56, 157. *See also* militarists
newspapers: articles on NPR, 124–25, 127; circulation, 161; criticism of NPR, 70–71, 129, 131; public opinion polls, 140–43
Ninigi no Mikoto, 115
Nippon Times, 160
Nisei interpreters, 85–86
Nishiura, Susumu, 63, 64–65
Nixon, Richard M., 172
noncommissioned officers: in Imperial Army, 99, 127; in NPR, 102, 127, 139, 178
North Atlantic Treaty, 11
North Atlantic Treaty Organization (NATO), 12
North Korea, 8, 51–52, 107–8. *See also* Korean War
Nosaka, Sanzō, 115

NPR. *See* National Police Reserve
NSF. *See* National Safety Force
nuclear weapons, 43, 181

O'Brien, John W. A., 24
occupation: accomplishments, 5–7, 160, 171–72; American staff, 6; bureaucratic resistance, 49; conqueror's mindset, 53–54, 85; effects of Korean War, 9, 21, 146; end of, 158–65; Japanese bureaucrats and, 48–49; life of American troops, 17, 18; MacArthur on, 6–7; military oversight of government, 171; mistakes made, 172–77; objectives, 4–5, 35; political parties and, 175–76; public opinion on, 57, 143; tasks, 17–18; troop levels, 19. *See also* supreme commander for Allied powers
officers, Imperial. *See* Imperial forces, former officers
officers, NPR: appointments, 50, 69, 89–90, 100–101, 176; arrogant, 127–28; captains, 100, 103, 127–28, 129–31; from civilian backgrounds, 101, 102, 103; democratic commitment, 139–40; differences from Imperial officers, 105–7; experience, 81–82, 91, 105; former Imperial officers as, 105–7, 117–18, 130–31, 148, 150–51, 154, 176; General Group, 91–92, 96, 98; from National Rural Police, 82, 90; noncommissioned, 102, 127, 139, 178; purged officers ineligible, 29, 56–57, 61, 69, 100–101, 102, 103–4, 105–6; recruiting, 60–62, 65–66, 69, 103; relations with troops, 178; small-unit leaders, 99–100, 102, 103, 129–30; staff, 100; training, 99–100, 103, 104, 105, 129–30; uniforms, 91–92
Ōhashi, Takeo, 31, 47–48, 97, 100–101, 136, 168
Okazaki, Katsuo, 31, 84
Ōkuma, Shigenobu, 149
Ōsaka, 1, 4, 9, 14, 68, 161, 175–76

pacifism, 157
patriotism: American, 110; Japanese, 46, 112, 113, 119–20
peace treaty: hopes for, 7; negotiations, 12, 13; ratification, 166; unilateral, 13, 20, 162–63
Percy, Charles, xix
police forces: expansion, 25–27; municipal, 25, 28, 167, 168; rearmament through, 24–27, 45–47, 137–38, 172. *See also* National Police Reserve; National Rural Police
Potsdam Declaration, 38, 56, 146
Progressive Party (Kaishintō), 138, 162
protests, 14–15, 166–69
public opinion: on disarmament and rearmament, 29, 52–53, 139, 140–43, 165; on NPR, 141, 173; on occupation, 57, 143; polls, 140–43
Public Safety Division, 31, 60
Pulliam, Howard E., 31, 60, 61, 62, 63, 66, 68–69, 70
purge: benefits, 57; exceptions, 62–63, 65, 100–101; order for, 35, 56; people included, 5, 57, 59–60; supporters, 148
purged officers: ineligibility for NPR, 29, 56–57, 61, 69, 100–101, 102, 103–4, 105–6; number of, 148; removals from purge lists, 104–6, 130–31, 146–47, 148, 154. *See also* Imperial forces, former officers; militarists

radicals, 3–4. *See also* communism
Ratcliff, Clifton E., 30, 31, 75–76, 80, 81
rearmament: constitutional change needed, 165; denial, 132–33, 173; inoffensive, 181; legality, 10, 27, 32, 46, 172; MacArthur's order, 10, 25–26, 55; mistakes made, 172–77; of NPR, 27, 43, 101, 132–33, 135; pace of, 27, 179–80; through police forces, 24–27, 45–47, 137–38, 172; public discussions, 135–39, 140;

public opinion on, 29, 139, 140–43; Socialist opposition, 52, 132, 136, 137, 138, 140, 166, 173–74; supporters, 54, 152, 153, 157; through police forces, 24–27, 45–47, 137–38, 172; U.S. pressure, 140, 144, 152; women's opposition, 52–53, 142, 143, 165; Yoshida on, 52–53, 136–38, 141–42, 143–45, 163. *See also* weapons

Republic of Korea (ROK) Headquarters, 21–22

rice, 3–4, 159. *See also* agriculture; food supply system

Ridgway, Matthew B., 78, 104

rightist organizations, 148–50, 151–54, 155–57. *See also* militarists

Roberts, William L., 107

Robertson, Frank, 111

Russia. *See* Soviet Union

SACB. *See* Subversive Activities Control Board

safes, 94–95

Saitō, Noboru, 68, 69, 86

Sakhalin, 82–83, 136

samurai, 111–13, 131. See also *bushidō*

Sauer, Colonel, 99

SCAP. *See* supreme commander for Allied powers

seishin kyōiku (military spirit), 109–14, 119–20

self-defense, right of, 33, 39–40, 41, 42, 136–37, 138

self-defense forces, 40, 53, 139, 173. *See also* Japan Self-Defense Forces

self-sacrifice, 118–19

seppuku, 130, 158

Shellenberger, Colonel, 91–92

Shepard, Whitfield P.: at CASA headquarters, 75–77; as chief, Civil Affairs Section, xviii, 21; interpreter, 60–61, 85, 86; Kowalski and, 21, 22–23, 47, 52; MacArthur and, 75; Masuhara and, 84–85, 86, 88, 104, 125, 126; National Police Reserve and, 23, 28–31, 60–61, 63–65, 66, 67, 73; personality, 75; Yoshida and, 45, 48

Shidehara, Kijurō, Baron, 36–37, 39, 165

Shiga, Yōshio, 4, 14

Shimbun Yoron Chōsa Renmei, 142, 143

Shintō, 112

Socialist Party (Nihon Shakaitō): American view of, 175–76; criticism of NPR, 133–34; criticism of positions, 174; Diet members, 31, 43, 133–34, 169; end of occupation and, 162; left and right wings, 162, 166; opposition to rearmament, 52, 132, 136, 137, 138, 140, 166, 173–74; on peace treaty negotiations, 13; Yoshida and, 174

soldiers. See *heitai*; *yobitai*

South Korea, 20, 107–8, 127. *See also* Korean War

Soviet Union: Cold War, 11, 12, 146, 162; Japanese peace treaty and, 12, 13, 164; Japanese rearmament and, 53; military forces in Far East Asia, 136; representatives in Japan, 16–17; Sakhalin, 82–83, 136; total diplomacy against, 12, 13, 16–17, 20

special vehicles, tanks as, 81, 94, 173

spirit. See *seishin kyōiku*

State Department, U.S., 35, 162

State-War-Navy Coordination Committee (SWNCC), 34–35, 37

Stevens, Kenneth, 79–81

student protests, 14–15, 167, 169

Subversive Activities Control Board (SACB), xix–xx

Subversive Acts Prevention Bill, 166, 169

supreme commander for Allied powers (SCAP): anticommunist campaign, 14–16, 20; authority, 32; Initial Post-surrender Policy for Japan, 35, 56–57; objectives, 4–5. *See also* General Headquarters; MacArthur, Douglas; occupation

Suzuki (chief of police), 68–69
SWNCC. *See* State-War-Navy Coordination Committee

Takayanagi, Kenzō, 37
tanks, 81, 94, 134, 135, 136, 153, 173
tennō. See emperor
Thoulton, Colonel, 100
"Three Human Bombs" story, 118–19
Tōhoku University, 14
Tōjō, Hideki, 62, 63, 156, 157
Tōkyō Maritime Training School, 30–31
Tōkyō Metropolitan Police, 25, 167
total diplomacy, 12, 13, 16–17, 20
training: Advisory Group role, 99; criticism of, 153; of NPR officers, 99–100, 103, 104, 105, 129–30; of NPR recruits, 79, 83, 93, 98, 99–100, 101, 104, 106–7, 129–30; of U.S. Army, 17, 18
Truman, Harry S, 11, 13, 78, 147
Truman Doctrine, 11
Tsuji, Masanobu, 155–56, 157

uniforms, 91–92, 125–27
United Nations, 12–13, 46
United States: ambassadors to Japan, 50, 158; Asian involvement, 7, 8–9, 19–20; bases in Japan, 41–42, 166, 181; civilian control of military, 89, 179; economic power, 19–20; foreign policy in Cold War, 11, 12, 13, 16–17, 20; military cooperation with Japan, 85, 93; military officer appointments and promotions, 89, 176; military readiness, 19–20, 153–54; patriotism, 110; peace treaty with Japan, 13, 20, 162–63; presidential power, 118; security pact with Japan, 163, 180–81; Truman Doctrine, 11. *See also* occupation
U.S. Army: 1st Cavalry Division, 9; 7th Cavalry Regiment, 30–31; 7th Infantry Division, 9, 82, 83; 24th Infantry Division, 8, 9; 25th Infantry Division, 9; cadre system, 82; divisions in Japan, 9, 17–18, 19; Eighth Army, 8, 99–100; Kowalski's career, xv–xix; organization, 93; training in Japan, 17, 18. *See also* Korean War
U.S. Department of Defense, 87
U.S. Military Academy, xv, xvi, 179

Walker, Walton H., 8
war, renunciation of. *See* Article 9
weapons: American, 93; artillery, 94, 132, 134, 135, 136; carbines, 28, 80, 81, 83, 93, 101; gradual armament of NPR, 27, 43, 101, 141; of Imperial Army, 92–93; Japanese production, 152; tanks, 81, 94, 134, 135, 136, 153, 173; training, 83, 104. *See also* disarmament; rearmament
Weetman, Harold R., 30, 100
Whitney, Courtney S.: as chief of Government Section, 28; constitution draft, 38–39, 40; MacArthur and, 28, 74; NPR officer screening, 60, 61, 64, 66, 67
Willoughby, Charles A.: former Imperial officers and, 28, 57–58, 59, 60, 61–62, 63–64, 69–70, 100–101; Hattori and, 61–62, 69, 153; Hayashi appointment and, 65–67; as Intelligence Section Chief, 28; MacArthur and, 28, 58, 74; reports on communist threat, 69–70; reputation, 58–59
women: coffee *sukoshi*, 76–77; support of disarmament, 52–53, 142, 143, 165; voting rights, 52–53, 143
World War II: bombings of Japanese cities, 1–2; conduct of Japanese soldiers, 116–17; D-day, xvii; Japanese surrender, 4, 158, 160. *See also* peace treaty

Yamaguchi, Yoshitada, 4
yobitai (new Japanese soldiers): choice of name, 121–22; combat boots, 81;

criticism of, 71; dignity, 127, 128–29, 178; former Imperial soldiers, 99; newspaper articles, 124–25; public perceptions, 123–25; recruiting, 60, 61–62, 77, 78, 83, 98–99; spirit, 108, 109–11, 130; suicides, 130; training, 79, 83, 93, 98, 99–100, 101, 104, 106–7, 129–30; treatment by officers, 178; uniforms, 125–27; volunteers, 98–99; voting rights, 139–40

Yoshida, Kenzō, 49

Yoshida, Shigeru: amnesty, 161; career, 48–50; Constitution Day ceremony, 170; constitutional reform and, 39–40, 50, 52, 173; dinner hosted by, 45, 47–48, 51–53; end of occupation and, 159, 163; family and marriage, 49; as foreign minister, 39, 50; on Korean War, 1, 4, 51–52, 55, 144; MacArthur and, 175; peace treaty negotiations and, 13; as prime minister, 1, 39–40, 50–51; on rearmament, 52–53, 136–38, 141–42, 143–45, 163; relations with SCAP, 49; "reverse course" program, 149, 151, 166, 169; Socialist Party and, 174; during war, 50, 54–55

Yoshida, Shigeru, National Police Reserve and: cabinet order, 31; depurging officers, 104; expansion, 72, 136, 180; goals, 51, 53, 55, 132; Hayashi appointment, 66, 67; MacArthur's order, 25–26, 41, 55; Masuhara's appointment, 84; officer appointments, 50, 90; rearmament, 135, 136–37, 143; support of establishment, 51; use in domestic disturbances, 168

ABOUT THE AUTHORS

COL. FRANK KOWALSKI, United States Army, member of Congress from Connecticut, died in 1974. He was chief, military government in Kyōto, Japan, 1948–49, and deputy chief, civil affairs section, GHQ in Japan, 1950–52. He retired from the Army in 1958.

ROBERT D. ELDRIDGE earned his PhD in Japanese political and diplomatic history at Kobe University and is the author of numerous works about U.S.-Japan relations, including *Fighting Spirit* (Naval Institute Press, 2011). He currently serves as the deputy assistant chief of staff, G-7 (Government and External Affairs), for Marine Corps Installations Pacific.

The Naval Institute Press is the book-publishing arm of the U.S. Naval Institute, a private, nonprofit, membership society for sea service professionals and others who share an interest in naval and maritime affairs. Established in 1873 at the U.S. Naval Academy in Annapolis, Maryland, where its offices remain today, the Naval Institute has members worldwide.

Members of the Naval Institute support the education programs of the society and receive the influential monthly magazine Proceedings or the colorful bimonthly magazine Naval History and discounts on fine nautical prints and on ship and aircraft photos. They also have access to the transcripts of the Institute's Oral History Program and get discounted admission to any of the Institute-sponsored seminars offered around the country.

The Naval Institute's book-publishing program, begun in 1898 with basic guides to naval practices, has broadened its scope to include books of more general interest. Now the Naval Institute Press publishes about seventy titles each year, ranging from how-to books on boating and navigation to battle histories, biographies, ship and aircraft guides, and novels. Institute members receive significant discounts on the Press's more than eight hundred books in print.

Full-time students are eligible for special half-price membership rates. Life memberships are also available.

For a free catalog describing Naval Institute Press books currently available, and for further information about joining the U.S. Naval Institute, please write to:

Member Services
U.S. NAVAL INSTITUTE
291 Wood Road
Annapolis, MD 21402-5034
Telephone: (800) 233-8764
Fax: (410) 571-1703
Web address: www.usni.org